Danny's adventures are a must-read for any outdoor enthusiast. No one has logged more miles in national parks or explored them so thoroughly. She asks tough questions and goes beyond the visitor center to uncover highlights and hidden treasures across seventy-one national park units across the South. At each park, she powerfully weaves together natural and human histories—including her own. This is not a superficial overview. Danny gets her boots muddy—and her hands dirty—clearing trails, viewing wildlife, and hiking deep into the region's wildest and most rugged terrain. It is a timely and critically important book that celebrates the South's enduring park legacies, delves deep into their storied past, and offers a candid, clear-eyed vision for their future.

Will Harlan, author of
*Untamed: The Wildest Woman in America
and the Fight for Cumberland Island*

––––––––––––

Danny's book—written from a true love of our national parks—reflects not only the author's enthusiasm for the special places preserved, but also the people and the stories reflected in those places, stories both past and present. The author as narrator weaves her own personal adventures about exploring the national parks with humor and wry observation. While revealing her own story, Danny never overshadows the true stars of the book, the national parks themselves.

It's as if Danny invites you along for the adventure, leading you throughout the South, from the castles of Puerto Rico to the Civil War battlefields to the Natchez Trace of Mississippi to the Smoky Mountains of North Carolina and East Tennessee, to smaller parks of which you've never heard, but will want to go after reading this book. And whether we are traipsing through a visitor center, along a trail, or visiting a pioneer cabin, with Danny in the lead, we learn tales of how and why these national parks came to be. Her conversational yet informative writing style leads you on a learning experience far removed from dull, dry historical textbooks. Grab this narrative! It will make you eager to experience these national parks for yourself.

Johnny Molloy, author of
over fifty outdoor hiking, camping, and paddling guides

———————

Danny Bernstein is an ideal National Parks guide. She loves the parks and believes in the public purpose they serve. She is insatiably curious about both their hiking trails and outdoor spaces and the complicated histories they preserve and tell. And she is ever mindful of the now century-long saga of the National Park Service as the agency that manages them. In this personal and intimate book, she blends these things in an engaging account that invites us to make our own journey through the parks of the southeast. I am eager to follow her.

Anne Mitchell Whisnant, author of
Super-Scenic Motorway: A Blue Ridge Parkway History

Forests, Alligators, Battlefields

Also by Danny Bernstein

Hiking the Carolina Mountains

Hiking North Carolina's Blue Ridge Mountains

The Mountains-to-Sea Trail Across North Carolina: Walking a Thousand Miles through Wildness, Culture and History

Contents

Map courtesy of the National Park Service, Southeast Region

To my granddaughters, Hannah and Isabelle,
in the hope and expectation that they'll
grow up to love and support their national parks

Girls, I'm leaving the national parks to you!

Kimberly Crest Books

Asheville, North Carolina 28804
www.kimberlycrestbooks.com

ISBN 978-0-9861932-7-9
LCCN 2015919240

Cover and Interior Designs: Diana Wade dwadegraphics.com

Author photograph: Anna Lee Zanetti

Forests, Alligators, Battlefields

My Journey through the National Parks of the South

Danny Bernstein

Kimberly Crest Books

FOREWORD

Our system of national parks, managed by the National Park Service (NPS), has often been referred to as one of America's best ideas. The conservation and protection of significant natural and cultural treasures was practically unheard of on the international scene. Now nations of the world regularly turn to the United States, and more specifically the NPS, for resource conservation guidance and training.

Danny Bernstein has penned an enjoyable read of her personal journeys to all the National Park Service units within the southeast region of the United States. The book is a mixture of travel guide and American history, with a generous dose of Danny's personal adventures at each location.

What makes this book unique, you might ask? If you're planning a visit to special places in the southeastern United States, you will find an excellent and concise description of more than seventy important destinations.

For each park, Danny begins by telling the reader the primary significance of the site, followed by good recommendations on how to get the most out of your stay. This approach is particularly useful if your schedule only permits a limited visit.

A most unexpected and pleasant surprise for me was a reacquaintance with so much of our American history. These are our stories told through NPS sites; they are preserved and interpreted for all to experience and learn.

We should not overlook the manner in which Danny organizes the book. The conventional approach would have been to simply arrange the book by sites in each state, or to place them in sequence by the date they came under NPS control, or even to put them in alphabetical order.

1

Instead, Danny arranges the sites into meaningful and clearly understandable themes, including Prehistoric America, The Europeans Are Coming, Revolutionary War in the South, Young America, The War of 1812, Coastal Defense, The Civil War, Twentieth Century Developments, Fighting for Equality, and The Great Outdoors: The Lowlands and the Mountains. This method of grouping helped me see the larger picture and follow the historical thread or natural history significance of each location within each broad theme.

Danny emphasizes the importance of her experiences with park staff at each site. She tackles the question of "what interpretation is" from the NPS perspective. Many park visitors have difficulty understanding the meaning of the term. In recent years, some NPS locations have moved away from this terminology and replaced it with resource education, as being more understandable. Not only does Danny explain what interpretation is, she underscores the skill NPS staffers develop and utilize to make each site come alive for the visitor by providing firsthand examples of inspiring interactions with NPS interpreters.

Danny Bernstein ends the book with sections providing sound, common-sense answers to a series of recurring questions that are heard at almost every park, followed by a passionate appeal to the reader to not only visit parks but to help our parks. It makes a lot of sense for those who love and enjoy these special places to join one or more of the nonprofit national park support organizations and to buy something from the bookstore in the park visitor center, as all these purchases support that particular park.

I hope you enjoy this book as much as I have. In 2016, we celebrate the 100th anniversary of the creation of the National Park Service by Congress. The NPS is in the midst of a yearlong celebration of our past one hundred years of park creation and development, but more importantly, NPS is focused on engaging the next generation of park visitors. I hope that you will be inspired to go "Find Your Park" here in the southeastern United States or elsewhere!

On a personal note, over the last several years, I have come to know Danny Bernstein on a professional level. Something that enhanced my reading of the book and I did not expect was hearing Danny's voice in my head, as though we were having a casual conversation, sitting on the porch at the Oconaluftee Visitor Center in Great Smoky Mountains National Park.

Terry Maddox
Executive Director 1990-2015
Great Smoky Mountains Association
August 2015

Why Am I Visiting All the Southern Parks?

I grew up in Brooklyn. You know that one tree that grows in Brooklyn? I didn't even live close to that tree. My husband, Lenny, grew up on Miami Beach, which at the time was called New York's southernmost borough. Brooklyn and Miami Beach were not the outdoor centers of the United States. And neither of us grew up with a car.

After we moved to New Jersey to work, we found an announcement for a hiking club in the local newspaper. I didn't know that adults hiked in groups without children, but it sounded like a great idea. We went on our first hike with people closer to my parents' age and were barely able to keep up. A sunny April day at the meeting point in town turned into a cold, rainy hike in the mountains, and I hadn't brought a rain jacket. But I was hooked on hiking and hooked on hiking clubs. I went out on local trails most weekends. With only two weeks of vacation a year, we started exploring national parks, going first to the iconic western parks.

The Statue of Liberty was probably my first national park site. Because I lived in New York, I took several visitors up the lady. Prior to 9/11, you could go up the crown by just being willing to stand in line—no reservations needed. As you went up the narrow, winding stairs, you were literally cheek-to-cheek with the person in front of you while you waited. At the time, I didn't know that this was a national park. Like many visitors, I thought of national parks as large expanses of land somewhere out west, not Liberty Island in the middle of New York Harbor.

In 1974, we visited Great Smoky Mountains National Park on a driving vacation from New Jersey. We thought we could do both Shenandoah National Park and the Smokies in just two weeks with our fifteen-month-old son strapped in the back seat. Little did we know that each park probably takes a lifetime to understand.

While I carried a pack filled with food, water, and diapers, Lenny backpacked our son up to Ramsey Cascades. We marveled at the huge hemlocks and the profusion of blooming red bee balm. Past the old Jeep road, the trail became rocky, wet, and precarious, but we reached the waterfall. I still wonder how we made it to the top, and just as important, how we made it back down to our car.

Seven years later, we returned to the Smokies and hiked the same trails. By then, our son was a great hiker—the kid had no choice—but we still had to entertain him on the trail. We sang "Ninety-Nine Bottles of Beer on the Wall" and sometimes we got down to zero before returning to the trailhead. Now we're taking our granddaughters to parks, and we've updated our repertoire of trail songs.

You don't need to have an outdoor childhood to love and support our national parks. My hiking friends who grew up in rural areas remember that they had unstructured time outside but never actually went hiking or camping with their families.

I don't own any land personally. I share our parks, forests, and trails with all Americans; we're all owners. I've more of a chance to pass on the battlefields, forts, and trails to my grandchildren than if I had acres of private land, tied up in deeds, trusts, taxes, and lawyers. The Smokies and the Blue Ridge Parkway are mine and I don't even have to mow the lawn. I own the paths, creeks, waterfalls, and historic structures. I can't do everything I want in the park, but that's true on private land as well.

I know that the national park standards—factual, forthcoming, and friendly—will be met, whether in the half-million acres of the Smokies or in the William Johnson House in downtown Natchez, Mississippi. No matter how many questions I have, a patient ranger will have the answers or make every effort to look them up. Rangers answer the phone and call you back, if needed.

What business can boast the same? The rangers in green and gray produce magic out of what may look like an ordinary place. They're teachers, historians, naturalists, law enforcement, and at times, EMTs. Every place has a story, and park rangers are the best when it comes to interpreting that history and making it come alive.

Parks offer the best recreational value for your time and dollars. Compare them to Disney World, which doesn't even have trails. I don't just pop in to the visitor center, get my National Park passport stamped, and fly out. The Passport to Your National Parks program, as it's formally called, offers passport-like booklets, which enables you to keep track of national park visits. At every visitor center, you can stamp your passport with the name of the park and the date of your visit.

At the visitor center, I watch the movie, study the exhibits, and pick up a park pamphlet. I walk a trail or two and read the inscriptions on monuments. I ask myself, *Why is this place worthy of permanent protection?* Then I return to the visitor center with more questions. I can't absorb more than one place a day.

ॐ◆ॐ

In 2016, the United States celebrates the 100th anniversary of the National Park Service, currently with 410 park units, including fifty-nine scenic national parks and many historic sites, battlefields, and national monuments. Every national park unit has a human story as well as great scenery. As shorthand, I call them all parks. A few years ago, I decided to visit all seventy-one national park units in the Southeast, where I now live. I needed to understand the history, the flora, and the fauna, but I also wanted to meet rangers, volunteers, park partners, and visitors. I adopted the National Park Service definition of the Southeast—Louisiana to the west, Kentucky north, the US Virgin Islands south, and the Atlantic Ocean east.

I've hiked all the trails (803 miles) in Great Smoky Mountains National Park, now my home park. The Blue Ridge Parkway runs right through Asheville, North Carolina, where I live. I've taken my granddaughters to see the goats at Carl Sandburg Home. I completed the Appalachian Trail in 1998. So when I got the idea for this book, I had four down and another sixty-seven to go. Visiting the national parks in the Southeast is much different from a once-in-a-lifetime trip to Yosemite or Yellowstone. Here, almost everyone lives close to a national park and keeps going back to their park. Many treat it as their local village green where they jog or walk their dogs. When I travel, I like to let locals know that I came to visit their national park and watch their puzzled faces. "Huh? We have a national park here?"

The Organic Act, enacted in 1916, gave the National Park Service a clear mission:

> *to conserve the scenery and the natural and historic objects and the wild life therein and to provide for the enjoyment of the same in such manner and by such means as will leave them unimpaired for the enjoyment of future generations.*

But the National Park Service doesn't just preserve and protect our resources. It interprets as well. Rangers explain the significance of the place so that visitors will care about the resources such as rivers, monuments, chimneys, and alligators.

In my previous life, I worked in computer science for thirty-five years, way before computing was cool, first as a software developer and then as a professor of computer science. I love computer users. You don't need to major in computer science in college to use computers. Why should it be different in other fields? I'm an amateur historian, but I prefer to call myself a history user. I read mostly secondhand sources, many from the National Park Service.

A few years ago, I walked the Mountains-to-Sea Trail (MST), a 1,150-mile state trail, to understand North Carolina. Now I figure that visiting all the national parks in the southeast region will help me become a southerner, even if I still sound like I grew up in Brooklyn.

1

THE GREAT OUTDOORS: THE MOUNTAINS

"In Wildness is the preservation of the world," Henry David Thoreau said. I wonder what he would think about the southeastern parks today. Should we make a distinction between untouched wilderness, like certain parts of Alaska, and wildness, land that's returning to its natural state and feels wild?

People have affected every area in the Southeast. Native Americans have lived here since time immemorial. Europeans settled and built houses and towns. They hunted, cleared the land, farmed, extracted minerals, and put in roads wherever they could. A combination of drought, logging, and wildfires denuded the mountain slopes.

When you discover a chimney or a house foundation on a trail, you realize that park visitors are not the first ones here. Still the national parks and preserves feel wild and green. Congress designated parts of the Everglades, Congaree, and Cumberland Island National Seashore as official wilderness areas, giving them an even higher level of protection.

We go to national parks for the great outdoors. Visitors expect mountains, trees, rivers, and great tracts of empty land. Most people admire the mountains from far away, but few climb them. In short, they think of Yosemite and Yellowstone. I like to refer to them as YY, the most testosterone-fueled parks. That's not as far-fetched and fanciful as it sounds, since Yellowstone was the nation's first national park in 1872. Congress granted Yosemite to the state of California in 1864 with the condition that it "shall be held for public use, resort, and recreation." In 1890, Yosemite became a national park.

People lived in Great Smoky Mountains National Park, the Everglades, and the Virgin Islands before they became national parks. For the most part, they weren't empty stretches of land. They have a human history. Acadia National Park in Maine, the first national park in the East, was created mostly of land donated by twentieth-century conservationists. The Smokies, authorized by Congress in 1926, was one of the first nature parks in the southeast region. At the time, logging companies and individual families owned the land, which the states of North Carolina and Tennessee purchased. Great Smoky Mountains National Park was created to protect the mountains, streams, and wildlife, but park management soon realized that they needed to save the cultural history as well.

At first glance, grouping this set of parks together may seem strange, but the mountain parks are arranged roughly in order of maximum altitude, the highest first. The mountains of the Smokies and the Appalachian Trail reach over six thousand feet, while Island Ford at Chattahoochee River National Recreational Area isn't even at nine hundred feet. However, you'll recognize that many plants are similar. People come to Mammoth Cave National Park to explore the caves. Yet there are miles of trails around the caves similar to those of the Smokies, though they're less rugged.

In the Southeast, you can't separate the wildness experience from its cultural history. So what would Thoreau think?

❦ Great Smoky Mountains National Park
Returning to wildness on Hazel Creek
North Carolina, Tennessee

Leading hikes for several outdoor groups has become my volunteer day job. The Smokies are my home park and I seem to be in one section of the park or another every week. The Smokies is the most visited national park in the country, but you wouldn't know this by walking the trails around Fontana Lake. Today I'm leading twenty people on the Hazel Creek Trail for the Great Smoky Mountains Association. The fastest way to get here is a thirty-minute boat shuttle across the lake to Proctor, an old logging town. We cross Hazel Creek on a solid bridge and start walking.

Fontana Lake, in the southwest corner of Great Smoky Mountains National Park, has been in the news for over seventy years. Few people know how to find it, fewer come here, but the regional media continues to write about the Road to Nowhere. A few years ago, even the *New York Times* sent reporters here.

Moses and Patience Proctor, the first white settlers, arrived on Hazel Creek in the early 1830s from Cades Cove. Maybe Cades Cove was too crowded for them even at the time. The Proctors built a cabin on what is now Proctor Cemetery, close to where they

13

lie under a modern granite gravestone.

By the turn of the twentieth century, logging companies were well established in the southern Appalachians. W. M. Ritter Lumber Company arrived in 1902 and started to log the Hazel Creek watershed a few years later. They built a railroad to bring timber from high up the cove. This was industrial-scale logging, and Proctor prospered. The town had electricity by 1907. At its height, Proctor had more than a thousand residents, with pool halls, barbershops, cafés, and a movie theater.

Ritter's loggers clear-cut the woods as quickly as they could, with no attempt to manage the forest in a sustainable manner. By 1928, having cut every tree worth logging, Ritter left the area, taking with them the infrastructure they had installed. Many logging families followed them to the Pacific Northwest. Those who stayed behind went back to subsistence farming.

We pass remains of the lumber mill, concrete foundations, and bits of large batteries from small-scale electrical storage. Yet, wildness permeates the trail. Hazel Creek flows free and clear. Anglers praise it as a great fishing spot. Rhododendrons have filled in every bit of land. On this warm August day, Solomon's plume is starting to fruit. White milkweeds line the trail, and asters proclaim that autumn is coming.

The trail is managed as an administrative road because park employees use it to maintain the Hall Cabin, our destination. Since the trail climbs ever so gently, I'd hoped that the group would stay together. However, by midmorning, some hikers have shot ahead of me. Others fall back. Marti Smith, the hike sweep, makes sure that everyone is OK.

When the United States entered World War II, demand for electricity to produce aluminum exploded. Alcoa transferred its land along the Little Tennessee River to the Tennessee Valley Authority (TVA) for the Fontana Project in exchange for future electric power. TVA built Fontana Dam to create electricity for aluminum smelting. The resulting impoundment flooded NC 288, the only road into the area, along with five communities now lying on the bottom of the lake. Residents had to move out of their homes, though many stayed in the area to work on Fontana Dam. Families lived in cabins, now part of Fontana Village, where our hiking group stayed last night. TVA then gave the land north of Fontana Lake to enlarge Great Smoky Mountains National Park.

If you walk a small section of the Lakeshore Trail, part of NC 288, you'll see several old car bodies sitting just off the trail. A tree has grown through one of them. Two cars are probably Fords, built in the mid-1930s. Another with the starter button on the floor could be a Plymouth, a budget car in those days. These cars probably weren't running very well ten years later. With gas and tire rationing, men off to war, and many women not able to drive, families left their cars behind when they moved out.

After walking five miles, we turn on Bone Valley Trail, a short trail leading to the Hall cabin, built in 1892. The Halls took in tourists who wanted to fish in the area before it became a park. We cross five minor streams, about calf deep on me, but I'm short. Each person takes the crossing a different way. I walk into the water without hesitation. My boots and socks get wet, but I've protected my feet from rocks, roots, and anything else that I can't see at the bottom of the stream.

Others change into water shoes, which offer less protection but keep their boots dry. A couple of hikers use flip-flops, which seems dangerous to the ankles. The rest just walk barefoot. A woman slips and falls in. When she gets up, it doesn't matter how wet her feet are.

By now, we've split into fast and slow groups. Everyone arrives at the Hall Cabin, our lunch spot, and we take the "class picture." I lead five hikers to the Bone Valley Cemetery. John, who's never been to a park cemetery, is almost speechless.

"How did these graves get here?" he asks.

"Well, this was a community," I say. We're all quiet and it sinks in. People lived here.

In 1943, the federal government promised to build a road to Bryson City on the North Shore of Fontana Lake after World War II, if Congress appropriated the money. While this promise lay dormant, NC 28, a modern highway, was constructed outside the park. Less than a mile of the North Shore Road was constructed on the western side. Outside of Bryson City, the park built six miles of road known as the Road to Nowhere, which ends in a tunnel. In 1971, the park stopped construction when they hit acid-bearing rock, because runoffs from the rock would pollute streams and Fontana Lake.

For years after TVA flooded NC 288, there was no practical way for descendants to take care of the graves left behind across the lake. The former residents and descendants had their first reunion in 1976 in the Bryson City area. Superintendent Boyd Evison asked visitors not to leave plastic flowers or other nonbiodegradable containers in the cemeteries in the park because there was no way to dispose of them. This type of pronouncement gives outsiders and the federal government a bad name.

According to knowledgeable locals, "That's what started the whole cemetery issue." The group created a cemetery association and demanded free transportation across Fontana Lake to the cemeteries on specific days. These occasions turned into Decoration Days, when families visit graves and keep in contact with each other.

The North Shore Road issue was revived again in 2001 when Congressman Charles Taylor, a Republican from western North Carolina, and Republican Senator Jesse Helms obtained $16 million to continue building the North Shore Road. This set off a process that evaluated the environmental impact of a thirty-five-mile road. The National Park Service held public input forums and accepted comments from anyone in the United States on various ways to resolve the 1943 agreement. Thousands of pages of testimony were generated, reviewed, and discussed. Descendants of the original settlers were the only ones who wanted a road in the park. Almost all comments were against the road and for a financial settlement with Swain County, where Fontana Dam is located, one of the four parties to the original agreement.

In December 2007, the Department of the Interior decided on a $52-million monetary settlement to Swain County instead of a road through one of the most pristine and untouched areas in the East. Though the park is now protected and the North Shore Road will never be built, Congress still has to approve all the funds to settle the 1943 agreement. As of now, compensation to Swain County is slow in coming.

We climb to Higdon Cemetery on the way back. Cemeteries were often placed on hilltops, saving the best bottomland for farming. Decoration Day here must have occurred recently because the graves are all neatly mounded, a Southern Appalachian tradition, and fresh plastic flowers stick out of the ground.

We walk at our own pace. The fast hikers have gathered in front of the Calhoun House, a frame house that is falling apart.

"Have you folks been inside?" I ask.

"No, we're waiting for you."

Today the Calhoun House, built in 1928, is the only structure left standing in Proctor. A broad covered porch runs the length of the front of the prim white-frame house. Granville Calhoun bought the house just as Ritter Lumber was leaving the area. Calhoun was a larger-than-life entrepreneur who took in visitors for fishing and exploring. A room off to the side with no access to the main house offered hospitality to tourists, a visiting preacher, or a teacher. The house had electricity, a hot water heater, running water, and even an indoor bathroom. The kitchen has the standard prewar cabinets; it looks a lot like my mother's kitchen in our inner-city apartment.

I give at least three separate tours inside the house as hikers arrive. Some are afraid to go into the house by themselves.

"No, there are no ghosts," I assure a woman, "but there are a couple of bats hanging from the ceiling."

Ken, our friendly boat captain, shows up on time with a huge cooler full of alcoholic drinks and sodas. I would kill for a hot cup of tea, but I'll have to wait until I get back to Asheville and make it myself.

༄ Appalachian National Scenic Trail
Maintaining a section of the A.T.
Georgia to Maine through fourteen states

The Appalachian National Scenic Trail (A.T.) may be the most famous hiking trail in the world, but what most folks know about it can be summarized in one word: thru-hiking. Many people who hike the A.T. in a year—the definition of thru-hiking—do it at a point of transition in their lives: graduation, retirement, losing a job or a life partner. The A.T. may be the most documented trail in the world with its books, movies, blogs, websites, and myths. Hikers come from around the world to walk it. A significant part of the experience is the people you meet and the friends you make on your hike. You won't be walking alone.

Yet, the A.T., currently estimated at 2,189 miles, is much more than a procession of hikers going from Springer Mountain, Georgia, to Katahdin, Maine, the classic, but not the only, way to walk the trail. Many others, including my husband, Lenny, and me, hike it in sections over many years. Once you complete the trail, you'll be forever known as a 2,000-miler and can put this achievement on your transcript and your tombstone. In 2014, 906 hikers reported completing the A.T., 783 of them as thru-hikers. The rest completed the trail as section hikers. Still many more get on the trail for a weekend or just a day.

Though the A.T. was declared complete in 1937, it wasn't until 1968 that it became the first National Scenic Trail under the National Trails System Act. The National Park Service delegated management responsibility for the trail to the Appalachian Trail Conservancy (ATC). A governmental body that owns the land, usually a national park or national forest, manages the land that the trail goes through, but the entire trail from Georgia to Maine is maintained by volunteers belonging to one of thirty-one trail maintaining clubs affiliated with ATC.

Lenny and I have been maintaining a section of the Appalachian Trail for over twenty-five years, first in New York State and now on the North Carolina–Tennessee border. For many years, we've been the proud adoptive parents of 4.9 miles from Devil Fork Gap to Rice Gap, located north of Great Smoky Mountains National Park and south of Hot Springs, North Carolina.

It's not a spectacular piece of trail. It has no historic cabin, shelter, or outstanding view. However, this plain duckling has some unusual features. The section wiggles south, even though you're hiking the A.T. north toward Maine. In May, the trail explodes with wildflowers. I've counted over forty-five species, and I'm hardly an expert. It's clear that people lived here. The trail has a two-grave cemetery and barbed-wire fences to contain cattle. Remains of two cabins that have been taken apart sit off the trail. Their logs have tumbled down over white metal kitchen cabinets. We've had to take out a toilet. A nameless waterfall has a large log across it, guaranteeing that its photo will never grace the pages of an outdoor calendar.

Our section of the A.T. goes through Cherokee National Forest. When their biologists want to create a clear-cut for wildlife management or need to burn a section, they might discuss it with ATC, but then they go ahead and do what they feel is right.

It's a long piece to maintain, though it doesn't seem like much when we hike it. At least four times a year, we drive two cars and put a car at each end. We don't want to walk our section twice, loaded down with clippers, Weed eater, shears, handsaws, and garbage bags. This section has little trash, compared to the bags and bags that we hauled out from our New York section. Clippings and branches are thrown off the trail. I feel good about breaking up campfire rings that have been built illegally right on the trail.

Carolina Mountain Club (CMC), my local hiking club, maintains ninety-two miles of the A.T., including nine shelters. The club takes its trail maintenance responsibilities seriously. Though we have only about one thousand members, we treat trail maintenance like a large hierarchical company. Lenny and I are among those who do the grunt work. We clip brush, clean water bars, pick up garbage, and take out small blowdowns. We also paint blazes using glossy white exterior paint. Though the label on the can says its paint is guaranteed for twenty-five years, we have to refresh the blazes every few years.

When we encounter a downed tree too big for our Silky Saw, a handsaw with a long handle, we call in the reinforcements, the CMC trail crew that wields chainsaws. CMC crews go out Mondays, Wednesdays, and Fridays year-round to do the heavy trail work. Most of these guys—and they're mostly guys—are way past retirement age with an average age of seventy.

When spring finally arrives, Carolina Mountain Club's A.T. coordinator sends out our first instructions.

"It's time to do the spring walk-through, clean water bars, and report problems on your A.T. section. We know that we have many fallen trees. Your input is going to be valuable for the crews to coordinate tree removal. The thru-hikers are coming. So get out there."

Bears have been active, prowling around several A.T. shelters, so Howard McDonald, our trail facility manager, put a volunteer crew together to install bear cables, similar to the ones in the Smokies. "We received a grant from North Carolina A.T. license plate money to cover the costs of equipment," he explains. "Frustrated bears and hikers playing Tarzan have caused some cable damage, but we're fixing and strengthening them to prevent this from happening again. We have a very good system that will last for many years. Hikers like it."

By early summer, blackberry canes may overwhelm the path by projecting their thorny lateral branches in all directions. Since we live in a temperate rainforest, we can't leave a trail alone. In a couple of years, the trail would be so overgrown that we couldn't find it again. We need to use a Weed eater to keep the growth in check. Blackberry bushes might be easy to grow in a garden because the plant doesn't demand much sunlight or good soil. Those qualities make the same plant a nuisance on the trail. In the Southern Appalachians, poison ivy also grows like it's on steroids. But I'm thankful that there's none on our A.T. section.

Adopting a trail is like adopting a highway. You get your own piece of real estate with magnificent views. You don't need a lot of experience or powerful tools. You're the eyes and ears of the trail crew. You do what you can and report what you can't do. You work at your own pace. In our hiking club, adopting a piece of the A.T. is quite prestigious. If a trail maintainer gives up his or her piece of trail, another member on the waiting list snaps it up almost immediately.

This is not episodic volunteering. We don't have a trail

maintaining day for the whole club, followed by a barbecue and a band. Rather, section maintainers, as we're called, usually work by themselves, tending the same piece of trail for years. I don't particularly enjoy trail maintenance; I'd rather be hiking. Maintaining is slow and tedious. By evening, my back is usually stiff and sore; I sleep on the floor and maybe take a couple of aspirins. But I do it because it's part of my hiking life. I don't like cleaning my boots either, but that's also part of hiking.

I get my reward for all this work when I meet hikers on our section. I stop them long enough to introduce myself. "We're your happy trail maintainers. Trails don't maintain themselves," I say. "Volunteers maintain trails. That's how the whole A.T. gets taken care of." They probably never thought about how and who keeps their trail clear.

In exchange for listening to me, I volunteer to take out their garbage. They're surprised because they expect a piece of chocolate or a granola bar. But I remember that when I hiked the A.T., getting rid of trash was the most annoying part of the trail routine. And hikers are grateful.

✢Appalachian National Scenic Trail
Ridgerunning on the Appalachian Trail
Georgia to Maine through fourteen states

"I started my ridgerunning season this year on February 26 at Cosby Knob Shelter. It was four degrees," Billy Jones says. This is Billy's third year as a ridgerunner on the Appalachian Trail in Great Smoky Mountains National Park.

You can think of a ridgerunner as an A.T. concierge. "I stop and talk with all hikers on the trail, whether backpackers or day hikers. Basically, I'm a steward and an ambassador for the trail."

Billy Jones, fifty-three years old, is slim and sturdy, with a neatly trimmed beard and mustache. His uniform consists of tan zip-off pants and a light green button-down shirt with an Appalachian Trail patch on his left shirtsleeve. Billy grew up in middle Georgia. After graduating from Auburn University with a degree in industrial management, he had a long career in medical insurance. In 2006, after he was downsized, he took the opportunity to thru-hike the A.T.

"There are no guarantees in life. If you have the means, go and do that thru-hike now. Don't wait until you retire," he says. A thru-hike makes you focus on what's important.

"I had a friend with MS who gave me a bandanna for my A.T. hike," Billy says. "I carried that bandanna the whole way. If I was facing another uphill slog or rainy day on the trail and having a pity party, I would look at the bandanna and remember how lucky I am." When Billy got home, he simplified his life very deliberately.

After reaching Katahdin, in Maine, the northern end of the A.T., Billy went back to work for a while to make sure his two daughters would have enough money for college. Once the girls graduated and dropped off his personal payroll, Billy's thoughts returned to the A.T. and becoming a ridgerunner.

"You're going to do what? You're crazy," his friends said. But he was looking for a simpler, more enjoyable life. Now, ridgerunning is his dream job.

"I go from shelter to shelter during the thru-hiking season, which is usually March 15 to May 15. A.T. hikers have been starting earlier and earlier. In mid-March, I met forty-four thru-hikers in the park. Then you have the college students who start on Springer Mountain in May and feel they can race through 2,189 miles, be up in Maine in three months, and back at school by September."

From Wednesday through Sunday, Billy walks about fifty-five miles from Spence Field to Davenport Gap, where the A.T. leaves the Smokies and heads north. The next week, he hikes southbound. Fletcher Meadema, a second ridgerunner, follows the same route going the opposite way. A third ridgerunner, Carl Goodman, walks from Fontana Dam, where the A.T. enters the park from the south, to Spence Field. Carl, seventy-three years old, has been walking this route for thirteen years, still using an old-fashioned external frame pack. After the end of the thru-hiking season in the Smokies, Billy is the only ridgerunner in the park. He works through October and has the longest season of any A.T. ridgerunner from Georgia to Maine.

Billy checks backcountry shelter permits. "I can give out shelter permits on the spot, if a hiker forgot to get one in advance, but I don't handle money," he explains. "Hikers have seventy-two hours to pay for their permit after they leave the park."

He's also a garbage man. "I take a lot of trash out of shelters. Hikers leave food and clothing in shelters, thinking someone might be able to use the stuff, but all that stuff is trash that I have to take out," Billy says. "In the park, there's little litter actually on the trail."

At the start of his five-day stint, Billy carries twenty-eight pounds on his back. But his pack might grow to thirty-five pounds by the time he finishes because of all the trash he picks up. "I may be the only hiker whose pack is heavier at the end of my back-packing trip than at the beginning," he jokes.

And those outhouses you encounter along the trail? Someone has to service them. "I do what's called privy management," Billy says, explaining that he cleans the seat, sweeps the floor, and fills a bag with mulch. A cup or two is tossed into the privy after each use to help break the waste down. He also disperses the mulch cone—cone deposition, as it's delicately called—that tends to build up. Each privy has a long-handled shovel used to remix the waste matter.

"Some shelters in the national parks still don't have privies and it's disgusting. I'm on a campaign to have a privy at every shelter. When a shelter doesn't have a privy to concentrate human waste, backpackers use whatever spot they can find."

He's also a teacher and a cheerleader. Billy instructs hikers on how to use the bear cables that enable backpackers to hoist their packs out of reach of the park's black bears. Friends of the Smokies (FOTS) funds the installation and care of bear cables, along with many other park projects.

At shelters, he sometimes helps people go through their packs. Inexperienced backpackers bring industrial-sized toiletries, huge boxes of talcum powders, and large tubes of toothpaste. "They also like to look inside my pack to see what I carry."

Ridgerunners do their best to teach Leave No Trace principles and ethics to hikers they meet without seeming as if they're lecturing to them. "Most hikers listen and try to comply, but it's a constant battle, which is one reason we're out here," Billy says.

To handle the crowd that often shows up at backcountry shelters, Billy tries to reach a shelter no later than three p.m. "On a nasty day, everyone wants to be in a shelter," he says. "Once I had forty-two people at Tricorner Knob Shelter, a space meant for twelve people. The rest slept on the ground around the shelter."

Sometimes, though, personalities flare up among hikers looking to stay dry. A.T. thru-hikers are given preference for a handful of spots in shelters when the bulk of the hikers come through the Smokies.

"I'm not a law enforcement ranger, but I do have a radio," Billy says when asked about bickering that arises between thru-hikers and those simply out to enjoy a few days in the Smokies. "Thru-hikers have to stay in a shelter if there's room."

Billy had a major problem a couple of years ago during a heavy rain. Thru-hikers wanted to stay in the shelter another night. "When I got to the shelter, I told them that a new group was coming tonight and they'd have to move along." The hikers stood their ground and gave him grief.

"I called the law enforcement ranger, who said the hikers needed to leave the shelter. The hikers cursed me out. I told them that if a ranger had to walk three miles in the rain to talk to them, he wasn't going to be happy. They finally got the message, left the shelter, and got back on the trail."

After learning that Billy is on the trail for eight months a year, the subject always turns to food. "When it's cold, I don't like to mess with a stove. Instead, I buy a huge sub sandwich, cut it up, and make a few dinners out of that. I buy single servings of fruit like mandarin oranges and a dessert, usually a granola bar," Billy says. When it's warmer, he carries a stove to boil water and rehydrates a meal in a ziplock bag.

When it comes to food, Billy is a real Southerner. He'll eat an oatmeal cream pie or a MoonPie and a granola bar for breakfast. He also loves Willy Wonka SweeTARTS jelly beans and stocks up on them after Easter for the rest of the season.

On days off, ridgerunners can stay at the Soak Ash Creek House, close to Gatlinburg, Tennessee. The comfortable house, donated to the park by Friends of the Smokies, even includes a washer and dryer. Here, Billy writes his report, outlining his encounters on the trail, goes through his email, cleans up, and rests. However, Holly Scott, his fiancée, often wants to go hiking or kayaking on her day off. Billy met Holly, the marketing manager at FOTS, when he dropped off pictures that she could use.

He's obviously smitten by Holly. He even gets along well with her dog. On their second date, Holly met him at the Mount Collins Shelter. She borrowed some backpacking equipment and walked up the trail carrying a pizza, a huge Mountain Dew, and homemade lemon bars. "It's nice to know someone who understands what I do," Billy says.

FOTS has supported the ridgerunner program since 2004. The park requested $37,600 on their 2014 Needs List to fund the program, which includes the long-season position, Billy's job, and the two short-season positions. The Friends group provides funding to the park that in turn passes the money to ATC to hire the ridgerunners and pay their salaries.

The ATC ridgerunner program started in the Northeast in 1970 and in the Smokies in 1992. Now there are over thirty ridgerunners along the A.T. And yes, there are and have been women ridgerunners. Susan Powell was the long-season ridgerunner in the Smokies in 2009.

Though spending so much time in the mountains hiking might seem odd for someone who had a well-paying career, Billy Jones takes delight in his life. "So many people are scared to do what they want to do. When I got my finances in order, I asked why I wanted to slave away at a desk. I eliminated clutter. Now I do what I want to do."

Blue Ridge Parkway
Building a trail at 6,000 feet
North Carolina, Virginia

The Smokies is a hiker's park, but the Blue Ridge Parkway is dubbed "America's favorite drive." The Parkway, the second most visited park unit in the country after Golden Gate National Recreation Area, is enchanting in October, when leaf color is at its best. Visitors drive up to Waterrock Knob, an overlook on the Blue Ridge Parkway at milepost 451.2, and photograph the layers of overlapping ridges. Some walk the half mile to what is the highest trail on the Parkway. Little do they know the work that is going on just below them. It's another world that Parkway visitors probably can't imagine.

The Carolina Mountain Club (CMC) trail crew cuts down trees, crushes rocks, removes roots, and moves earth to build 2.2 miles of the Mountains-to-Sea Trail (MST) out of forest land that winds along the Blue Ridge Parkway. Almost all the volunteers are over sixty years old, many much older. They come out week after week to work on this piece. Most trail workers aren't hikers and have no desire to walk other sections of the MST. They're here to build, not hike.

The MST stretches over a thousand miles across North Carolina. It starts on Clingmans Dome in Great Smoky Mountains National Park, takes various trails through the park, and continues on the Blue Ridge Parkway. Though the public thinks of the Parkway as a recreational road through the mountains, there are miles of walking trail as well. Hikers and visitors recognize the ubiquitous white circles used to blaze the MST.

The Blue Ridge Parkway meanders through the Appalachian Mountains, from the southern end of Shenandoah National Park in Virginia at milepost 0 to the entrance of Great Smoky Mountains National Park in Cherokee, North Carolina, at milepost 469. The scenic road was started in 1935 during the Great Depression, and finally completed in 1987. Most people drive a section of the twisty, curvy Parkway, stopping at overlooks and picnicking in the small parks just off the road. Since the maximum speed limit is 45 miles per hour, and truck traffic isn't allowed, the Parkway attracts road bikers. Besides the MST, the Parkway has miles of trail, emanating from the road. The Blue Ridge Parkway is considered a park, not a commuter thoroughfare, so the road isn't salted or sanded when it snows. The dangerous section is just gated and closed until the snow melts.

Building the 2.2-mile piece of the MST on Blue Ridge Parkway land from the east side of Waterrock Knob to Fork Ridge Overlook required over six thousand hours of work over a six-year period.

Volunteers cut through the rocks, roots, and trees so hikers can walk comfortably. It's not easy to build trail at almost six thousand feet above sea level. The season is short, May to October, and depends on the Parkway being open. In the winter, the freeze-thaw cycle plays havoc with the trail surface. Rocks pop out, trees fall, and water and ice are all over the trail. The first job in the spring is to clean up after winter.

CMC volunteers constructed and now maintain over 140 miles of the MST. Once the sections on either side of Waterrock Knob are completed, you'll be able to walk over 350 miles on footpaths zigzagging on the Parkway to Stone Mountain State Park. The trail ends at Jockey's Ridge State Park on the Outer Banks. The MST is a North Carolina state trail and ultimately under the responsibility of the NC State Parks system. But the state isn't building the trail. It's an all-volunteer effort.

When the crew finished this section of the MST, they invited Kate Dixon, Executive Director of Friends of the MST, from Raleigh to see the new piece of trail. "You know, it's a royal visit, like when the queen visits her far-flung colonies," I explained to Ann Hendrickson, our host, when I told her that Dixon and I were coming to their work site.

We walk the section to admire the trail work, while Hendrickson, one of only two women on the crew, explains the effort. From the ramp on the Waterrock Knob Trail, we climb down 120 steps made out of locust wood. Trail builders love locust trees since the wood is hard, strong, and virtually impervious to fungal decay.

Trail designing and building is a craft, mostly learned by the apprentice method from more experienced volunteers. Building a trail out of a side hill is slow and laborious. The small, narrow-track bulldozer used by professional construction crews, while acceptable for trails in a housing development, doesn't work here because these earthmovers destroy too much forest. The MST trail crews don't use mechanized tools, other than chain saws.

To ensure that the trail will last, the builders put down a layer of crushed rock. They don't bring in material from the outside. Every rock has been moved and broken up on-site. A layer of dirt is placed on top of the rocks. All the while, the crew studies the landscape to see if a tree on the high side of the trail is compromised and could fall in the next storm.

The crew moves boulders, some as big as VW Bugs. "You better trust your crew members if you're moving a rock downhill," Hendrickson emphasizes. The rocks look like they've always been here. "These rocks are like my children. I know them all." And she does. As we walk down the trail, she points out a flat-looking rock where I'm standing, which was pried out of the left side of the hill.

"It was that flat? Or did you chip away at it?" I ask.

"We did reshape it a little, but we placed the pointy end down, so hikers would have a smoother surface to walk on."

Hendrickson has been part of the CMC Friday Crew for over six years. She retired from doing wildlife research in developing countries, though she occasionally still takes on an interesting assignment. After the trail-building season is over, Hendrickson will be off to Bhutan. She was a serious athlete as a child and young adult, first as a gymnast, then as a speed skater, culminating in her participation in the Winter Olympics in Lake Placid in 1980.

"I work like I skate," she likes to say. "I'm not the fastest, but I can go all day." Trail workers need endurance.

CMC is the oldest and largest hiking and trail maintaining club in Western North Carolina, probably in the whole state. The club, with over a thousand members, celebrated its ninetieth anniversary a couple of years ago. They offer three or four hikes a week, year round. Seven trail crews go out regularly to maintain the MST and Appalachian Trail and other trails in the mountains.

Every Friday, the Waterrock Knob gang leaves Asheville at

eight a.m. and drives an hour to the site. They work for five hours and are back at three p.m., exhausted, muddy, and happy. The first concern is always safety. The second objective is to have fun so that volunteers will want to come back week after week. And oh yes, they also want to get some work done.

Why do volunteers come out every week? Digging in the dirt is good, fulfilling work, where you can see results. Most crew members had stationary jobs during their career years and now want to build stuff. But trail builders keep stressing the camaraderie. Several drive almost three hours one way from Charlotte to work for the day.

As we walk down, Dixon and I meet the group members and learn their specialties. Skip Shelton, the crew leader, gave out assignments this morning. Some build a couple of steps. Others crush rock to cover bare ground. The third crew completes the last bit of construction in the middle section. At the end of the day, they'll pull out their tools and walk them down to the cars. Next Friday, they'll blaze the trail with the familiar white circles. Another 2.2-mile section on Parkway land will be ready for hikers.

Skip Shelton has been the crew leader for three years. Originally from Minnesota, he worked as an engineer for DuPont Imaging Systems most of his career, much of it locally, before the site became DuPont State Recreational Forest. He's a big man who knows how to uproot a rock and move it safely. Skip shows us a digging bar, which weighs twenty-five pounds. On the trail, digging bars are used to pry rocks out of the ground and pound down the soil.

"There's lots of muck when you move rock and build water bars. We were in mud up to the tops of our boots a while back," Skip says, pointing to a water bar. A water bar is a diagonal channel across the trail that diverts surface water off the walking path.

But it takes more than strength and trail-building knowledge to motivate a volunteer group. Since trail crews accept all comers, it's up to the leader to assign work that a person can handle safely. But no mollycoddling.

In his lecture this morning, Skip said, "This is our last day to work on this piece. Don't walk by a problem. Fix it." Professional volunteer coordinators might blanch at this straightforward order.

Wayne Steinmetz specializes in rocks. "Rocks need to fit in just so," Steinmetz says. *Steinmetz* in German means stonemason. "Probably my ancestors in the middle ages were stonemasons."

Bob Lindsey pries a loose rock from the top of the trail. He calls himself a mentee of Lee Barry, a CMC member who still holds the record for the oldest person to thru-hike the Appalachian Trail. Barry was eighty-one years old. In turn, Barry was a protégé of Earl Shaffer, the first person to thru-hike the A.T. in 1948. Hikers and trail maintainers have their own rock stars.

When Lindsey comes to the work site, he picks up older maintainers who may have stopped driving. The senior man here today is over ninety-one years old. He's no longer able to move rocks, but he rakes leaves onto the trail, which gives it a finished look and protects it from the elements.

Water gushes out of four springs onto the trail. Long-distance hikers need regular, dependable water sources. However, water is an enemy of the trail and must be diverted to prevent erosion. The crew has built innumerable water bars out of logs and stones.

Piet Bodenhorst, a CMC crew elder, is a burly man with baby blue eyes who wears a red bandanna to catch the sweat off his head. "This section will require a lot of maintenance because of the water. It was a great challenge to build," he says. Besides working on the MST, an access trail was cut in the middle of the section so that the crew could get to their work area faster. "We'll have to close the access trail in the middle so that hikers don't get confused. I hope the winter will heal the trail, that is, make it less visible."

"You remember the piece of trail that you personally built. Trail work gives me a sense of accomplishment." Bodenhorst is a manager through and through. A retired chemist and VP for a carpeting company, Bodenhorst has worked on a trail crew since 1999. "What are we going to build after next year? We're thinking about Fork Ridge to Scott Creek Overlook."

"It's only a half mile long. Hikers can walk it on the Parkway," I say. When I walked the MST across North Carolina, I was on the Blue Ridge Parkway for eight miles in this area.

"But the hiking experience is so much better when it's in the woods," Bodenhorst says. "Right now, Parkway land in this half mile is so narrow, it's just a cliff. It would be impossible to build trail. The Parkway needs to acquire land here from private landowners."

"The skill and artistry of the trail is extraordinary," says Dixon. "So many people drive the Parkway and stop at Waterrock Knob. Even if they don't hike one thousand miles across North Carolina, they can walk a mile and get a good feel for the trail."

As we leave, Ann Hendrickson calls after us. "Remember to tell them this is a true team effort."

❧ Little River Canyon National Preserve
Up and down to the river
Alabama

I rarely have a companion on my national park expeditions, other than my husband on occasion. But Beth Ransom, a hiking buddy, was curious about the mountains in Northeast Alabama and joined me for a day at Little River Canyon. I warned her that I spend a lot of time at the visitor center, reading the exhibits, but she promised she would be patient.

Little River Canyon is a hotbed of activity. The Little River starts at Lookout Mountain near Chattanooga and flows on top of the Cumberland Plateau. The eleven-mile Canyon Rim Drive follows the western side of the twisty canyon, with several overlooks and trails to the river. The Little River ends at Weiss Lake, south of the park.

The Canyon doesn't have its own visitor center. Jacksonville State University Field School operates an information center, open from ten a.m. to four p.m. Beth and I appear at the gates two hours early and decide to come back after we finish the Canyon Rim Drive.

Our first stop, Beaver Pond Trail, takes us on a flat loop, where we find the remains of an encounter between a snake and a bird. A pile of bones, which look like chicken bones, are scattered on the ground. A backbone lies close by. I shoot several close-ups like a police photographer but without the high-quality camera or skill. Jewelweed, wintergreen, and aster line the trail. It turns out to be the only flat trail in the park.

Farther on the drive, we stop at Mushroom Rock, a group of huge boulders with a pattern like a rhinoceros. The rocks form a small maze. One rock sits between the two lanes of Little Canyon Drive. No one can miss this stop.

Several trails, such as the steep Lower Two-Mile Trail, take us down to the river. At the bottom of one river section, two couples have backpacked their small children. The parents get ready to go back up with their precious load. Good for them! They aren't waiting until the kids grow up, when it might be too late to get them interested in the outdoors.

Trees discreetly camouflage a few private houses. Dirt roads take off from Little Canyon Road. Because Little River Canyon is a preserve, bow hunting and trapping are still allowed. It's probably the other way around; it was declared a preserve so that people could continue to hunt and trap. Little River was designated an Alabama Wild and Scenic River in 1969, giving it a lot of protection. It became part of the National Park System in 1992.

After the Eberhart Point trailhead, the road is rougher, steeper, and less traveled. Several back roads and driveways emanate from here, along with more private houses. The drive ends at Canyon Mouth Picnic Area, with a gentle trail up the canyon, where Beth and I meet our first rangers of the day.

Once at the southern end of the canyon, we drive back up Shinbone Valley to Little River Falls. Most visitors congregate here because the parking area is on a main road with the waterfall only a few minutes' walk away. A park volunteer, stationed in the parking lot, gives us a map. She's wearing dressy slacks and a sweater, with a Volunteers in the Park (VIP) patch pinned to her sleeve. She tries to explain how to get to the falls, but her instructions are very confusing. Looking at her stylish open-toed sandals, I imagine that she's never gone down to the falls herself. Nevertheless, she's a volunteer, so she must care about this park.

Little River Falls drops forty-five feet into a large pool, starting Little River Canyon. The top of the falls is rocky and flat. Everywhere, signs in several languages tell you not to get too close to the falls or cross rushing streams. However, a large family sits close to the edge, watching their teenage son and daughter cross and recross a side stream for a perfect picture. I hold my breath as I watch. The area could use a roving ranger in uniform.

By the time we get back to the parking lot, the information center has long been shut tight. Beth and I may not have learned all the intricacies of the preserve, but we descended into the canyon at several points and felt the power of the river. The next river unit is so large that it has several information centers and available rangers to answer questions.

∽✦∾

ᏣᎪ Big South Fork National River and Recreation Area
Exploring the Cumberland Plateau
Kentucky, Tennessee

I learned a while back that when you're a Smokies hiker, trails in every other Southeastern national park seem easy. The hills are rolling, not as steep as in the Smokies or on the mountain section of the Mountains-to-Sea Trail. Each park has to be taken on its own merits. You can't compare Great Smoky Mountains National Park, with a maximum altitude of over 6,600 feet at Clingmans Dome, with Big South Fork National River and Recreation Area (BISO), which protects the south fork of the Cumberland River and the canyon it created. Here, the maximum altitude is only 1,745 feet. It's not the absolute altitude that counts but the relative change between the top and the valley. Even so, the climbs here are shorter and gentler.

BISO is not a national park but a recreation area, which means it's more macho. You can hunt, run around in your ATV in selected places, raft, kayak, mountain bike, and even take your dog on hiking trails, if it's leashed. But I didn't try any of these other activities, except for petting a couple of dogs, since I stuck to hiking trails. The park was established in 1974, but it was years before there was enough infrastructure for visitors.

At Bandy Creek Visitor Center, Ranger Mary Grimm is eager to share her park with me. She grew up in the BISO area.

"My great-great . . . I lose the number of greats . . . grandfather Jonathan Blevins built the first hunting camp here in 1817," she says.

This camp eventually became Charit Creek Lodge, a walk-in lodge in the park. She offers several hiking suggestions. "My favorite is Angel Falls Overlook Trail to the view." And she doesn't even warn me that the trail is labeled as strenuous. Thumbs up for Ranger Grimm.

I drive back down to the river, park, cross the bridge, and follow the John Muir Trail, which some refer to as "the other John Muir Trail." In 1867, Muir walked about one thousand miles from Indiana to Florida, a journey he wrote about in his book *A Thousand-Mile Walk to the Gulf.*

Spring has arrived at BISO with sessile (maroon-colored) trillium, bloodroot, trout lilies, and hepatica. The trail, blazed with a blue outline of Muir's face, meanders between steep rock walls and the river. After a series of switchbacks, I reach the rocky overlook with an expansive view of the curve in the river. But where are the falls? Two backpackers, father and son, eating lunch up here are just as puzzled.

Together, we figure out that the falls must be the rapids in the river. It turns out that in 1954, before the park was established, a couple of local fishermen blasted huge boulders in the river to improve boating and fishing. Instead, they created a dangerous rapid. I'm still amazed at people who feel they can damage property that isn't theirs.

At the end of my hike, I check back with Ranger Grimm to let her know that I found the falls. And who should be there behind the desk with her? Ranger Bill Herman, who worked at Oconaluftee Visitor Center in the Smokies, is now a permanent ranger here. This is not the first time that I've run into rangers I met in other parks. That's why I always wear a shirt or hat that says Smokies.

BISO, with four hundred miles of trail, isn't just about the river. The appeal is the isolation that you feel in the gorge, which is lined with high rock walls. On my second day in the park, I see no one on Twin Arches Loop Trail, probably the most popular trail in the park.

The magnificent Twin Arches are just as impressive as the rock formations out west. The difference is that here the arches aren't in the desert, where they stand out. Our arches have trees in the way, so they don't photograph as well. I head to Charit Creek Lodge, a walk-in lodge that can be reached in 1.8 miles from the trailhead.

I get here at about eleven o'clock, in time to have coffee with Matt Peterson, who works at the lodge. Charit Creek Lodge, which they describe as a hostel, serves meals with alcohol, offers a place to sleep, and even has showers. While guests have to walk in or ride a horse, the lodge is serviced by a dirt road. Therefore, the staff can go into town—probably Jamestown, Tennessee—and resupply as often as necessary. With new ownership, the emphasis is on farm-to-table food, which, as Peterson points out, is what it was in the old days.

Charit Lodge used to be a hog farm and hunting lodge. Unlike the Smokies, which found itself with a hog problem not of its own making, here previous owners brought in hogs for hunting, albeit before BISO became a park. Wild hogs root for food in the dirt and leave the ground churned up as if it had been run through with a rototiller.

On the continuation of the loop, the rock shelters and cliffs really pop out. The trail runs above Charit Creek. Native Americans, settlers, and miners digging for saltpeter used rock shelters. Water drips through pocket canyons and down rock ledges, creating multi-colored streaks. I could be here for a week, photographing each rock formation. But I need to move on to a different part of the park.

After two days of hiking in BISO, I head for Blue Heron Mine, or Mine 18, an abandoned coal-mining town. Most visitors take a tourist train from Stearns, the same train route that miners used to get in and out of this isolated place, but the train doesn't arrive until almost noon. So I drive down the serpentine road and get here about nine a.m. as Ranger Chelsea Lauber opens up the tiny visitor center and bookstore.

"Are you here from the Smokies?" Ranger Lauber asks. Oh my gosh, have I been visiting parks this long? Not only do I recognize rangers, but they recognize me. She also worked at Oconaluftee Visitor Center in the Smokies for Supervisory Ranger Lynda Doucette for several seasons. Now, Lauber is here in a permanent position, and I congratulate her.

I'm the only visitor this morning, so I enjoy a great introduction to the Blue Heron mining site.

Blue Heron was one of many coal camps in the BISO area, owned by Stearns Coal and Lumber Company, this one active from 1937 to 1962. The tipple, one of the few original structures, is a sorting mechanism, which crushed, separated, and sized coal from nearby mines. The park didn't want visitors to explore old coal mines, so they collapsed and closed them.

The coal company decided that this mine was no longer profitable and moved on, taking many buildings with them. The structures were only meant to last fifty years anyway, and most lapsed into decay. There are no original houses, schools, or churches. When the park recreated the community in the 1980s, it built open metal shells, which they call ghost structures. Each shell is built on the approximate site of the original buildings, replicating the size and orientation of the first structures. The shells contain displays and an oral history program told by the original residents of the Blue Heron community.

The concrete outline of the original bathhouse remains. It was important for the miners to have a place to clean up before going home. Enough coal dust was flying around in the camp that the men didn't want to bring any extra dirt in their houses.

Blue Heron has all the conventional trappings of the isolated coal camps that you read about. The school had one teacher for eight grades and about thirty students. Few children went beyond eighth grade since the high school was in Whitley, accessible only by train. I went to high school by train as well, but it was a Brooklyn subway, which ran very frequently. The Southern Baptist church was the center of community life. Strong faith and coal mining seemed to go together because mines were isolated, dangerous, and dark.

The camps didn't have medical facilities—a glaring omission. A sick person had to go by train to Stearns. The camp probably had informal emergency treatment but no building or nurse. The company store took scrip money. The displays even quote its most famous line: *I owe my soul to the company store.* Life was tough on women, who kept cleaning coal dust, nurturing few aspirations beyond wife and mother. Even so, women had more freedoms in mining camps than on the farms because here they were less secluded and belonged to a community.

As I walk around, I keep thinking about the end date: 1962. I was in high school in 1962. Where were you in '62? I know, most of you weren't born in 1962.

ᘒ Obed Wild and Scenic River
Keeping it wild
Tennessee

Every national park unit I visited has some unique characteristic that sets it apart. It seems that Obed is the only wild and scenic river managed by the National Park Service and located in the Southeast. Little River Canyon in Alabama, though scenic, certainly isn't wild. There we walked to the dam and saw houses above the river. If you look at a picture of both rivers, they look like they're at the bottom of a canyon, but it's the surroundings that count.

The Obed and its tributaries are pristine. The flow of the river carved amazing gorges for thousands of years. Only portions of the four streams that make up the Obed unit are in the Wild and Scenic program. The National Wild and Scenic Rivers System, created by Congress in 1968, preserves certain rivers with outstanding natural, cultural, and recreational values in a free-flowing condition for the enjoyment of present and future generations. Note that I'm only including rivers managed by the National Park Service. Rivers like the Chattooga are wild and scenic, but managed by other agencies. If you make the category small enough, everything can be the only or first.

The visitor center in Wartburg, Tennessee, northwest of Oak Ridge, is not on the river. Because the park unit is so spread out, with only a few access points to the streams, the park probably decided to make the visitor center accessible. I wonder how many people stop at the visitor center and never make it to the river itself.

The narrator in the orientation film, *The Obed—Find Yourself Here*, says, "God made three beautiful places: Garden of Eden, Obed . . . ," and I never catch the third place. The video stresses the climbing, paddling, and fishing opportunities here. While rock climbing, a woman slips, gets caught by her rope, but recovers nicely. I gasp, but not as loudly as when I watch a girl, maybe six years old, walking on the river rocks, barefoot. What was the park service thinking, showing a visitor barefoot on slippery rocks?

The Obed River and its two main tributaries, Clear Creek and Daddy's Creek, cut into the Cumberland Plateau of East Tennessee, providing some of the most rugged scenery in the Southeast. Paddlers come from all over the world to run this river.

I drive down to Lily Bridge across Clear Creek. Like a true New Yorker who's always anxious about finding a place to park, I stop at the first parking area I see and grab my pack. A steep trail takes me on a historic bridge to the overlook. When I walk past the overlook, I realize that I could have driven a little farther and walked a flat trail to the view. But I would have missed the layered boulders, which look like an uneven multi-tiered cake, where climbers have left metal chains with hanging loops on the end.

At the overlook, if you gaze up and out, you'll see no sign of civilization. Maybe this is what Daniel Boone saw when he walked through this area heading west.

⌖Chattahoochee River National Recreation Area
Atlanta's playground
Georgia

I feel really silly. I planned for a day at Chattahoochee River National Recreation Area just north of Atlanta, but the morning looks like a complete washout. The forecast predicts 100 percent rain and a good chance of thunderstorms. But I'm in the park on a wet Sunday and I can't wait for perfect weather. I have nothing else to do but to continue with my plans.

I'm still questioning what it means to visit a national park unit. It's somewhere between getting my passport stamped at the visitor center and hiking all the trails, but that's a wide range. I knew that the visitor center was going to be open at nine a.m., rain or shine. I can rely on a prompt opening in almost any park. But was I going to be the only visitor?

The park is a forty-eight-mile linear series of stops, on both sides of the Chattahoochee River from Lake Sidney Lanier to the northern outskirts of Atlanta. Created in 1978 during the Carter administration, the park protects the river and gives Atlanta folks another place to get outdoors. President Jimmy Carter used to enjoy kayaking down the river.

I head to the park headquarters at Island Ford Visitor Contact Station. As soon as I drive into the park, it's obvious that I'm hardly the only one visiting on this cold, wet day. A woman in no-nonsense rain gear pounds an Orienteering Today sign into the ground. Cars with kayaks on their roofs turn off on side roads.

The visitor center was the summer home of Samuel D. Hewlett, a prominent Atlanta attorney. Built between 1936 and 1941, the house was sold to the Buckhead Century Club in 1950 and became, in part, a gambling club. When Georgia changed its gambling laws, the club couldn't make a go of it and sold the house to the Atlanta Baptist Assembly for a camp. How's that for a switch in purpose? A conservancy acquired the building and land in 1979, and passed it on to the park service. But that's only the story of the Island Ford section. Each section has its own history of how it became incorporated within the park.

I can only spend so much time talking to the ranger and looking around the beautiful building. A man, dressed for rain, invites me to orienteer with their group, but I decline since they're not starting until eleven a.m. I don't want to wait around and drink coffee for the next two hours.

I walk about three to four mostly flat miles. The trail follows the twists and turns of the Chattahoochee River, climbing past over-hanging rocks. Canada geese seem to thrive in the rain. As I circle back toward the parking lot, I meet orienteers running, walking, or ambling with their map and compass. It's a busy place on a wet, gloomy day. I'm going to have to return on a sunny Sunday.

᪣ Mammoth Cave National Park
Working a crowd
Kentucky

Mammoth Cave is much busier than the Chattahoochee Recreation area, maybe because it's the oldest tourist attraction in North America. The first people probably entered Mammoth Cave about four thousand years ago. Tourists started coming in

1816—before Hot Springs, Arkansas, and before Niagara Falls became popular—attracted by the mystery and grandeur of the seemingly endless underground passages. In the visitor center, an LED display says "400 miles of passageways in the cave, as of 2013." Cavers, scientists, and adventurers keep discovering more. It's a shallow cave with many mysteries.

"There's no end in sight. Mapping and exploration are never ending," says an explorer in the visitor center film.

I'm on a Star Chamber tour, one of many National Park Service cave tours. Tonight, I'm seeing the cave as nineteenth-century visitors might have experienced it. We carry lanterns instead of depending on the usual overhead electric lights. Ranger Shannon Hurley, who lives locally, is our guide. He preps us with all the usual no-nos before we go into the cave—no smoking, eating, touching rocks. But there's a new one.

"If you hit your head on a low rock, watch your language. We don't want to increase children's vocabulary in a negative manner." That's followed by warnings of how difficult this tour is: "260 stairs with an elevation change of 160 feet. If you have heart or lung trouble, knee or back problems . . . It's very difficult to rescue someone in a cave." But no one backs out of the tour.

We walk down the Historic Entrance, a natural entrance, where prehistoric people first entered the cave. Skeletons were found in the cave. One man was crushed by a rock. The first explorers may have gone in for gypsum, now used mostly for drywalling.

"The old Hostess Twinkies had gypsum as well," Ranger Hurley says. "It was supposed to make the cupcakes light and fluffy."

One day, at the turn of the nineteenth century, John Houchins went out hunting. At the top of the ravine, he saw a black bear and took a shot but missed. "He was obviously not a native Kentuckian," Ranger Hurley says. But Houchins chased it until he found himself at the cave entrance. We don't know if Houchins got his bear, but he gets credit for rediscovering the cave. Unfortunately, now the bears are all gone from the park.

Mammoth Cave became important when saltpeter, a key ingredient in gunpowder, was discovered in the cave. The "unpleasantness with Britain," as the park brochure calls the War of 1812, was brewing, and the United States could no longer import foreign gunpowder. Cave owners found saltpeter production very profitable because they were using slave labor. You can still see the large wooden vats and pipes used to bring water into the cave. The soil was washed away to get at the saltpeter. Because Mammoth Cave is a dry cave, so many artifacts that would have decayed with water are still here.

When the War of 1812 was over, demand for saltpeter petered out—that's where the expression originated. An owner had the bright idea that tourists might pay money to see the cave. Stephen Bishop, a slave, became a guide and the first explorer of the cave trail system. He crossed the Bottomless Pit by throwing a ladder across the chasm and crawling across. On another tour, I cross the same pit on a good bridge with a handrail.

The cave kept changing owners, who brought new ideas of how to capitalize on this wonder. One of the owners, Dr. John Croghan, thought that the constant fifty-four-degree temperature and cave air would cure tuberculosis. In 1842, he invited more than a dozen TB patients underground to live in wooden and stone huts. Servants cooked meals and took care of patients' needs. Visitors kept coming to the caves, going right past the patients, who they described as walking skeletons. But the cave air didn't work too well and all the TB sufferers died. Three are buried in the Old Guide's Cemetery behind the Mammoth Cave Hotel. Croghan himself died of TB soon after. The stone huts are still here for modern visitors to see.

I've been here two full days on two different occasions. By

concentrating on the cave, I've only walked a few of the eighty miles of trail aboveground. According to Ranger Hurley, "Mammoth Caves is mostly a day trip. People come through from the Midwest and stop for a tour on their way to Florida." That's why there are no large gateway towns, like Gatlinburg outside the Smokies.

Also with I-65 so close, people get off the interstate, take a tour, and get back on the road, even though there's lodging next to the visitor center. I'm staying at the Mammoth Cave Hotel, run by a concessionaire. It feels like a 1950s hotel, with a tiny bedroom and even smaller bathroom. You can't beat the location, and it's a shame that part of it will be torn down soon.

By the 1920s, there was a clamor to protect the caves and the land above them. In 1926, Congress authorized Mammoth Caves as a national park, along with Great Smoky Mountains National Park and Shenandoah National Park in Virginia. The Kentucky National Park Commission was established to start buying land from individuals. The park was dedicated in 1946.

On each tour, I listen to entertaining stories of what happened in the caves. The rangers are funny as well as factual, and they each write their own material. The tours are led by park rangers, not by volunteers. I find it amazing that so many tours are offered day in, day out, and they're almost all sold out. The easy tours can have up to 120 people, but they're orderly. If you pay attention, you aren't going to miss a thing.

At some point on every tour that I've been on, the ranger turns out the lights and asks for quiet. The silence and utter darkness would drive anyone crazy after a short while. But here even young children stop chattering and marvel at the quiet. The rangers know how to work a crowd and are masters in interpreting the caves to visitors.

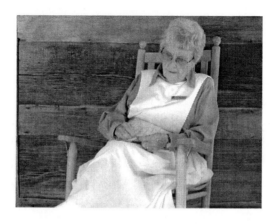

2

INTERPRETATION, NOT JUST INFORMATION

In National Park Service lingo, interpretation is the process of providing every visitor an opportunity to connect personally with a place. Rangers and volunteers interpret informally when they greet people in the visitor center, the trail, or battlefield, and formally when they give a program. When I volunteered in the Smokies, I took a course on resource education and learned a little about the theory and practice of interpretation.

"The chief aim of interpretation is not instruction but provocation," Freeman Tilden wrote in *Interpreting our Heritage.* His basic tenet was that information per se is not interpretation, though interpretation should contain information. Though Tilden didn't invent the concept of interpretation in national parks, his book, published in 1957, is still a classic on the subject.

Interpreting in the national parks is a skill that's taught, not something you can do just off the cuff. Visitor contact is highly personalized. An interpreter, whether a ranger or volunteer, evaluates the visitor and uses a well-crafted, personalized response.

If you sign up for a program in any national park, you'll follow a ranger or volunteer as she or he talks casually about what you're seeing and the science or history behind the scene. But the program isn't designed casually. The interpreter sets out themes, goals, and objectives for what ends up being an hour's walk. The interpretive program needs to be place-based, which means it can't be presented anywhere else. Then a supervisor approves the details and maybe dry runs it. This all sounds like creating a lesson plan for elementary school teaching. The only difference is there's no formal assessment. You're not going to test visitors. Somewhere in the National Park Service, educators and interpreters work on these guidelines, and there are PhD dissertations on park interpretation.

Learning to Interact with Visitors

"Much like Disney World, we're in the business of exceeding expectations," Mike Meldrum, an interpretive ranger at Cades Cove, explains in my course on interpretation. "The visitor wants to know 'What's in it for me?' and that's what we have to answer."

We listen to several audio quotes from Michael Eisner, former head of Disney. Some in the audience grumble that the park service had interpretation standards way before the amusement parks were around.

Ranger Meldrum loves Disney World and goes there every year.

"You need to be committed and passionate." He applies Disney techniques to the park. We need to:

- Make eye contact and smile.
- Greet and welcome every visitor.
- Seek out visitors and ask, "Can I help you?"
- Use appropriate body language.
- Preserve the positive visitor experience.
- Thank each visitor for coming to the park.
- Avoid personal conversation with other park personnel when visitors are around.

Ranger Meldrum reminds us that "Visitors are always watching you. So if you're wearing a uniform, be careful because you're on stage." That's my biggest take-away from the course.

Kent Cave, supervisory interpretive ranger at Sugarlands Visitor Center, who grew up in North Carolina, is well versed in negative Appalachian stereotypes that visitors may bring to the Smokies. Cave discusses two stereotypes of Southern Appalachian residents. One is the inbred, moonshining, barefoot hillbilly. To understand this image, Ranger Cave first plays a video called *Moonshine,* with Jim Tom Hedrick, which plays up every antic that you can think of. Jim Tom has an Appalachian drawl and missing teeth. He drinks the hard stuff continuously as he tries to explain how he makes moonshine. It's hilarious.

The next documentary, *The True Meaning of Pictures: Shelby Lee Adams' Appalachia,* is disturbing, not funny. Adams, a photographer and videographer, focuses his camera on Appalachian stereotypes. He often aims for the house at the top of a hollow to find the most isolated families. We watch a short clip of an old woman smoking a pipe surrounded by a family with several handicapped children. The implication is that these folks were inbred.

The second stereotype of Southern Appalachia is that of the self-made man, the hell-of-a-fellow mountain man type, embodied in the movie *Sergeant York*, starring Gary Cooper. The movie is based on the true story of Alvin York from the Tennessee hills, who became one of the most decorated soldiers in World War I.

Some visitors think that the national park was plopped here by the federal government, without any connection with the people around the park. They'll ask, "Why were so many Civil War battles fought in national parks?" and "Was the Cherokee Indian Reservation placed close to the national park so they could get more tourists?" Part of an interpreter's job is to dispel stereotypes and focus on the actual history.

The Smokies was home to more than two hundred communities before the land became a national park. Interpreters enjoy getting into costumes and talking about former residents. To learn how to do that, we walk to the Ownby Cabin on a nature trail close to Sugarlands Visitor Center. Ranger Lisa Free, dressed as Mary Ownby, who lived in the cabin over one hundred years ago, is weaving a basket.

We have to find problems with her setting. Some are very easy. A plastic water bottle lies close by. Ranger Free wears modern sneakers and uses scissors and a screwdriver with plastic handles. Other inconsistencies aren't so obvious. Ranger Free has rolled up her sleeves above her elbows. In many religious traditions, a woman keeps her arms covered to below her elbows.

Ranger Free started out by doing a first-person interpretation, i.e. playing Mary Ownby, sometimes called Living History. But that's not done much in the Smokies. There's not enough training in this technique and it makes it tough to answer visitor questions when the interpreter can't break character. Instead, Ranger Free quickly switches to third-person interpretation, where she can talk about the owners of the house and the times. It's easier to interact with visitors in the third person. The ranger feels a strong sense of responsibility to respect the former residents by getting the details right.

ℬ✦ℭ

Mike Maslona, supervisory interpretive ranger at Cades Cove, who leads the next session, enjoys acronyms. He starts with EIEIO. In another order, EIEIO becomes:

- Orient the visitor—Where is the bathroom?
- Inform the visitor—How many bears are in the park?
- Educate the visitor—What can you teach beyond basic facts?
- Enlighten the visitor—Why is this story important?
- Instill in the visitor—How can we inspire good stewardship?

The concept of stewardship, to preserve and protect for future generations, is a holy one. An interpreter needs to make visitors feel that they own the park resources. The mountains, bison, Liberty Bell, Civil War artifacts, cabins, belong to all of us. Inspiration and significance are more important than just facts. Rangers imbue programs with internal meanings so that visitors see connections and want to protect the resources. This is a very optimistic view of the world—just educate people and they'll protect the parks and not litter, harass a bear, or carve their names on a cabin wall.

Interpretation goes beyond just a lecture and uses appropriate techniques, such as questions and answers, old photographs, quotes, audience participation, jokes, and even silence. Maslona takes us on an interpretive walk to Cataract Falls behind Sugar-lands Visitor Center.

"When you get to a waterfall, let the resource talk to the visitor," Ranger Maslona says.

I need to hear this because I am prone to letting my enthusiasm overtake the visitor's experience. When I lead a hike to a historic site, I'm tempted to say, "Look at this marvelous chapel, built in . . ."

In designing our program, we might start with a tangible item—thing, place, or event—and then connect it to intangible meanings—old, utilitarian, home. An old-fashioned hand bell could be a dinner bell, cowbell, school bell, or a garden bell to warn someone that a bear was in the garden.

To build on those tangible objects and their roles, Ranger Maslona introduces his wife's favorite movie, *The Wizard of Oz*. From the characters, we can hone various aspects of our program.

- Scarecrow wanted a brain. We need information.
- Tin Man wanted a heart. We have to have an emotional connection with our subject.
- Lion wanted courage. We give visitors opportunities to do things they wouldn't do by themselves, like walk a trail or canoe a creek.
- Dorothy wanted home. Make a connection between what visitors know, like home, and what they experience in the park.
- Wizard. That's us presenting a program.

Back in the classroom, we each give a three-to-five-minute version of a potential visitor program. The talks range from the night sky to Cades Cove as a state of mind, fishing, cooking at the Mountain Farm Museum, and bird songs.

The course on interpretation is really geared to seasonal rangers and interns, the folks who are in college or just graduated. I'm very impressed with the group. Putting aside my park volunteer hat for now and looking at them from the perspective of a retired college professor, I note that they're all prepared, eager, and not afraid to show how excited they are about this opportunity to work in the Smokies for the summer. They're not interested in mixing with volunteers, maybe because we're so much older than they are. The seasonal rangers are in their early twenties while most volunteers are past fifty. Maybe we remind them of their parents. Maybe they think that we can't help them on their way up the NPS ladder.

Most seasonal rangers didn't graduate from academically selective universities. They studied a variety of subjects from history to biology, though forestry seems to be the major most associated with working for the National Park Service. These newcomers obviously have tremendous drive, ambition, and the willingness to plan. And that will carry them forward more than the prestige of the college they attended. I feel excited for them and I wish them well.

As I travel through the parks, I'm still amazed by how much rangers and volunteers care about their parks. They are passionate about sharing their knowledge with anyone who takes the time to listen. And I like to listen.

Gee Interprets a Settler in the Smokies

Sarah Gee Phillips isn't Mrs. Sarah Davis; she just plays her on the Mountain Farm Museum at the Oconaluftee Visitor Center in the Smokies. Right now, Gee rocks on the porch of the Davis House while working on a quilt pattern. Today Gee, eighty years old, wears a blue dress, white apron, and black tie shoes.

"Mrs. Davis wouldn't be quilting on a Monday. She would probably be scrubbing her laundry on a washboard," she explains to visitors. For the past twenty years, Gee has traveled from her home in Dayton, Ohio, to volunteer in the Smokies. She arrives for the Mountain Life Festival held at the Mountain Farm Museum the third Saturday of September and stays for six weeks during the height of the fall colors, when the park gets a great number of visitors. She works four days a week, Fridays through Mondays, and has three days to hike, visit, and do her shopping and laundry outside the park. While she volunteers here, she shares an apartment with a seasonal ranger.

The Davis house was built in 1900–1901. John E. Davis, Sarah's husband, was a cooper (barrel maker), so the family was quite well off. He and his sons built the house from American chestnut trees. The boys gathered stones in the stream for the chimney. The park moved the house from Thomas Divide above Deep Creek. The barn is the only structure that was originally here. "Not every farm would have all the buildings that are here in this museum," Gee says. "This is just to give visitors an idea of what a farm could have." She reminds visitors that settlers wouldn't build a house on bottomland because that land would be reserved for growing crops.

Gee greets visitors with, "Come on here and sit down a while." Her East Tennessee mountain accent comes back when she returns to the Smokies. Gee encourages children to quilt with her. "So there are a few stitches that are bigger than others. No big deal."

Each day Gee decides what needs doing. One day, she makes soap. Another day, she bakes cornbread over an open fire, and later reheats some lunch for herself. The kitchen is in a room separated by a wall from the rest of the house. You have to go outside and back into the kitchen. Visitors can look inside clearly, but Gee doesn't want visitors actually in the tiny kitchen, especially while she's cooking.

On the first crisp day in October, I ask how Mrs. Davis would have kept warm in winter. "To begin with, we would have kept the door closed," Gee explains. "I would be dressed in wool and not synthetic. Also people didn't shower every day. They sponge bathed. You needed to be careful with your water because you had to carry it all from the stream."

A bucket of water with a ladle sits on a side table. She doesn't bring water into the house from the Oconaluftee River close by, the way it was done at the beginning of the twentieth century. A barrel hides a pump situated on a sand pipe, a tubular cavity several feet deep filled with gravel and sand. This system prevents the water pipe from freezing in winter. The pipe is hooked up to the water supply at Oconaluftee Visitor Center nearby. In other words, Gee uses treated city water like the rest of us.

Sam Reed, a retired construction worker and local volunteer, works on the farm the same days as Gee and helps her out. He now sports a long beard and wears blue overalls. Sam brings water to the kitchen and builds a fire. Even in Mrs. Davis's time, great-grandmothers like Gee depended on others to deal with the heavy lifting. When he's not helping Gee, Sam works on farm chores.

Gee was born and raised in the community of Wheat in east Tennessee, now part of Oak Ridge National Laboratory. She remembers people from all over the country moving into her town during World War II and living in prefab houses.

"My husband and I wanted to volunteer on the farm because we both grew up close by. I've been coming to the Smokies since I was a little girl. This Farm Museum is like my early childhood," she says.

"We were on vacation in Glacier National Park. I met a volunteer at Logan Pass who spent three months doing volunteer work," Gee says. "So my husband and I decided to come down here and find out about volunteering."

Her husband died six years ago, but Gee keeps coming back. "The people here are like my extended family. Volunteer service is the reward, the way I can give back to the national parks," says Gee. "I've been to many parks. But here I feel a childhood connection to the farm." She says that she'll keep coming back as long as she can.

While the park can provide specific training on visitor services such as interpretation, they can't teach lifeway skills like quilting, blacksmithing, open-hearth cooking, heirloom gardening, and broom making. Most current volunteers have gained those skills on their own and come to the park with them already developed. Gee had help with the history of the Davis family. Tom Robbins, a retired ranger-historian, gave her a printout of the farm's history. There's also a large notebook of articles on the farm and farm skills in the Oconaluftee Visitor Center library. Gee met the youngest daughter of the Davises and entertained some of the Davis grandchildren.

Gee may be in uniform, but she's not cautious about giving her opinion on the state of the world. "The only drugs we had in our days was when your mama lined up all the kids and gave us medicine on Saturday night—cod liver oil and castor oil," she tells a woman who's a regular visitor in the Smokies.

Unlike Western parks that might be a once-a-lifetime experience for most visitors, many people vacation in the Smokies year after year. "We've watched other children grow up while they've watched ours do the same," says a woman. They may stay in the same place each time and expect the same attractions, such as watching and listening to Gee.

Lynda Doucette, the park's supervisory interpretive ranger on the North Carolina side of the Smokies, explains what Gee contributes to the Farm Museum.

"Gee brings the past to life by allowing visitors to connect with the meaning found in the Mountain Farm Museum exhibits. She takes these treasures from the past and enables one generation to connect to another. We certainly would love to have staff and volunteers at the Mountain Farm Museum throughout the visitor season (spring, summer, and fall) to interact with visitors. Our biggest challenge is that we don't have enough housing available, or the funding to pay for housing, so we need to look for volunteers who live in the local community. The most important skill set a volunteer needs to have is the ability to speak with a variety of people, enjoy public contact, and a willingness to serve."

Gee always leaves visitors with, "So happy you stopped by."

Once a visitor asked her where they could find real hillbillies.

"You're looking at one," she replied.

3

PREHISTORIC AMERICA

When historians talk about parks that protect prehistoric America, they mean before there was contact with Europeans. If there's no written record, you're dependent on the skill of archaeologists to dig deep, literally, and tell the stories of ancient people. There may be thousands of sites in the southeast, but there are only three national park units in the region devoted to this topic.

Archaeologists have established a general cultural sequence, which I should have remembered from school but relearned at Ocmulgee National Monument in Georgia. So here goes:

- Paleo-Indians Period. 17,000 years to 11,600 years ago. They hunted big game. Archaeologists found Clovis points (arrowheads) on the site.
- Archaic Period. 11,600 years ago to 3,000 years ago. These people were hunter-gatherers, who used more specialized tools, such as knives, drills, and choppers.
- Woodland Period. 3,000 to 1,100 years ago. Now inhabitants started to cultivate crops and make pottery.
- Early and Late Mississippians Period. 1,100 to 650 years ago. They built large ceremonial lodges.

The specific dates may differ, depending on what you read, even if the information all comes from the National Park Service. But to me what matters is how these early North Americans lived. The inhabitants at Russell Cave hunted big game. In contrast, the Mississippians at Ocmulgee built large mounds and cultivated crops. Archaeologists attempt to reconstruct the life of people long gone from whatever remains can be found today. From tools, bones, and sometimes earthworks, they work out how and where ancient people lived, what they ate, and how they made their tools. They also attempt to reconstruct a prehistoric society and government, because it takes a lot of people, organization, and arduous labor to build mounds.

ᴄ҂ Russell Cave National Monument
Protecting an old civilization
Alabama

Oh, the places I'll go, chasing down national parks of the Southeast. I'm glad that I committed to visit them all, independent of how interesting they seem on the website. I wouldn't know about these national park sites otherwise. The hills of northern

Alabama may be low when compared to majestic Clingmans Dome in the Smokies. But when you're here, they're fascinating. Beth Ransom and I drive from our cabin in DeSoto State Park to find Russell Cave.

Russell Cave National Monument, in northeast Alabama just south of Tennessee, protects one of the most complete archaeological records in the eastern United States. Native people lived in the cave for almost nine thousand years, mostly in fall and winter. Researchers found evidence of burials, pottery, bows, and arrows. They unearthed stone points, which were used as weapons and multipurpose tools. The park doesn't seem to use the term *arrowheads*.

A display in the visitor center asks, "What did prehistoric people do for fun?" Like many of us today, native people played games and music. They made musical rasps, which look like tiny washboards and sticks, from bone.

A boardwalk takes us to the cave, but we can't go inside very far because water flows into the cave from an underground stream. Tableaus of Indians attending to daily tasks have been set up. An artificial fire burns in the center. A woman swaddles a baby lying on a board that looks like a snowshoe while an older brother looks on. When Europeans came in the sixteenth century, they found Mississippians in Russell Cave living a prosperous life. In contrast, by the time Europeans found the Ocmulgee mounds in Georgia, all the Indians were gone.

People knew that the caves were here from the first. Thomas Russell, a Revolutionary War veteran, owned the property in the 1800s, but the Tennessee Archaeological Society didn't conduct the first dig until 1953. The National Geographic Society funded a second expedition and bought the cave and the land around it from private owners. They donated the land to the National Park Service. President John F. Kennedy declared Russell

Cave a national monument in 1961.

We walk a steep asphalt trail for 1.5 miles. The asters and oak trees are similar to those in the lower parts of western North Carolina, but the rocks are distinctive. Large slabs line up like a layered wedding cake, reminding me a little of the Obed River. In other areas, rocks have tumbled helter-skelter down the mountain on the side of the trail. The area is considered the southern terminus of the Appalachian Mountains. Some advocate that the Appalachian Trail should really end here instead of Springer Mountain, Georgia, but that's not going to happen anytime soon, if ever.

Who created the paved path? Park literature says that the loop trail is over fifty years old. It couldn't have been the Civilian Conservation Corps (CCC) because the trail was built long after the Corps was disbanded. A ranger mentions that it might have been the Youth Conservation Corp (YCC), which some compare to a modern CCC with less publicity. But it was too early for the YCC. If the trail was created after Russell Cave became a park, why was it built so steeply? Not only does it discourage hikers, but also it creates erosion.

It remains a mystery to me until I find Ranger Larry Beane, who explains. "The trail was built in 1962–1963 by the National Park Service to explain how Indians used the mountain's ecology. It was built so steeply because it was the only place to put a long trail in the park. The park does not own much of the bottom land."

◐ Poverty Point National Monument
For extra credit
Louisiana

Finding Poverty Point is its own mystery. I wanted to see the rural back roads of Louisiana, and I sure have. The only sign of commerce or people on my way to Poverty Point is the occasional gas station and mini-mart, an oasis for drivers. A few times, I need to slow down for a cluster of houses. In Europe they use the word *village*, but here there's no word for tiny town.

The land has been rising since I left the Louisiana bayous. You can tell because here cemeteries have underground graves, where in New Orleans and even farther north, bodies are buried on the surface. The altitude here is about one hundred feet. Finally, I reach Poverty Point, east of Monroe and close to the Mississippi border.

Poverty Point protects an archaeological site, now selected as a World Heritage Site, where prehistoric people lived from 1730 to 1350 BCE. They moved soil to level the land, and then created mounds and ridges. Without domesticated animals or wheeled carts to help, they shaped the earth by hand. Archaeologists have never given a name to these prehistoric people.

The museum displays artifacts from the site. Like a lot of visitor information in Louisiana, pamphlets at Poverty Point are available in French as well as English. Visitors can sign up for the tram ride through the mounds. Instead, I pick up a twelve-page trail booklet describing a 2.6-mile walk.

"If you don't want to walk in the trees," the woman behind the desk says, "you can walk on the road." Are people that afraid of forests?

The trail is well signposted and mowed since there are no trees on which to paint blazes.

The first stop is Sarah's Mound, named after Sarah Wilson Guier, who's buried in the mound. Sarah and her husband established Poverty Point Plantation and planted cotton. Names like Poverty Point and Hard Times Plantation suggest that here plantations weren't luxurious. The park has placed stairs up Mound A, which they think was a ceremonial site. The top is at the dizzying height of 172 feet. I feel like the Kenyans who come to the United

States to race. The trail is so flat that I only stop to read the plaques.

So what happened to these people? Archaeologists speculate that the Mississippi River changed course and may have flooded out the community. The residents then dispersed. On the National Park Service website, Poverty Point is shown as a National Park unit, though operated by the state of Louisiana. When I get here, it's obvious that Poverty Point is a Louisiana state park from the signage around the visitor center to the ranger uniforms.

"Now that it's become a World Heritage Site," the state ranger says, "it will never be turned over to the federal government." Louisiana will want to keep the park. So I just got some extra credit.

Ocmulgee National Monument
Mysterious Indian mounds
Georgia

When I walk into a park visitor center and the person behind the desk, whether ranger or volunteer, is eager to give me the basic facts of the park, I know it's going to be a great visit. What the actual site offers is almost secondary. "It's all good," as they say.

Ocmulgee National Monument, established in 1936, is 702 acres and hosted almost 123,000 visitors in 2014. Though it's located along the northeast edge of Macon, Georgia, a city of more than ninety thousand people, the park feels remote and rural. The Ocmulgee River separates the main section of the city from the park.

Ocmulgee, which means bubbling water in the Muscogee or Creek language, protects seven Indian mounds. That's what attracts visitors, but the area has evidence of people living here for more than seventeen thousand years. The visitor center displays a collection of archaeological artifacts, including early Clovis points (arrowheads) through colonial bells and a three-hundred-year-old sword. The park staff is proud that their collection demonstrates the historic connection to all cultures "from Stone Age to Space Age." The Mississippians built the earth mounds, the park's star attraction.

The beautiful visitor center was refurbished in 2009. Ranger Jim Branan is keen to give Lenny and me a rundown of the various cultures that lived on the Macon Plateau. The exhibits on the archaeology and prehistoric people go through the four periods: Paleos, Archaic, Woodland, and early and late Mississippian.

Mississippian culture is a general term for a people that may have come from the Mississippi River and practiced sophisticated cultivation techniques. The Mississippians farmed a fertile land, growing corn, beans, and squash, crops known as "the three sisters." The Indians built large ceremonial earth mounds, maybe influenced by Central American cultures, as a sign of wealth and power.

Without an understanding of why and who built these structures, the earth mounds could look like small garbage mountains or bad replicas of Mount Fuji. The seventeen-minute film on the *Mystery of the Mounds* explains what you'll see on the property. The park built the visitor center close to the large Earth Lodge. You can go into the Earth Lodge by yourself, but nothing beats a tour with an enthusiastic ranger.

On a dry and warm November Sunday morning, we're the only visitors on the Earth Lodge tour. Ranger Angela Bates starts the tour in the visitor center by showing us the yaupon holly bush, *Ilex vomitoria*, a native evergreen bush that wouldn't look out of place in my front yard. The leaves are very high in caffeine. Native people brewed it into a black tea and used it in purifying ceremonies by fasting and vomiting in the Lodge.

We walk less than five minutes to the Earth Lodge, the only

mound you can enter. The Mississippians built the original lodge in 1000 CE as a council chamber. Only men could participate in ceremonies and discussions. The building burned down fifteen years later; the dates were confirmed by carbon dating. The original floor has lasted more than a thousand years.

The tunnel entrance has such a low ceiling that even I have to bend down to my waist to walk in. The walls and roof have been reconstructed. This space, forty-two feet in diameter, is ringed by the original clay seats pressed into the floor. A simulated fire hole lies in the center. An effigy of an eagle-like bird on the floor has become the symbol of the national monument.

Ranger Bates points out that Mississippians designed the entrance to the mound so that the sun shines right through the Earth Lodge and lands on the bird figure twice a year: October 22 and February 22.

"If the sun is out, it's blinding in here on these two days. Maybe the February date was time to get the fields ready for planting and October 22 was the time to harvest the crops," Bates speculates. The Mississippians abandoned the Ocmulgee site by about 1100 CE and the fate of its inhabitants is still a mystery.

The Creek Indians moved here, attracted by a British trading post and good farmland. Most of the Creek Nation were forced to Oklahoma after the Creek War ended in 1836. Much of their original land had already been ceded to European settlers, creating the town of Macon.

"So who discovered the mounds?" I ask.

"People always knew the mounds were here," Ranger Bates explains.

Hernando de Soto passed through in 1540, bringing diseases to the Creek people. The Spaniards baptized two natives in the Ocmulgee River.

A six-mile network of trails takes us to other mounds. The

Great Temple Mound, about a half mile from the visitor center, is the highest. The park constructed an elaborate wooden staircase to the top of the mound where we get a clear view of Macon and the Ocmulgee River. The trails lead to a boardwalk and the riverbanks. On the way, you pass swamp areas with birds and otters. The park mows selectively to attract wildlife and remove invasive plants like tallow trees.

Naturalist William Bartram visited twice in the 1770s and wrote about the Creek and the mounds in a book with a long title now available as *The Travels of William Bartram*. Railroad tracks cut through the mounds in 1843. The Civil War came to Macon, creating further damage. A second cut for a railroad still in use was excavated through a large portion of the Funeral Mounds. Now the tracks bisect the park.

"It's lucky that we still have all this stuff," says Bates. In the early part of the twentieth century, a group of concerned Macon residents wrote to the Smithsonian Institution and encouraged its staff to come down and look at the mounds. The Civilian Conservation Corps and others engaged in public works projects excavated here on a large scale. In 1934, Congress passed a bill to authorize establishment of Ocmulgee National Park, but two years later President Franklin D. Roosevelt declared the site a national monument. Some are still trying to make the unit a national park.

Along with all this archaeology and history, the visitor center includes a food pyramid exhibit, comparing a typical Mississippian diet with the foods we eat today. It points out that the early Mississippians exercised for one to ten hours a day. The message is clear: go walk a trail. They're short and flat. For a more sustained challenge, the sixteen-mile Nene Kerretv Trail connects several trails inside and outside the national monument. A wayside panel explains the health benefits of exercise.

Back at the visitor center, I have one more question for Ranger

Branan. "How long do you recommend for a visit?"

"About ninety minutes," he says.

It took me almost ninety minutes just to read the exhibits and talk to Branan. It's about three p.m. and we've been at Ocmulgee for almost six hours. I drop some money in the collection box set up by the Ocmulgee National Monument Association, the Friends group for the park. When we say goodbye, Ranger Branan gives Lenny and me each a Junior Ranger badge. Even though we didn't fill out a booklet or answer questions, he feels we earned them.

4

THE EUROPEANS ARE COMING

A lot happened in the New World between 1492 and the American Revolution. It seems that every powerful European country wanted a piece of America. Actually, they wanted the whole thing, not that they knew at the time what the whole thing was. Mostly, explorers looked at the Southeastern United States as a gateway to the riches of South America. Only much later did they think about actually settling here.

Christopher Columbus came to the US Virgin Islands in 1493 on his second voyage, looking for water. That's enough to preserve the remote beach as a national historical park. Hernando de Soto looked for riches when he overran Indians, spread diseases, and died in the New World. Later the Spanish built forts and castles. But the fortunes here were tied to the wars in Europe between the Spanish, French, and British.

Protestants in Northern Europe had a good public relations machine during religious strife with Catholics. They devised the Black Legend, *La Leyenda Negra*, to demonize the Spanish empire and its Catholic conquerors. Engravings showed the Spanish feeding Indian children to their dogs. Britain, in particular, tried to say that their colonialism was kinder and gentler.

Later the Danes came to the Virgin Islands to grow sugarcane and make rum. The United States bought the islands in 1917, but visitors still find evidence of their Danish past, from food to reading material.

A Voyage Long and Strange: On the Trail of Vikings, Conquistadors, Lost Colonists, and Other Adventurers in Early America, by Tony Horwitz, traces the era between Columbus's voyages to the New World in 1492 and the Pilgrims landing at Plymouth in 1620. Horwitz goes back and forth between the history and his own modern travels. He visits several locations that became national parks, though that's not his focus. Horwitz's books are always an entertaining mixture of history and his own adventure—sort of like this one, but his trips involve a lot more booze.

☙ Salt River Bay National Historical Park and Ecological Preserve
Columbus's men landed
St. Croix, Virgin Islands

Sometimes a national park stirs up the imagination and the senses so much that it doesn't really matter what's actually here. That's certainly the case with Salt River Bay National Historical Park and Ecological Preserve in St. Croix, the US Virgin

Islands, a long name for a tiny place. Salt River is the only place in the United States where Columbus's men landed.

Salt River became a historical park in 1992, yet the literature says that the park is still in its developmental stage. It may look like it's just another lovely, deserted beach in the Virgin Islands, but it has a long, documented history. The area has been continuously occupied since about 400 CE. A series of people from South America settled here. The Taino Indians built a village and ceremonial ball court for games, but by the 1400s, they had been conquered and enslaved by the Caribs.

On November 14, 1493, men from Christopher Columbus's second expedition to the New World landed here. The Spaniards needed fresh water and took Taino slaves. A party of Carib Indians in a canoe intervened. The resulting fight left one man dead on each side. This was the first altercation between Native Americans and Europeans. The Spaniards later ordered the extermination of the Caribs.

St. Croix, now a United States territory, lived under seven flags: Spanish, British, Dutch, French, French Knights of Malta, Danish, and now American. Several public buildings fly the flags to show the island's history. Some people might think that there's nothing here, while others will say *Wow!* I'm so amazed that I can walk a beach with such an illustrious history.

Salt River Bay, on the north central part of the island facing the Caribbean Sea, isn't easy to find. Though the directions are clear on the map, the corresponding road signs are missing. On the US mainland, some park units display their reassuring brown signs for miles before the actual entrance, but on the way to Salt River, there's nothing, not even a street name.

With a couple of maps, a compass, and stops to ask for directions, Lenny and I find ourselves on the beach where Columbus landed. According to park statistics, Christiansted National

Historic Site, the fort in the center of Christiansted, St. Croix, had over 109,000 visitors in 2014. In contrast, the same year brought only about five thousand people to Salt River, one of the ten least-visited parks in the country. I wonder how many people just gave up the search.

The beach is beautiful and mostly free of people. Owners of upscale beachfront houses have erected fences around their property and posted lots of Keep Out signs. A few local families come to swim and picnic on the beach. If you're looking for an empty beach, you'll enjoy Salt River. There are no visitor facilities, other than a parking area.

You can discern the remains of a British fort by the raised ground against a tree. Mangrove forests, with their complex, tangled root system, border the bay. The roots filter the water, protecting the coral reefs and offering shelter to turtles, fish, and shrimp. You can snorkel or stay above water and kayak in a much larger preserved area underwater. For something different, take an evening kayaking tour to see bioluminescent single-cell organisms that look like underwater lights.

A VIP (Volunteers in Parks) offers an interpretive program a couple of days a week, but I'm not here at the right time. The visitor center for the three St. Croix parks is in Christiansted National Historic Site, where you can pick up a brochure for Salt River.

If you want to find the park, take the North Shore Road, also known as Route 80, from Christiansted. Turn right immediately after the Salt River Marina. The Columbus landing beach is at the end of the road.

80 ✦ CR

❧ San Juan National Historic Site
A place of war
San Juan, Puerto Rico

"Columbus didn't discover the New World. The Indians found a bunch of lost Spaniards," Ranger Emmanuel Rodriguez says in his introductory tour at San Juan National Historic Site.

Though there's no written account of Christopher Columbus ever landing in Puerto Rico, the explorer must have heard enough to report to his Spanish benefactors that Puerto Rico was a place worth exploring and colonizing. This historic site constitutes the oldest European structures in the National Park Service. Puerto Rico is located in a strategic spot in the Western Hemisphere. During European exploration and colonization, trade winds easily blew sailing ships here from Europe. The island was the first major spot for ships to resupply with food, clean water, rest, and probably women, though the ranger didn't mention that last one.

All the major European countries, hell-bent on conquering the rest of the world, vied for Puerto Rico, but Spain got here first and fought for four hundred years to hold it. At the time, Puerto Rico, which means rich port, was the gateway to the New World. From the island, they could explore the Western Hemisphere, where they found gold, silver, spices, and jewels by the ton. "By the ton," Ranger Rodriguez repeats several times.

Ponce de Leon founded the Spanish colony in 1508. To help them hold this precious land, the Spaniards started constructing Castillo San Felipe del Morro in 1539 at the headlands of the island. The Castillo protected the entrance to the Caribbean and controlled access to South American gold and wealth. Later, Fort El Cañuelo, a half mile across the mouth of the bay, was built to create a crossfire if an enemy tried to enter the harbor. Though *castillo* can mean castle, these forts were places of war.

73

Other European countries tried to wrest Puerto Rico from Spain. Sir Francis Drake first attacked in 1595. The second English attack was successful, but they "died of bad hygiene" (dysentery) and left. The Spaniards understood the importance of clean water and didn't allow animals in the fort. All construction work was done by hard hand labor. The Dutch came next in 1625 and attacked by land. They managed to burn San Juan, causing total devastation, but they too left eventually. The Spanish built a wall around the city and started building Castillo San Cristobal, on the east side of Old San Juan, to ward off another land attack. Great Britain attacked again in 1797, but the Spanish held on.

"If England had won the war, I'd be speaking like Benny Hill instead of like Ricky Ricardo," Ranger Jose L. Gonzalez says while leading the San Cristobal tunnel tour. Ranger Gonzalez walks us up and down secret passages and stairs that we might have missed on our own exploration. The final tunnel can only be accessed on a ranger tour, limited to fifteen people. He opens the rusty low gates with a large key. We each take a flashlight and silently enter the tunnel. Then he closes the gate so that another visitor can't wander in randomly. This is creepy. What if the ranger loses the key or his way? Who will find us?

We walk single file through the narrow, dark tunnel. At the end, we find two slits in the walls where the Spaniards looked out for enemy ships. The tunnel was a potential minefield and a lookout, considered a masterpiece of eighteenth-century engineering. The openings, called loopholes, provided the only air for the soldiers.

"Imagine a soldier with a lit torch in one hand and explosives in the other," Ranger Gonzalez says. "They had better keep their two hands apart." This was not a great assignment for the soldiers; it was probably considered a punishment.

Castillo San Cristobal was the site for a TV movie, *Wizards of Waverly Place: The Movie*, with Selena Gomez, a popular teen celebrity. Since a couple of teenage girls are on the tour, Ranger Gonzalez points out every single place where Selena Gomez stood. It's obvious he has studied the movie. The girls are so excited to hear his anecdotes. I suppose that's one way you get children interested in national parks and history.

A mile-long walk on the city street takes us to El Morro, a six-level fort, older and smaller than Castillo. We go up and down circular steps and ramps to towers and plazas. The magnificent view of Fort El Cañuelo across the mouth of the bay makes you appreciate the damage that crossfire can cause. Here couples have their pictures taken with the Atlantic Ocean as background. We do the same.

Each fort has a chapel because Spanish colonization encouraged the spread of Catholicism and, in many cases, forced religious conversions. In Cristobal, Saint Barbara, the patron saint of people in danger of fire or explosion, protected soldiers working with dangerous cannons. A Virgin Mary stands in the El Morro fort. In front of each statue is a donation box, encouraging visitors to support the national park. Am I donating to the park or the chapel? Though it's a weird place to put a donation box, the park may get more money this way.

How did the forts go from Spanish control to national park? To support Cuban independence, the United States declared war against Spain in 1898. The Navy bombarded San Juan to prevent Spanish troops and supplies from reaching Cuba, but the Spanish forts were no match for nineteenth-century naval firepower. Spain agreed to give Cuba its independence and ceded the remaining colonies—Puerto Rico, Guam, and the Philippines—to the United States. Because of the strategic location of the port, the United States didn't want to give up Puerto Rico.

"Temperance was looming, and Americans needed a place to drink," the ranger points out.

The Spanish-American War established the United States as a superpower. This is the war where Teddy Roosevelt charged up San Juan Hill, but in Cuba, not in Puerto Rico. The forts were used in both World Wars.

On an outside wall at the El Morro site, a plaque marks Copeland's Corner, which honors a woman who contributed to golf in San Juan. When the military administered the forts, they brought golf to Puerto Rico and built a nine-hole course around the walls of the fort. The golf course is long gone from the historic site, but golf can be played in many resorts around the island. The forts were incorporated into the National Park Service in 1949, though the Army didn't move out until 1961.

After my visit, I check Facebook for the historic site. The page's cover photo shows a man driving a dogsled through heavy snow. I doubt if San Juan has any snow, but San Juan National Historic Site is one cool place.

ᕦ De Soto National Memorial
Pillaging the South
Florida

Hernando de Soto was a brutal man. In his four-thousand-mile trek, he and his men overwhelmed Indian villages, took countless Indians as slave porters, and destroyed native cultures. In 1539, de Soto sailed from Cuba into present-day Tampa Bay on the west coast of Florida. His goal was to explore Florida, but mostly to find gold. He brought with him more than seven hundred men, two hundred horses, war dogs, and two women.

De Soto was the ultimate entrepreneur; he planned and financed the expedition himself. He was already a rich man, having taken part in the Spanish conquest of Peru. But the wealthy, idle life in Spain didn't suit him, and he was ready to invest his whole fortune to plunder Florida. He was driven to succeed. If he returned to Spain without gold, he'd be a failure. His fortune would be gone as well.

De Soto National Memorial outside of Bradenton, Florida, interprets this history in a lively manner on a site that covers less than thirty acres. Since there's nothing left from the expedition, the challenge is in the interpretation. It's also not clear exactly where the De Soto expedition actually landed. As Ranger Diana Bauman explains, "You can't put an X on a map where they landed."

Even so, there's a lot to do at the site. A twenty-one-minute film recounts the expedition using first-person historical accounts. It starts as De Soto's party lands on May 30, 1539. Indians watch the Spanish come ashore. In their metal armor, the soldiers crash through the mangrove swamp. Early on his march, De Soto comes upon a Spaniard who had been taken prisoner by Indians years earlier, and can now act as an interpreter. How's this for a lucky break?

De Soto and his men keep going north, looking for gold and fighting Indians. They aren't searching for gold mines, but for treasures that the Indians already possess. Why work hard digging the ground when you can steal someone else's wealth?

The film reminds us that "There was cruelty on both sides." De Soto's route shown on a map looks like a long strand of cooked spaghetti. They went up to present-day Tallahassee, into South Carolina, traversed the Appalachian Mountains in North Carolina, down to Mobile, Alabama, and eventually crossed the Mississippi River.

De Soto, who died of fever in 1542, was buried in the river. The survivors eventually floated down the Mississippi and made their way back to Cuba. The film sums up the expedition this way: De Soto didn't find gold or create a settlement, but his accounts of nature and native people encouraged future explorations.

At the Living History Camp, under a thatched roof stand, a

volunteer in Spanish colonial dress demonstrates various weapons and tools of the times. A conch shell on a stick was used as a hammer or hatchet. She blows into the conch as Indians might have done to alert the villagers. "A kind of telephone of the times," she explains. A long musket called an arquebus was the Spanish weapon of the era. The volunteer explains that this gun was made up of a lock, stock, and barrel—hence the expression, "lock, stock, and barrel."

Another volunteer dresses visitors in Spanish war garments. Lenny puts on a chain mail pullover. The steel armor is the next layer. He's helped into metal gloves called gauntlets. On his head, he wears a cabasset, a metal helmet.

"Now I understand why the soldiers needed to have others carry their supplies," Lenny says. "This is heavy."

The site offers a one-mile interpretive trail along the shoreline of the Manatee River and the mangrove swamp. Benches and wayside signs explain the expedition and the natural environment. The trail ends just outside the park where the Catholic Diocese of Venice, Florida, erected a Holy Eucharist monument and memorial cross dedicated to all priests who served in Florida, starting with the twelve priests who came with Hernando de Soto's expedition.

A magnificent gumbo limbo tree near the visitor center spreads its branches. It's known as the tourist tree because "it stands in the sun, turns red, and peels." The Colonial Dames of America erected a commemorative stone under the tree in 1939, the 400th anniversary of the De Soto landing. The stone was placed over an Indian burial mound to preserve it. In 1948, Congress created the De Soto National Memorial.

"Women who were married to influential men preserved a lot of land," Ranger Bauman explains. The Colonial Dames and Daughters of the American Revolution organizations are part of the early history of national parks in the South. The De Soto Trail, a driving route to thirty-four sites in Florida connected with the expedition, starts here. That's a lot of activities to pack in a thirty-acre site.

Historians David and Anne Mitchell Whisnant, who wrote the administrative history of the park, explain the challenges of interpreting the events that occurred in the vicinity. The history of the encounter between conquistadors and Native Americans is "difficult." The Hernando de Soto site is probably not where the Spanish landed. The park also has to deal with eroding shoreline and encroaching development. The Whisnants have high praise for the park staff.

The site gets a large number of visitors for such a small place. Locals use the site as a town park for dog walking and jogging. It's probably also popular with school groups from Tampa and surrounding cities.

De Soto National Memorial may be the national park unit that interprets the earliest instance of Europeans on the North American mainland. This distinction might not be enough for most visitors to make De Soto National Memorial a destination park, but if you're driving the west coast of Florida, it's definitely worth a few hours of your time.

Castillo de San Marcos National Monument and Fort Matanzas National Monument
Protecting St. Augustine
Florida

European settlement of North America didn't start with Jamestown in 1607 or Plymouth Rock in 1620 but with St. Augustine, established in 1565. Standing near the northern tip of Florida on the Atlantic coast, St. Augustine is the oldest continuously occupied European-established settlement in the country.

While the historic part of the city is filled with T-shirt and coffee shops, two fascinating national monuments, Castillo de San Marcos and Fort Matanzas, interpret Florida's origins.

Ponce de Leon was the first European to come to Florida's east coast in 1513, and he named it La Florida, the land of flowers. Later, when the Spanish brought gold and silver from Central and South America back to the mother country, they needed an outpost close to their trade routes, and St. Augustine was established. The French also had designs on this new land and built Fort Caroline, located forty miles north of St. Augustine, in an attempt to break the Spanish monopoly. The two powers clashed and the Spanish captured Fort Caroline, ending the presence of the French in the area.

This was no small Spanish victory. The word *matanzas* means slaughter in Spanish, which pretty well describes what happened to the French. The word was later used as the name for a Spanish fort, placed where the French were massacred. France never again strongly challenged Spanish claims in North America.

St. Augustine prospered as a Spanish holding for almost twenty years, but in 1586, the town almost lost its foothold. War had broken out between Spain and England, and Sir Francis Drake was in the region looking for England's share of the New World. With a huge fleet at his disposal, Drake attacked St. Augustine, and his men burned the city to the ground. While the Spanish held on to St. Augustine, the residents struggled with Indian raids and pirates over the decades. In 1669, Queen Mariana of Spain ordered that a fortress be built to protect Spanish interests in the New World. Though called the Castillo, the Castle of St. Marcos, no royalty lived here. It was simply a way to protect St. Augustine, but it was quite a stronghold.

The Spanish castle was built of coquina, a limestone made up of broken shells. Nine previous wooden forts erected by the Spanish in the same area hadn't survived. However with coquina, the enemies' cannonballs just seemed to be swallowed by the walls, as if they were made of taffy. They started building this fort in 1672. But the inlet into the Matanzas River was still unprotected. So the Spanish built Fort Matanzas (1740–1742) to defend the back door to St. Augustine. The structure is more like a watchtower, not a real fort.

"It sat as a deterrent, like a police car on the side of the road," a park ranger explains. The castle withstood each new attack and was never conquered by force. The British occupied Florida in 1763 at the end of the Seven Years War, known as the French and Indian War in the United States. But twenty years later, the treaty that ended the American Revolution returned Florida, and therefore the castle and fort, to Spain.

By now, Spain couldn't really control its territory and in 1821 ceded Florida to the United States. The castle became a prison for Seminole Indians and later Plains Indians. The structures were decommissioned in 1899, and both became national monuments in 1924.

෨✦ଓ

A visit to the two monuments is a child's dream come true. Castillo de San Marcos has a moat, thick walls, a courtyard, cannons, and lots of rooms to explore. Fort Matanzas looks like a classic fort on an island. It's best to visit Castillo de San Marcos first and then drive about fifteen miles south to Fort Matanzas. If you plan to arrive at Castillo de San Marcos when it opens, you can visit both monuments comfortably in one day. This makes a good winter trip.

Before entering the castle, we sit on a bench and look out at the channel that was protected by the cannons. The large cannons had a three-mile range. We walk around the outside perimeter of the castle, where an old Spanish flag flies overhead. The castle is configured as a square with five-sided bastions at each corner. The outline is difficult to see from the ground, but it means there were no blind spots when sentries patrolled on the upper level. We take the self-guided tour in the castle and feel the block of coquina in the exhibit rooms.

We stoop down to crawl into the original magazine, built to protect precious gunpowder from enemies or fire. In a short film, volunteer reenactors dressed as Spanish soldiers of the time demonstrate how to load and fire a cannon and musket. Their instructions are given in Castilian Spanish with English subtitles.

A ranger recounts the history of the castle. Forts were military bases, not homes. During the Spanish period, soldiers walked to work from their homes in town. Only soldiers assigned to guard duty stayed in the castle overnight. And unlike castles in the Middle Ages, the moat around the castle didn't have any water. Cattle, needed to feed the soldiers, grazed in the moat.

"This storming the castle thing went out with the Middle Ages," the ranger says. "When the British burned St. Augustine yet again in 1702, all the people living in the town came into the castle. The smell of people was bad enough, but think of the livestock living with you."

At a cannon-firing demonstration, volunteers wear costumes made of twenty-five pounds of thick wool, even on the hottest summer day. But roving VIPs wear appropriate uniforms for the region: a polo shirt, khaki pants, and a wide-brim hat. When I volunteered in the Smokies, I needed to wear a heavy button-down shirt and long trousers.

We drive to Fort Matanzas Visitor Center on Anastasia Island. The fort itself is on Rattlesnake Island, reached by a five-minute free ferry ride operated by the park. With binoculars, we see pelicans, snowy egrets, and other shore birds. Once at the fort, we climb to the top of the tower via a well-secured ladder and note the old Spanish flag. Modern hoodies hang on hooks on the bottom floor where soldiers slept. You can only stay at the fort for forty minutes, but the site is small and doesn't take long to explore. You need to leave the island with the same group you came with.

From the visitor center, we walk the 0.6-mile nature trail through a maritime forest. The trail, mostly on a boardwalk, goes through live oaks, saw palmettos, and red bay trees. Great horned owls nest close to the visitor center. A pair of owls was spotted a few years ago, and then disappeared. They may be nesting again in the same spot.

❦ Fort Raleigh National Historic Site
The Lost Colony
North Carolina

The owls at Fort Matanzas may reappear on their own, but archaeologists are still struggling with the fate of the Lost Colony. How does the National Park Service interpret a site when there's almost nothing left to see? Fort Raleigh National Historic Site protects the site of the Lost Colony that settled here in 1587, but by definition, the site doesn't have much to show. Fort Raleigh, located on Roanoke Island between the Outer Banks and the North Carolina mainland, is the island where Virginia Dare, the first child born in the Western Hemisphere of English parents, came into the world on August 18, 1587.

I always try to arrive at the visitor center just as it opens. Almost no one else is here and I can get the staff's full attention. Explaining this site takes enthusiastic interpreters like Ranger Rob Bolling and Robin Davis, an Eastern National bookstore employee who's lived on the island for over thirty years. Davis takes me aside to tell me the story of the Lost Colony.

Sir Walter Raleigh sponsored several expeditions into the New

World, but he didn't join this trip because Queen Elizabeth I didn't want to lose him. She had already lost Raleigh's half brother when his ship sank on an expedition and he drowned. The purpose of the first trip was a reconnaissance voyage meant to explore the coast and find a place for a settlement. On the second trip, the men were supposed to find precious metals and possibly raid Spanish ships. Their interaction with the Roanoke Indians didn't go too well. The colonists became too dependent on the Indians for food, and the Indians died of European diseases. The second expedition left fifteen men to hold the fort, literally, for England, and the rest went home.

On the third voyage in 1587, 117 people, including women and children, crossed the Atlantic Ocean to settle in the Chesapeake Bay. The ship made a stop on Roanoke Island to find the fifteen men they'd left behind, but they had disappeared. The captain said that he wasn't going any farther, and dumped the colonists here. It sounds like the equivalent of "you'll figure it out." But the colonists weren't self-sustaining and asked their leader, John White, to return to England to get more supplies. White didn't get back to the colony until three years later because of England's war with Spain. He found no one. Nothing but the letters CROATAN carved on a post. Did that mean that the colonists went with the Croatan Indians? Archaeologists are actively working on this baffling history, but have not come up with a clear, accepted answer. The mystery remains.

While mulling over this story, I follow the Thomas Hariot Nature Trail down to Albemarle Sound with its small beach, passing an earthen fort along the way. This fort, dating from 1584 to 1590, has been excavated and studied since 1895. Recent digs have uncovered plenty of artifacts from the late 1500s, including Indian and English pottery pieces and glass beads. The interpretive trail emphasizes that the colonists were not self-supporting.

One sign on the trail says, "STOP—Could you survive in these woods without outside supplies?"

The sixteenth-century military expeditions to the New World were about profit for England. The leaders didn't seem to think about their own survival. The first voyage had sent too many mining and military experts but not enough farmers and artisans who could support the expeditions. Didn't the military realize that they needed support personnel?

Since there's not much to see here, the Fort Roanoke website mentions other local sites that are worth a look. In the summer, the Waterside Theatre, on Albemarle Sound, performs *The Lost Colony* drama, a play by Paul Green, inspired by a 1921 movie. Roanoke Island Festival Park, a North Carolina state site in Manteo, has a replica of a sixteenth-century sailing ship named *Elizabeth II*. There's an American Indian town and a settlement site, all with costumed interpreters.

The Elizabethan Gardens, a couple of miles from Fort Raleigh, features two acres of manicured gardens. The Elizabethan layout was inspired by Italian design, popular in the day, but the plants are modern, some grown and sold on site. In the middle, the Sunken Gardens have a fountain in the center with an enclosed walkway.

The Garden Club of North Carolina officially opened the Elizabethan Gardens in 1960, on Virginia Dare's birthday. Sculptor Maria Louise Landers imagined Virginia Dare as a sexy, voluptuous grown woman. I've been asked if it's worth visiting Fort Raleigh. Yes is the short answer. If you're staying on Cape Hatteras National Seashore or visiting the Wright Brothers National Memorial, plan to spend a couple of hours at the Fort Raleigh Visitor Center and walking the grounds. The site will quickly clarify a lot of history. And that's a goal of National Park Service interpretation.

಼◆಼

⚔ Fort Frederica National Monument
Oglethorpe ruled here
Georgia

Unlike Fort Raleigh, Fort Frederica has plenty of artifacts to explore. Visiting Fort Frederica National Monument reminds me that learning history in school was never as much fun as walking around this site. Fort Frederica is a small 250-acre unit in the middle of St. Simons Island off the southern Georgia Coast. After driving on a causeway past restaurants, high-end gated communities, and stables of pampered horses, I arrive at a historic sign explaining the Battle of Bloody Marsh. The entrance to the monument is just a little farther up Frederica Road.

In the 1700s, Britain and Spain seemed to be fighting constantly. Spain controlled what is now Florida and tried to move north into Georgia, while the British tried to move south. At this point, both sides claimed South Georgia—debatable land, as it was called. James Edward Oglethorpe, who founded Savannah, had a hunting camp on Cumberland Island. He created a colony in 1736 for the deserving poor, bringing over drifters and unemployed folks who had landed in debtors' prison in England.

The colonists built a fort, which protected Savannah, only seventy-five miles to the north. They created a replica of an English village. You can still see the brick outlines of many houses along with the magazine that stored gunpowder and other equipment.

Two battles ensued here between Great Britain and Spain: the Battles of Gully Hole and Bloody Marsh. In 1742, the Spanish advanced toward Frederica. Oglethorpe's men met them at Gully Hole Creek and fired, causing the Spanish troops to retreat. The British then pursued the enemy. The next skirmish lasted only an hour before the Spanish fell back again. It was said that the marsh was red with blood, hence the name, Bloody Marsh.

This was the last stand for the Spanish in Georgia. Both battles were won by the Brits, of course, and this land remained in British hands until the American Revolution. After the future of Georgia was set, the army disbanded and the community died out. In 1748, one thousand people lived in Fort Frederica. By 1757, barely a hundred called it home.

A fire finished off what was left of the village. "There was nothing suspicious about the fire," says Ranger Cynda Carpenter. "When you have a lot of wood, you're going to have a good chance of fire."

The Colonial Dames of America, which works to preserve historic locations, started buying land and petitioned the National Park Service to protect the area. It became a national monument in 1936. The site is now a quiet grassy area with several sets of ruins, a museum, and many live oaks dripping with Spanish moss.

A sign outside the visitor center helps to plan your visit. It reads: "Museum 20 minutes, Film 25 minutes, Self-Guided Tour 45 minutes."

The small museum has several tableaus of settlers going about their daily lives. Highlanders with rifles are shown marching in formation. Glass cases display nails, bits of leather, chains, and pottery shards. The film shows a reenactment of the two battles, Bloody Marsh and Gully Hole Creek. The narrator reminds us that we're only seventy-five miles north of St. Augustine and Castillo de Marco.

I walk around the site for much longer than the forty-five minutes the park suggests. In 1947, archaeologists started exploring the remains of the village. This must have been a dream job. History was uncovered, literally, as archaeologists excavated the foundations of the houses and barracks and then focused on the colonial lifestyle and even diet of the villagers. They worked from original records, because the British know how to document. Francis Moore, Oglethorpe's secretary, had published *A Voyage to Georgia* in 1744. The archaeologists worked to match descriptions and maps from this journal to what they found on site. The doctor and the tavern keeper shared a common wall. These were the first houses to be identified. From those two dwellings, they could figure out where other colonists lived.

Outside the visitor center, I cross a moat and enter the town within the walls of the fort. Street signs have been erected. I walk on Broad Street to see several house foundations that have survived. A plaque explains who lived in each dwelling. The houses were built on a foundation of bricks and tabby—like coquina, a mixture of lime, sand, and oyster shells. Now the outlines of the house sites are filled with shells.

Oglethorpe brought over skilled craftsmen and merchants. You can see where the doctor, the baker, and the candlestick maker lived and worked. Presentation cases contain plastic replicas of artifacts, bits of spoons, pottery, and nails found on site. Local Yamacraw Indians cleared the site of all trees, but residents planted Seville orange trees that are still bearing fruit. The ruins of a magazine, which stored guns and ammunitions, stand close to the Frederica River. Cannons protected the entrance to the fort.

The fort wasn't self-sufficient but depended on supplies from England. For the first year, a man could get one pint of strong beer per day when he worked, but not otherwise. He was also entitled to 312 pounds of beef or pork a year—that's almost a pound of meat per day. There's no information on what women were given to eat.

There was no church when the colonists lived in this village. But Oglethorpe brought John and Charles Wesley, two ministers from England. John Wesley visited Fort Frederica from Savannah several times to conduct Anglican services. After he went back to

England, he had a religious experience, which led him to found the modern Methodist Church. Every community needs a cemetery, here located past the visitor center. A period herb garden tended by volunteers is just outside the cemetery. It shows what settlers might have grown at the time.

On this trip, I reread *Ecology of a Cracker Childhood* by Janisse Ray, a nature writer. She writes about her childhood in South Georgia interspersed with discussion of environmental problems in the area. She describes herself as a descendant of Oglethorpe's debtor prisoners. The first time I read the book, the phrase didn't make an impression, but now I know what she meant.

૯ Timucuan Ecological and Historic Preserve
The French try to move in
Florida

The debtors that Oglethorpe brought over tried to recreate England in the New World. The French, however, came to Florida, hoping to profit from some of the riches that Spain had obtained here. When Jean Ribault and his men arrived at the mouth of the St. Johns River in 1562, they wanted to find gold and silver, though this expedition didn't seem to match the brutality of Hernando de Soto's expedition. Ribault must have liked what he found, because he erected a monument about ten miles east of present-day Jacksonville. Like many modern adventurers, Ribault published a book on his trip.

Two years later, René de Laudonniere established the first French colony in the New World, attracting Huguenots, French Protestants looking to get away from religious persecution by Catholics. But the colony wasn't successful. The Timucua Indians, friendly and helpful at first, got tired of propping up and feeding the Europeans. Just as the French were about to give up and return to France, Ribault came back with supplies for the struggling French colony.

In the meantime, the Spanish felt they owned Florida. In 1565, five hundred men led by Pedro Menendez sailed up the St. Johns River and massacred the French. This was the first battle between European nations for control of North America. The slaughter was the end of the French in Florida, and Spain would control the area for the next two hundred years. As the displays at the visitor center explain, the French had little impact on the environment in Florida. The Timucua Indian culture also fell apart and disappeared.

Nothing original survives on the ground from the French expedition and colony. Fort Caroline National Memorial was created in 1950, at the urging of Representative Charles Edward Bennett from Jacksonville. Over the years, the site has expanded to become the Timucuan Ecological and Historic Preserve. The visitor center displays nets, baskets, and adzes from the Timucua Indians. It also features famous men who had an impact on this part of Florida. Napoleon Bonaparte Broward, a governor of Florida in the early 1900s, encouraged the draining of the Everglades swamps, creating the South Florida boom and its environmental problems. William Bartram, a naturalist from Philadelphia, traveled through the South and popularized the image of Florida as paradise.

A mile-long loop leads to a Timucuan hut and to a reconstructed fort. As the interpretive signs state, the size and location of the colony and fort are still a mystery to historians. But the National Park Service built a fort with a moat, ramparts, cannons, and high walls. The rest of the loop explains the salt marsh habitat that the French would have found at the time. Live oak trees drip with Spanish moss, which is neither Spanish nor moss—it's an air plant.

One sign talks about the importance of muscadine grapes for the Timucua Indians and the French colony. The French managed to make over one thousand gallons of wine while they were here. "Of course," remarks a fellow walker. "They were French."

The Ribault Monument stands close to where Ribault might have landed on his first visit. An elaborate entrance and set of steps lead to a view of the St. Johns River. In 1924, the Florida Daughters of the American Revolution erected a stone column, similar to the marker placed near this spot by Ribault. The group wanted to commemorate the first landing by Protestants on American soil, allowing religious freedom in the New World. The marker also reminds Americans that this colony was established half a century prior to the Plymouth Colony.

಄✦ಆ

Across the road from the entrance to Fort Caroline lies a six-hundred-acre gem that shows off the natural environment of Old Florida. Willie Browne grew up in a house overlooking the salt marsh where he fished and explored shell mounds. His parents moved away, but he and his brother stayed. They farmed, fished, and operated a sawmill.

After his brother died, Browne lived in a cabin by himself and encouraged people to visit his land as a refuge. Browne could see development coming. Builders offered him millions, but Browne turned them down. Instead, he donated his property to the Nature Conservancy with the stipulation that they keep it wild. Because Browne was a great admirer of Theodore Roosevelt's conservation effort, the land was named the Theodore Roosevelt Area after the first conservation president. The park acquired the property in 1990.

I park at Spanish Pond to walk the well-marked nature trails. When Menendez camped here before attacking the French, there must have been plenty of water. Now Spanish Pond has become a meadow filled with vegetation after modern-day neighbors of Fort Caroline drained the pond. The boardwalk leads to the red trail, passing the remains of the Willie Browne cabin and a fresh gravestone for John Nathan Spearing, a Confederate soldier.

On the bird viewing platform overlooking the marsh, I can identify white egrets, bald eagles, and great blue herons. But the view also includes a smokestack, beach, homes, and ships. I'm close to working Jacksonville.

Two young rangers return after retrieving a sweater that a visitor left on the trail. That's really above and beyond the call of duty. I ask if I could take a picture of them.

"Hey, where's your flat hat?"

They pull out green knit hats from their pockets and put them on, to be in proper outdoor uniform.

"It's winter," one says, "and this is part of our winter uniform."

Winter? It's about seventy degrees. But it's Florida.

Under the birding platform, a sign explains that the platform was built as part of the Recreation Fee Demonstration Program. When Congress allowed the National Park Service to charge entrance fees to certain parks, they decided that the individual parks could keep 80 percent of the collected funds. The other 20 percent is distributed to parks that don't collect fees. In this park, the money went to build the platform. But why place this explanation in such an obscure spot?

In Jacksonville, I tell several locals, a waitress in a chain restaurant, the hotel clerk, and the guy making our Subway sandwiches, that I'm here to visit Timucuan Preserve. "You know, Fort Caroline?" I get a blank look from each one.

Fort Caroline is a fun place for the family. The Jacksonville tourist industry should really promote it better. Now with a Timucuan Trail Parks Foundation, maybe the park will attract more visitors.

✒ Virgin Islands National Park with
Virgin Islands Coral Reef National Monument
Tropical America
St. John, Virgin Islands

Virgin Islands National Park is the one park that most people have heard about in the territory of the US Virgin Islands. They picture flawless beaches, drinks, sun, and sand on the island of St. John—and they're right. That's why people visit the island. The national park takes up more than half of the island, retaining wide-open beaches without the trappings of Coney Island. It takes a long time and some planning to get here. You need to fly to St. Thomas, take a forty-five-minute taxi ride to the ferry terminal, and then the passenger ferry to St. John.

St. John is not untouched wilderness. The islands making up the US Virgin Islands were a Danish colony for over two hundred years. Denmark was a late arrival in the European race for colonies and profits in the New World. It occupied the uninhabited islands of St. Thomas from 1671 and St. John starting in 1718. The Danes, with the help of enslaved labor, built the sugar works. They grew sugar cane and turned it into sugar and rum. Sugar was big business in the 1800s, because Europeans wanted their sweets. Ruins of sugar mills dot the island. Remnants of walls, towers, and houses are disintegrating in plain sight, most covered by creeping weeds.

Annaberg is the most famous sugar mill preserved by the park service, partly because you can drive to the site. If you're lucky, a volunteer with Friends of Virgin Islands National Park will offer a tour. The windmill tower provided the power to crush the sugar cane, but work animals were also needed. It turns out that donkeys are perfect animals in this setting because they need little water in an area that can be quite arid. Sugar mills stopped operating a long time ago, but donkeys, now gone feral, walk the roads. You can pick one up for free. How you get it back home is your problem.

We stay in the campground on Cinnamon Bay, a paradise of a place. Our tent, the type that some call a FEMA tent, is huge and only a couple of minutes' walk from the beach. If you really want to save money, you can bring your own camping equipment: tent, sleeping bag, and cooler. Some people do figure out how to get all their stuff on the plane. However, Lenny and I have rented a tent with all the trimmings. The large canvas tent, the kind summer camps used to stuff kids in, comes with cots, clean bedding, and two large coolers. A lantern and all the cooking equipment you could want to feed a family are part of the deal. This is luxury.

"Huh, most of us wouldn't consider cold showers a luxury," Lenny says. True, the bathroom building, a few minutes down the trail, doesn't have hot water. To take a shower, I hold a chain with one hand while trying to soap myself with the other. Still, the campground is paradise to me.

We fix breakfast and lunch but go out to dinner in Cruz Bay. That's called marital compromise. But on the evening of the ranger program, we eat dinner at T'ree Lizards Restaurant, the campground eatery. As we walk in, we place our order from a limited menu. A waitress painstakingly writes our selections in beautiful cursive writing. Cats roam the floor of the outdoor restaurant. The food is good, and it's a quick meal so we can listen to the ranger.

Outside the restaurant, a small sitting area holds the only electric outlets. The campground charges over thirty dollars for Wi-Fi access. Campers twist themselves in knots to plug in and check their email. We can live for a few days without Internet or electricity. We're camping after all. This area offers a place to meet fellow campers as well, a big benefit of staying here.

Cinnamon Bay attracts many family groups. In the campsite next to us, a Danish family with three young children seems to spend all their time around the picnic table. We see them here when we leave in the morning and still sitting when we return. The two elementary-school-age children do homework, supervised by the father. The mother bathes the six-month-old girl in a dishwashing bucket.

One evening, I go over and introduce myself.

"How long are you here for?" I ask.

"We're taking several months to visit the three islands," the father says. He's a college professor on a sabbatical. The mom smiles but doesn't speak much English.

"Looking for your ancestors?"

"No," the dad says. "Just showing our children their heritage."

After talking to several visitors, I realize that Lenny and I are an anomaly because we're only staying in St. John for three days. Everyone we meet is on the island for least a week, most for a couple of weeks to a couple of months.

"But what do you do for two months?" I ask.

"We relax, swim, and putter."

I can't see lingering here for two months, even in a rented house with reliable Wi-Fi. The island has less than twenty miles of trail. What would I do after I walked all the trails?

The Reef Bay Trail takes us down 900 feet in 2.6 miles to Reef Bay Beach with its well-preserved sugar mill. As we walk down to the ruins, the terrain changes from lush tropical plants to dry, sparse vegetation. Along the way, we take the Petroglyph Trail. Archaeological records confirm that Taino Indians carved petroglyphs between 900 and 1500 CE. Circular faces with wide eyes reflecting in the spring-fed pool stare at me.

The Reef Bay Great House, just off the main trail, is considered one of the most important architectural monuments in the park. The owner of Reef Bay Estates lived here. Then the property went through several hands. The existing building dates from the early nineteenth century, but the stone foundation of an earlier wood building remains within its walls. After Denmark abolished slavery in 1848, the sugar industry was no longer profitable. By 1908, Reef Bay, the last operating sugar mill, stopped operation. The daughters of the last owner lived in the house until 1951. By then, the house was already deteriorating.

Now the building is boarded up and covered in ivy. The house is isolated and not easily accessible, other than on foot. The remote location has protected what's left but kept it from being rehabilitated.

You could write a bodice ripper or a mystery about the occupants of this house. Here's the start of a plot. *A young Danish woman doesn't want to go back home with her parents and stays in the big house with just her servants. They raise chickens and grow vegetables, but it's a meager, lonely existence. Then a strange man comes knocking . . .*

The United States had been trying to buy the Virgin Islands from the Danes since 1867. While World War I was raging in Europe, the islands became an American territory. However, Danish influence is still felt all over the islands. What happened to the Danes? Did they go home or integrate? Learn English? A Library of Congress publication notes that Danish Americans, more so than other Scandinavian Americans, "spread nationwide and comparatively quickly disappeared into the melting pot . . . the Danes were the least cohesive group and the first to lose consciousness of their origins." Still the Danish influence here can be felt in the architecture and street names. Many Virgin Islanders have Danish last names.

In 1956, Laurance Rockefeller, grandson of John D. Rockefeller, the co-founder of Standard Oil, bought land in St. John and donated more than five thousand acres for a national park. Now over fifteen thousand acres are protected.

In my obsessive quest to see every national park unit in the Southeast, we drive to Hurricane Hole to get to Virgin Islands Coral Reef National Monument. The Coral Reef Monument was created in 2001 to protect almost thirteen thousand acres of submerged marine life adjacent to Virgin Islands National Park.

This park is best appreciated from a boat or while scuba diving, but we find the only place to reach it from Centerline Road, the main road through the island. We pull off on a wide spot and get into the water. I maneuver around the mangroves. The trees are so intertwined in the brackish water that it's hard to distinguish the trunks from the roots. I swim out past the mangroves and lie on my back in the warm water, looking at the blue sky. We have the whole area to ourselves. This is the stereotypic view of paradise on earth. I can now say that I was in Coral Reef National Monument.

✒ Christiansted National Historic Site
Fascinating and underappreciated
St. Croix, Virgin Islands

What is the most underappreciated unit of the National Park Service? After my trip to the US Virgin Islands, I can answer with great conviction that the three intriguing parks in St. Croix—Christiansted National Historic Site, Buck Island Reef National Monument, and Salt River Bay National Historical Park—qualify for both overlooked and underappreciated.

After enjoying the trails, beaches, and donkeys of Virgin Islands National Park in St. John, Lenny and I fly to St. Croix, the most Danish of the three US Virgin Islands. The Danish West India Company purchased St. Croix from France in 1733 to increase its sugar mill operations. Of the three islands, St. Croix is the largest, flattest, and most suited to agriculture.

Christiansted National Historic Site, established in 1952,

consists of seven acres and six historic buildings in the middle of the town of Christiansted, named in honor of King Christian VI of Denmark and Norway. Its stated mission is "to preserve the historic structure and grounds within its boundaries, and to interpret the Danish economy and way of life in St. Croix between 1733 and 1917." During the height of the sugar cane industry, mid-eighteenth century to mid-nineteenth century, the island became wealthy, attracting international residents. At one time or another, the white population of Christiansted consisted of Danes, Norwegians, British, Germans, Dutch, Irish, and a few Sephardic Jews. There's still an active synagogue in Christiansted, though we decided to skip Friday night services.

Fort Christiansvaern, built in 1738, is the major historic building left by the Danes. The yellow building still has its cannons pointing out to sea, though I doubt if it could take on a hostile navy now. The location was protected by two smaller forts, forming a triangle. If an enemy ship came into the harbor, it would be caught in crossfire, but the fort was never attacked.

The small visitor center offers information for all three St. Croix national park sites. The historic site needs a lot of help. We're at the fort on a Saturday, hoping to join a scheduled ranger tour, but we're out of luck because there just isn't enough staff on duty.

Instead, Jazmyne, a smiling fifth-grader, approaches us and asks if we want a tour.

"Yes, please," we say.

Jazmyne starts with the dungeon for bad slaves.

"If you burned cane fields, they put you in solitary confinement." That was the worst crime that could be committed in those days. The cell is a small black hole. Jazmyne also makes sure we visit the urinals, where human waste went straight out to the sea.

Alexander Hamilton, born in the Caribbean island of Nevis, grew up in Christiansted with his mother, Rachel Lavien, and older brother. Lavien had left her abusive husband, who was much older and more socially powerful. He had his wife imprisoned in the fort for several months, claiming that she had committed "such mistakes, which for married people were indecent and very suspect." At least she had her own cell.

Lavien's life could inspire romance novelists. After being released from prison, she fell in love with a Scotsman, James Hamilton, and had two sons, though she wasn't free to marry. The family came back to Christiansted, but soon the Hamilton boys became orphans. Alexander trained as a carpenter.

As an exhibit states, "Hamilton was determined to make his way into the world, but not in St. Croix since he was not born to a plantocracy." Instead, he found his way to New York, where he became one of the Founding Fathers of the United States. The ten-dollar bill now displays the face of Alexander Hamilton.

In the fort, the officers had a day room facing the courtyard where they rested, played checkers, and wrote letters. The original Danish furniture dates back from the 1830s to 1850s. Upstairs, the cannons face out to sea.

Jazmyne has the singsong uptalk of a tween trying to recite important facts. She does a great job as a tour guide and saves us the trouble of figuring out the various rooms from a paper guide photocopied to death. As we leave the fort, we learn that she's the daughter of the ranger on desk duty.

"Jazmyne loves history," her mother says proudly. "She wants to be a ranger."

We continue the tour suggested in the park pamphlet. The town is laid out in a grid with imposing masonry structures, painted yellow. Christiansted's Danish heritage comes through in its architecture, arcaded sidewalks, and street names. The colonial capital was built on the backs of slaves and fueled by sugar and rum money. By 1917, the Virgin Islands were in a long economic decline. Denmark sold the three islands to the United States a few days before it officially entered World War I.

The other buildings, all within a couple of blocks of each other, are mostly closed, but a walk around offers a good feel for the wealth and gentility of the colonial era. The Steeple Building, built in 1753 as the original Lutheran Church, is now a museum. The Danish West India & Guinea Company Warehouse, where slaves were once auctioned off in the yard, has been turned into storerooms. The Custom House and post office dates back to 1844. Today the exhibit signs have faded. The Scale House is now used as offices, with outdoor exhibits on Alexander Hamilton's early life. Government House, owned by the Virgin Islands government, might be open to visitors on weekdays.

The last building on the tour, the Lord God of Sabaoth Lutheran Church, was first built as the Dutch Reformed Church before 1740. On Saturday evening, I hear music coming out of the open doors and slip quietly into the church. I'm wearing Bermuda shorts and a T-shirt but hope that other worshippers are also in casual dress. Almost all the parishioners are African-Americans. The pastor, a tall, rotund man, wears a white robe with a rope holding the garment closed. The congregation is up at the pulpit receiving the Eucharist, followed by energetic singing led by an inspirational choir. According to Garrison Keillor and a lot of others, Lutherans love to sing.

The president of the congregation makes his announcements and asks, "Are there any visiting Danes worshipping with us tonight?" Three couples stand up. They're wearing shorts as well.

"Are there other visitors?" I don't stand because I'm not worshipping, just observing.

The music turns lively. The congregation sways and takes a few side-to-side steps in the aisle. The minister and the female assistant minister, similarly dressed in a white robe, are dancing. The

Danes look around in amazement. We all sing "I Shall Not Be Moved." Even I know the words and join in.

℘✦℃℞

The national parks in St. Croix could use a lot of help and a Friends group. When I meet Ranger David J. Goldstein, chief of interpretation and education, I ask again about a tour.

"My priorities are the children on the island," Goldstein says. "They don't know about their own place. They don't know why they're here." So no resources for the public. I sympathize with him. Even the Eastern National bookstore is closed this weekend.

The St. Croix parks are underfunded and understaffed. I'm outraged at how little help the St. Croix national park gems are getting from their residents. This is not a poor area. We met rich retirees from the mainland with second homes or living here permanently. The upscale restaurants show that there's plenty of money on the island. These folks could be volunteers.

Where is the Friends group? Almost every national park has a Friends group, which raises money for the park, supplies volunteers, and in general increases visibility. The parks also need volunteers who will give tours, clean up the trails, and do a thousand things that the park staff doesn't have the resources to do. Heck, how about just writing a check? The parks can't do it all on their own. Even before budget cuts and sequestration, the National Park Service was never well funded. There has to be support from the local people.

And what about the Danes? St. Croix is the most Danish of the Virgin Islands. All park pamphlets are in Danish and English and so are the restaurant menus. A mother and daughter came from Denmark to celebrate the mother's sixtieth birthday. The mother had worked as a nanny in St. Croix more than forty years ago. Danish tours come here from November to April. I spoke to several Danes who said that they came in search of their country's history. Of course, visitors help the island's general economy, but not much seems to trickle down to the national parks. Shouldn't there be a Danish Friends of the St. Croix National Parks? Money, time, and effort could refurbish the fort and open up the other buildings.

Even the tourist brochures have very little mention of the national parks. The website visitusvi.com has an exhibit board in the center of town offering sightseeing suggestions. The Christiansted fort is only suggested on Day 5, maybe.

If you're in the Virgin Islands, visit St. Croix and its national parks, and drop a ten-dollar bill in their donation box.

5

REVOLUTIONARY WAR IN THE SOUTH

Why were all battles fought in national parks? This is one of many silly questions asked of park rangers.

To most visitors, the American Revolution seems clear and uncontroversial. The Americans won, the British lost, and the United States became an independent country. The Brits tried to reclaim the United States in 1812, but they weren't successful in that war either. Revolutionary war reenactors are just as passionate as Civil War buffs, maybe because the British costumes are so flamboyant. In the South, most battles were fought between colonists: Patriots—Americans who wanted to break away from Great Britain—and Tories or Loyalists—Americans loyal to the British

Crown. We associate South Carolina with the Civil War, because that war started here with the bombardment of Fort Sumter. Yet there are more Revolutionary War action sites in South Carolina than in any other state.

April 19, 1775. The first shots in Lexington and Concord, Massachusetts, were supposedly heard around the world when British troops tried to seize military supplies from the Patriots. In November of the same year, Loyalists besieged Ninety Six, a trading post in South Carolina, for a couple of days. A few months later, Patriots won the Battle of Moores Creek in eastern North Carolina.

But it wasn't until 1778 that British strategists decided to move to the southern colonies, still thinking that they could keep timber and agricultural products safe for the empire. The South was not the Loyalist hotbed that the Brits were counting on.

"In the South, the British found timid friends, and inveterate enemies," said Lt. General Charles Earl Cornwallis, commander of the British forces in the South.

Cornwallis, a career military man, had been in the Seven Years War, known as the French and Indian War in the United States. We keep meeting him in various encounters in the South. Though Cornwallis lost at the Battle of Yorktown, effectively ending the Revolution, it wasn't a career-breaking defeat for him. He became commander in chief and governor-general of India.

On the Patriot side, Nathanael Greene's name is everywhere in the Southern Campaign. In many places, his first name shows up misspelled. Regionally, he's most prominent at the Battle of Guilford Courthouse, in present-day Greensboro, and Cowpens, in upstate South Carolina. After the war, he fell deep into debt, but the states of Georgia and South Carolina generously thanked him for his service. Greene bought a plantation on Cumberland Island, though he didn't have time to enjoy his new estate because he died young. You can visit his grave on the island.

The first fort in what is now Fort Moultrie was built to protect Charleston Harbor from British occupation. It was named in honor of its commander, Colonel William Moultrie, who defended the harbor in a nine-hour battle. Four years later, the British captured Charleston and held it until the end of the war.

Fort Sumter, which we know best as the site of the first Civil War encounter, was named for Thomas Sumter, a patriot born in Virginia. When Charleston fell to the British and the South Carolina governor moved the state capitol to North Carolina, Thomas Sumter didn't give up. Instead he created a militia to renew the struggle against the enemy. South Carolina honored him as one of their own. Too bad that we only know Sumter from a Civil War fort instead of as the Revolutionary War hero he was.

♿ Ninety Six National Historic Site
Trading post and battle site
South Carolina

Some parks are not on the way to anything else. You just have to make them a destination. Ninety Six National Historic Site, two miles from the current town of Ninety Six, South Carolina, sits between Greenville and Columbia.

The name Ninety Six always raises a question. The trading post, on British maps since 1730, sold necessities such as rum, sugar, and gunpowder. English traders thought that this spot was ninety-six miles from Keowee, a principal town in lower Cherokee, close to present-day Clemson. The settlement morphed into a town with shops, a courthouse, and a jail. As the number of colonists grew, they impinged on Cherokee territory. Fort Ninety Six withstood two Indian attacks. However, this history alone might not have made it a national park unit.

Every military park claims a first. Ninety Six was the site of the first significant land battle in the South during the Revolutionary War. Fought on November 19–21, 1775, the confrontation ended in a truce between Loyalists and Patriots. But the bigger event occurred in the spring of 1781, toward the end of the war.

The British had fortified the town. Loyalists and slave labor built an eight-pointed-star fort, a showcase of military engineering. The Patriots, under the command of Major General Nathanael Greene, besieged the fort for twenty-eight days, the longest battle in the Revolutionary War. They dug a tunnel to set off explosives and open a breach in the wall. The tunnel was never finished, and the Patriots stormed the fort. That didn't work too well either. When the Continental Army heard that a British contingent was coming, they slipped away. Ninety Six brought out the Patriot stars. Besides Nathanael Greene, Henry Lee III, dubbed Light Horse Harry, Thaddeus Kosciuszko, and Andrew Pickens fought here—all names we encounter over and over again in the Southern Campaign.

What can you actually do at the site today? Visitors are always advised to watch the movie because it's a great introduction to the site. At Ninety Six, Trace Adkins, a popular country music singer, narrates the movie. Apparently, history is one of his passions. The star fort is remarkably well-preserved for its age, now exhibited in the center of a one-mile paved loop trail. The park service has outlined the boundaries of the tiny original town of Ninety Six. The site protects over one thousand acres of land, without much development outside its boundaries. A monument to James Birmingham, the first South Carolinian to die during the Revolutionary War, was erected, but in general, the historic site has remarkably few memorials. You feel you're seeing the battlefield site as it was two hundred years ago.

I walk the Gouedy Trail, site of a major trading post and several gravesites. The original Charleston Road, which led from the coast into the backcountry, takes off from the Gouedy Trail. Because of the large number of traders and settlers using this road, the path, now sunken and obvious, has been rehabilitated as part of a hiking trail. Hikers don't need blazes to follow this route.

Today, two groups of local schoolchildren visit the park. I find them at the Logan Log House, a settler's cabin built in the 1700s, moved here before the site became a park. It was used as the park's first visitor center. Now the cabin is outfitted as the Black Swan Tavern, where men gathered for food, a pint of beer, and the news of the day. After, the students walk around the fort. Over sixty-five thousand people visited the park in 2014, many of them probably with their classes.

☙ Moores Creek National Battlefield
A three-minute battle
North Carolina

Like Ninety Six, Moores Creek National Battlefield in the sandhills of North Carolina is not close to other tourist attractions. I know I'm going in the right direction when I turn on General William Howe Highway, named after the commander in chief of the British Forces in the American Revolution.

This quiet national park unit preserves the site of a short but important battle. The administrative history of Moores Creek says that the battle was to the southern colonies what Lexington had been for the northern colonies. Moores Creek, twenty miles northwest of Wilmington, North Carolina, is a slow-moving black-water creek. Cypress trees, with their characteristic knees, throw off their reflection in the water. A bridge has stood here since 1743.

On February 26, 1776, the Loyalists gave the Patriots an ultimatum. They could avoid combat if they laid down their arms and swore allegiance to the British Crown. When the Patriots refused, a short but significant battle ensued that had great consequences for the direction of the Revolutionary War.

Loyalists, mostly Scottish Highlanders with broadswords, marched to the coast and planned to join British forces under Lord Charles Cornwallis. First, they had to cross Moores Creek. Here was the Patriots' last chance to stop them. Once the British came after them, they knew they couldn't win. Colonel James Moore of the 1st North Carolina Continentals took charge of countering the Loyalists.

That night the Patriots partly destroyed the bridge across Moores Creek. Then they abandoned their camps and hid in the earthworks they had previously built. Loyalists waited for daybreak, then marched across the creek where they were surprised with artillery fire. Expecting a small force, the Loyalists found themselves facing about a thousand Patriots. The battle lasted three minutes. Loyalists lost thirty men, the Patriots only one.

This was the first southern victory of the American Revolution, which ended British rule in the colony. As a result, many believe North Carolina was the first colony to call for independence. The Patriot victory encouraged revolutionary fervor and helped beat back the British on Sullivan's Island off the coast of Charleston, South Carolina.

Today, Moores Creek National Battlefield is an eighty-eight-acre park with two short trails, perfect for families willing to take a detour. At the visitor center, four panels depict troop movements through the area: blue lights for Patriots and red lights for Loyalists. Other panels illustrate a timeline in two parts. Above the line, events focus on national happenings at the time, starting with the Stamp Act on March 22, 1765, a direct tax on colonists. Below the line are relevant North Carolina events. Governor William Tryon, North Carolina's first Royal Governor from 1767 to 1770, imposed taxes on liquor to fund the construction of Tryon Palace in New Bern.

The History Trail, a one-mile loop, leads to the battle site through savanna and swampland. Part of the trail, built from recycled rubber, looks like wood chips glued together. The park has rehabilitated the earthworks to help visitors understand the battle. I pass six monuments, including one for Private John Grady, the only Patriot killed in this battle. A memorial to the Loyalists sits under a spreading live oak tree with Spanish moss dripping from its branches.

The trail crosses the historic Negro Head Point Road, which linked the interior of North Carolina to the Wilmington coast, a key port in the slave trade. You can get a feel for colonial transportation by walking a small piece of the trail as it crosses the park. Negro Head Point had holding pens for the slave markets in Wilmington.

The Tar Heel Trail, a third of a mile long, goes through a stand of longleaf pine, a tree tapped for tar, resins, pitch, and turpentine. These products, known as naval stores, were sent to Wilmington and exported to the world to support the shipbuilding industry. Tar waterproofed ship riggings. Thousands of tar kilns were scattered throughout coastal plains. An example of a reconstructed tar kiln stands on the trail. Coastal North Carolina supplied a quarter of the world's naval stores. If you ran barefoot through the pines, you'd get tar on your heels, hence the nickname Tar Heel for North Carolinians.

Once steel ships came in and these naval products were no longer needed, longleaf pines were cut down throughout the area to make way for the faster growing loblolly pines. The park now has a program to plant longleaf pines throughout the site.

Protection of the site started formally on February 27, 1856, the eightieth anniversary of the battle. Two years later, a cornerstone was laid for what was to become the Patriot monument. The Moores Creek Monument Association, founded in 1899, protected the battlefield until 1926, when it was turned over to the US War Department. The National Park Service then acquired all battlefields in 1933. Moores Creek National Battlefield Association now has the distinction of being the oldest continuing operating Friends group in the National Park Service.

The Mountains-to-Sea Trail across North Carolina, a one-thousand-mile trail from the Smokies to the Outer Banks, goes into the battlefield. When I walked the MST in 2011, I took a completely different route through the coastal plains. But this fledging trail changed its route to make use of more public lands and now includes Moores Creek.

⌘ Historic Camden Revolutionary War Site
Worst Patriot defeat
South Carolina

"Spend a few peaceful hours where the British spent a rough year!"

That's the tagline of Historic Camden, South Carolina, located between Columbia and Florence. I drove two hundred miles to visit Historic Camden, a Revolutionary War site. To me, driving four hundred miles round trip from Asheville is in between a day trip and staying overnight. I spent over five hours at the site, which made it a long day.

Historic Camden is an NPS affiliate, not an official unit, but it's shown on the park service Southeast Region map. When I've worked on hiking challenges such as walking all the trails in the Smokies, I covered every trail on the map. It's no different with visiting all the parks in the Southeast. If it's on the map or on an official list, I have to go there. And I'm glad I did.

When I called the day before, Joanna Craig, Executive Director of the Historic Camden Foundation (HCF), warned that a swarm of fourth graders would take over the site. I pictured a swarm of locusts. Nevertheless, I go when I plan to go. Having children around is fine. It turned out to be a bonus.

A little history: Camden had been a frontier settlement since 1733. Later a merchant, Joseph Kershaw, opened a general store, and became prosperous enough to build a big house on Pine Tree Hill befitting a gentleman. After Charleston fell in May 1780, British General Cornwallis marched into Camden, fortified the area, and erected a large stockade fence.

General Horatio Gates, hero of the Battle of Saratoga, took command of the American troops in the South to clear the British from the Carolinas. The two armies met about eight miles north on August 16, 1780. The Americans were soundly defeated in what is called the worst Patriot defeat of the American Revolution. Many in the American militia panicked and ran. General Gates joined the fleeing troops and never recovered from this disgrace. Nathanael Greene then took over as commander of the Southern Continental Army.

Lord Cornwallis moved into the Kershaw house, shipping its wealthy owner to a prison in Barbados. When the British evacuated at the end of the war, they burned most of the town but not the house. Undeterred, Joseph Kershaw returned, and the town was rebuilt a couple of miles north of its original site. The house had several subsequent owners and eventually burned in 1865.

I arrive at ten a.m. to find forty children from a local school, divided into four groups, already engaged with the site. The visitor center is closed, so I attach myself to a group and listen to a description of the battle and the cannons in a barn. The resident cat plays with a dead bird in its mouth as it wanders around the children. The poor interpreter—never could figure out if she was staff or a volunteer—has to compete for attention with the cat.

The key to having children's attention is to keep them moving, and the program does this admirably. We all shift to the stocks, a colonial punishment for which guilty persons had to put their legs into large hinged wooden boards and endure public humiliation. For more major offenses, the head went into a pillory. Here the kids eagerly raise their hands so they can be imprisoned in these contraptions.

After the children let off steam playing colonial games, we watch an admittedly slow film on Camden history. The reconstructed Kershaw-Cornwallis house, the house on the hill, is the highlight of the visit. Historic Camden, now owned and managed by the HCF, rebuilt the house. Using archaeological records, the current structure is on the same foundation as the original. The inside has generic Georgian period furniture. Several other buildings of the period have been moved to the site and interpreted.

I thought we were going to get the usual house tour: *The table is eighteenth century oak while the bed is a reproduction . . .* Boooring, even for adults. But Jennifer Lee, the interpreter in the big house, gives a costume presentation.

"What did colonial men and women wear? Not jeans and a T-shirt."

Lee starts with a nightshirt and brings out Loyalist and Patriot uniforms and a male wig. Women also wore a nightshirt under all their petticoats and plumage. To involve as many children as possible, each kid wears only one piece of colonial clothing. In the eighteenth century, people bathed twice a year, at most. The rivers were so full of refuse that a person would end up dirtier and even sicker after a bath than before. This makes an impression on the kids. The group then moves on to quill writing. What a brilliant program!

This location only encompasses the old village of Camden. I drive to the battlefield, eight miles north on a 477-acre plot of land protected by the Palmetto Conservation Foundation (PCF), which also manages the Palmetto Trail, a South Carolina state trail. The battlefield is covered with rows of longleaf pines, similar to the terrain at the time of the battle. Several short trails have interpretive signs pertaining to the battle.

The site has been trying to become part of the National Park Service since 1983. Craig appeared before Congress, testifying on the importance of the site and advocating for veteran protection. "There are veteran Patriots who may be lying here without a proper burial."

The affiliated site doesn't receive federal funding and has no park rangers, though you can get your national park passport stamped. The passport is arranged by NPS regions, but it doesn't leave you room for too many stamps in each region. The Southeast section of my passport has long been filled, and I now use another notebook for my visits.

Several years ago, I visited Tule Springs in Nevada, when they were trying to become an NPS unit. They succeeded and are now Tule Springs Fossil Beds National Monument. My feeling is that Historic Camden and the battlefield will eventually become a unit of the National Park Service. They have the land, the site, and the passionate locals, who will probably morph into a Friends group. The only question is when. So does this park count as extra credit?

Kings Mountain National Military Park with the Overmountain Victory National Historic Trail
Where the New World begins
North Carolina, South Carolina, Tennessee, Virginia

Every American Revolutionary site might look the same on the surface. They all have a film, a museum, and a short walk around the battlefield. However, if you look below the surface, you'll find that each has its own flavor based on history, topography, and surroundings.

Kings Mountain, thirty-nine miles southwest of Charlotte, North Carolina, lies in a quiet, pastoral setting. The area, named for an early settler and not the British King George, encompasses almost four thousand acres. Winter is a perfect time to spend the day here, with mild weather and unobstructed views from the hilltop.

Summer, though, "gets pretty buggy here," says Ranger John Hambright. The ranger is the seventh generation grandson of Lieutenant Colonel Frederick Hambright, who fought at Kings Mountain, a fact that never fails to impress me. The present-day Hambright still lives in the area.

A few facts. Most Revolutionary War encounters in the South were fought entirely between Americans on either side of the independence issue. On Kings Mountain, on October 7, 1780, Patriots defeated the Tories in little more than an hour.

Kings Mountain was one of several battles aimed at reestablishing British rule in the South. At first, this strategy looked right for the Crown. In South Carolina, the British had captured Charleston in early 1780. Later in the year, they triumphed at Camden and at the Battle of Waxhaws. In the latter battle, the successful Tories under Colonel Banastre Tarleton continued killing after the Patriots waved the white flag of surrender. The Patriots didn't forget this massacre.

In 1780, Lieutenant General Charles Earl Cornwallis, commander of the British forces in the South, ordered Major Patrick Ferguson into western North Carolina to recruit and train Loyalists. Ferguson, the only Brit to fight here, sent a message to the backwater men, the overmountain settlers in the Appalachians, and warned them that he was going to kill them all if they didn't submit to him. The major didn't try to win hearts and minds. He operated by threats. Although he was a brave leader and considered the best marksman of his day in the British Army, Ferguson rubbed everyone the wrong way.

The Overmountain Men of Scots-Irish descent lived west of the Blue Ridge Mountains. They defied the 1763 proclamation of King George III that English settlers stay east of the mountains and out of Indian land. These tough men were well versed in guerilla tactics, having fought the Indians. Instead of being cowed by Ferguson's threats, the Overmountain Men from North Carolina, Virginia, and what is now Tennessee organized under three Patriot commanders at Sycamore Shoals, in present-day Elizabethton, Tennessee. They marched two hundred miles in fourteen days to Kings Mountain, where Ferguson and his men waited. Another group came from Elkin, North Carolina, and the two met at Quaker Meadows, close to present-day Morganton. The Overmountain Victory Trail commemorates this march.

To tell the groups apart, Tories wore twigs in their hats while Patriots stuck bits of paper in theirs. To quote the visitor center film, "These mountain men knew each other and they hated each other. Unrelenting civil war had scourged the South with partisan plunder, bushwhackers, and brutal massacres. Neighbors against neighbors, fathers against sons."

The Patriot commanders knew the intense independence of the Overmountain Men and didn't lay out an explicit battle strategy. Isaac Shelby called out:

> *When we encounter the enemy, don't wait for a word of command. Let each of you be your own officer, and do the very best you can . . . If in the woods, shelter yourselves and give them Indian play: advance from tree to tree . . . and killing and disabling all you can . . .*

In other words, "I trust you and you're on your own, fellows." That suited the Overmountain Men. They didn't take directions well. Like Indians, they hollered each time they fired a shot. Kings Mountain, a 150-foot rocky spur in the Blue Ridge foothills, was treeless at the time of the battle. Ferguson took to the hilltop, which should have been an excellent position. The Patriots opened fire from below and took cover in the trees. It didn't take much elevation gain to affect the battle. The Patriots ran from tree to tree to reach the summit.

In the thick of the battle, Ferguson used a whistle to command his troops from his vantage point. He was struck by several bullets and soon died at the battle site. After the Tories surrendered, the Patriots showed no mercy and continued the killing, yelling, "Give them Tarleton's quarter" as revenge for the slaughter at Waxhaws, the previous battle. Finally, the leaders took control of their men. The Overmountain Men had won against the Tories, effectively ending Loyalist influence in the Carolinas.

Sharyn McCrumb, in her novel *King's Mountain*, retells the story of the Overmountain Victory Men. The author humanizes Major Ferguson by giving him a mistress who describes what's happening on the Tory side. Ferguson, the second son of a Scottish aristocratic family, needed to make his name in the military. According to McCrumb, George Washington had shot him in the crook of his right elbow at Brandywine, making his arm unusable. By the time Ferguson reached Kings Mountain, he had learned to use his left hand. For some reason, he wore a red checked shirt in battle, making him an even more visible target.

The Patriots won. Then what? How do you clean up after a battle? What do you do with all the prisoners? How do you spread the food around? How do you supervise the only doctor on site, especially a doctor who happens to be a Loyalist? Most history books stop at the end of the battle and don't discuss these problems.

I spent several hours at Kings Mountain on the film, exhibits, and bookstore at the visitor center and walking the battlefield. The museum houses exhibits in large, open tree-trunk sculptures, meant to simulate the hilly landscape. When a visitor enters the tree trunk, motion sensors activate the exhibit. A pioneer woman of Scots-Irish descent stands in a typical Appalachian cabin and explains why her husband is going to fight the British. Her husband says that they live, "Not at the end of the world but where the new world begins." A battlefield panorama shows the movements of the armies. Fiber optic lights embedded in the map highlight the position and actions of both sides in the battle—red lights for the Loyalists and blue lights for Patriots.

The 1.5-mile paved Battlefield Trail gives a good feel for how the battle played out. If a visitor has a limited amount of time in the park, Ranger Hambright recommends walking the Battlefield Trail to understand the challenges the Patriots were facing. "They were being charged with bayonets and running from the enemy," Hambright says. Small hills that may be barely noticeable when you're out for a walk become major obstacles when you're dodging enemy bullets coming from the ridge top. On the walk, you can't see any modern infrastructure.

It's about at this point in my visits to Revolutionary battlefields that I start to look at monuments in detail and check out who sponsored these memorials. In 1815, Dr. William MacLean erected one of the earliest Revolutionary battlefield memorial markers in the country. You can barely see the writing on its free-form stone. A modern one with the same inscription stands alongside.

Two obelisks dominate the landscape along this loop trail. In 1880, the Kings Mountain Centennial Association erected a twenty-eight-foot monument known today as the Centennial Monument to mark the battle's 100th anniversary. In *Memories of War,* historian Thomas A. Chambers explains, "Not until the Revolution's centennial would governmental commemorative efforts begin in earnest, tied in large part to efforts to heal the Civil War's wounds by binding the nation together in what was depicted as a sectional past."

Through the persistent efforts of the Kings Mountain Chapter of the Daughters of the American Revolution, the federal government put up an eighty-three-foot-tall modern obelisk in 1909. The monument lists the dead and wounded, both officers and militia. However, the Kings Mountain battlefield was forgotten until 1930. At the 150th anniversary of the battle, President Herbert Hoover became the first president to visit an American Revolution battlefield in the South. Over seventy thousand spectators heard the President's address, broadcast coast to coast on radio. Kings Mountain became a National Military Park the next year.

The loop trail passes at least two monuments to Major Ferguson, the enemy. An old stone with the inscription "Here Col. Ferguson fell Oct 7, 1780" is barely readable. Major Ferguson is buried on the side of the trail under a big pile of stones. The "Citizens of the United States" erected his memorial gravestone in 1930. The passage of time and our friendship with the British allow for acknowledgment of this one-time enemy.

At Cowpens, the next major southern battle, the British didn't depend on American Loyalists but brought out their regular army.

ᴄ᷍ᴝ Cowpens National Battlefield
Fighting the British Army
South Carolina

After losing at Kings Mountain, the British sent in their army, the best in the world at the time. Cowpens became one of the turning points of the Revolutionary War in the South.

As its name implied, Cowpens was a field used by farmers to graze cows on their way to Charleston markets. The area around the park has remained very rural. On January 17, 1781, General Daniel Morgan, a southern Revolutionary hero, led a group of Continentals, paid army soldiers, and militia, real volunteers, to a victory against a large force of British soldiers.

Lieutenant Colonel Banastre Tarleton, fiercely hated in South Carolina after his troops cut down unarmed soldiers at the Battle of Waxhaws, was the British commander. The one-hour battle was meticulously designed with several lines of soldiers, each with its own strategy. It was as if the Brits and the American Army said, "I'll meet you behind the school yard. Bring your friends and be prepared to fight." The Patriot foot soldiers and cavalry used a double envelope technique that resulted in mass surrender of the British troops.

The visitor center houses an exhibit of soldier uniforms, a movie, and red and blue toy soldiers. Children can find other toys in drawers that say *Open me.* I loved the movie, a recap of the Cowpens battle told by a grandfather to his wide-eyed grandson.

"We were ready to die. We were willing to die," the grandfather says. He praises General Daniel Morgan as "one of us," even if he was born in New Jersey. In contrast, "Tarleton went to one of them fancy schools in Britain. He bought his commission."

After enjoying the visitor center and the funny and knowledgeable staff, Lenny and I walk the one-mile trail to see the battlefield in a pastoral setting. You have to imagine the land with almost no trees. It was a cow pasture after all. Robert Scruggs built a house in 1828 that still stands on the battlefield.

The Washington Light Infantry, a Charleston militia made up of the city's leading citizens, erected a thin spire on top of a concrete base in 1856, the seventy-fifth anniversary of the battle.

However, they did more than just leave their name at Cowpens. They attempted to unify the state of South Carolina by bringing white shells from the lowcountry at Fort Moultrie. Today the ground around the monument is filled with white pebbles.

The group had celebrated the Revolutionary War victory for over fifty years in Charleston, but now they vowed to make a pilgrimage to Cowpens. By then, with the division between North and South so pronounced, commemoration of Revolutionary battlefields could be used to invoke either the sectionalism of the South or the national unity agenda of the North.

After the monument was erected, a group of Spartanburg women bought a one-acre tract and gave it to the Washington Light Infantry. Cowpens became a National Battlefield Site in 1929 on just this small piece of land. The cabin remained private until the National Park Service bought it from a Scruggs family member. The park, now 846 acres, has graduated to a National Battlefield.

It wasn't easy to travel to southern Revolutionary battlefields before the Civil War. Cowpens was considered very remote and difficult to reach. Southern roads were unpaved and in poor condition. Lodging and restaurants were few and far between and certainly not the quality expected by the Charleston upper crust who contemplated making such a trip.

Today, the roads are decent and it's easy to find the park visitor center, thanks to the reassuring brown signs on the roads. But some things haven't changed. Accommodations are not available close to the park. Fast food is the rule, so I always take my lunch. Cowpens is no longer a multi-day trip. It's less than an hour from Greenville, a major city.

According to National Park statistics, the average length of a visit to Cowpens is forty-five minutes. But I talk to the ranger on duty, read every exhibit in the visitor center, and take a few notes, though I don't pretend that I retain it all. I walk the trails and try to imagine the battle. Then I circle back to the visitor center and ask the ranger some more questions. By this time, a new person is behind the desk, giving me a different perspective. Sometimes in the discussion, I realize that I missed something important and go back to check it out. At Cowpens, we spent over four hours at the site.

ᔕ Guilford Courthouse National Military Park
Victory or defeat?
North Carolina

Who would have thought there would be a national military park that recognizes a Revolutionary War defeat? Guilford Courthouse National Military Park in the North Carolina Piedmont commemorates a significant two-and-a-half-hour battle that ended in a tactical loss by the Americans. But the British suffered the most in the battle. As a critic of King George III said, "Another such victory would ruin the British army."

Tucked away among shopping malls and upscale residences, close to I-40, the 230 acres surrounding Guilford Courthouse in Greensboro offer a fascinating blend of entertaining history and footpaths that lead across the battlefield. You don't have to be knowledgeable in the details of the American Revolution or appreciate war strategy to enjoy a visit to Guilford Courthouse. The importance of the battle is well explained.

The British, feeling that the war was stalemated in the northern colonies, decided to head south, where there might be more support for the British cause. When the French joined the American forces, the Brits expected that American Loyalists faithful to the crown would take up arms to defeat the rebels. They soon discovered, though, that they had an inflated view of the support they would find in the South.

General Cornwallis received orders to secure South Carolina and carry the British campaign north. According to the visitor center film, not everyone in the British Parliament was in favor of fighting to keep the American Colonies. Some argued, "They will bleed us white," while others wondered, "How can we afford this war halfway around the world?" and "How can we ask the public to send their sons to war?" Does this sound familiar?

The British chased the Patriots all over the South, first at Kings Mountain and Cowpens, both in upstate South Carolina, and now in the small hamlet of Guilford County. General Nathanael Greene, the southern commander of the Continental Army, was ready. In Guilford County, Cornwallis wanted to defeat Greene much more than he needed to hold the land. The battle came to a sleepy little community of farms settled in the 1740s. Here, the Brits weren't depending on American Loyalists. As in Cowpens, they had dispatched the British Army.

The county of Guilford, formed in 1771, was near a Society of Friends settlement, Quakers who would play a role in the battle's aftermath. On March 15, 1781, about 1,900 British regulars met Greene and his 4,400 men, a force of both well-trained, long-term Continental Army soldiers and state militia, mostly from the south.

The battle itself was as choreographed as a classical ballet. Greene placed the North Carolina militia in the front line. The inexperienced volunteers were expected to fire one or two volleys and retreat. The North Carolinia militia ran as the British advanced. The second line was comprised of the Virginia militia; they were considered more experienced. They lured the enemy into deep woods, but the British broke through the second line.

In the third line, the veteran soldiers of the Continental Army shot at point-blank range. The British troops fired their cannons and the Americans retreated. Most of Greene's men survived. The general deployed his troops in a defensive posture and knew when to hold them and when to fold them.

The Americans slaughtered the Redcoats. The British lost a quarter of their men and a third of their officers. But the British captured the land around the Guilford Courthouse.

"So was it a victory or defeat for the Patriots?" I ask Ranger Dan Kahl, who's staffing the visitor center desk today.

"Well," Ranger Kahl says, "I'm a military man. The British took control of the land, so they technically won. But with the massive British loss of life, it's not so clear."

"The British said that it was a 'victory with all the hallmarks of a defeat,'" adds Nancy Stewart, a salesperson in the bookstore, who has steeped herself in Revolutionary War history.

When the Americans surrendered the grounds to the British, they abandoned their war dead on the battlefield, much to the disgust of British officers. The British took the wounded of both sides and brought them to the Quaker settlement. The Quakers, who abhorred war and avoided conflict, tended to everyone. After the battle of Guilford Courthouse, with a weakened British Army, Cornwallis abandoned the Carolinas. He hoped for a turnaround in Virginia but he didn't find it. At Yorktown, seven months after the battle at Guilford Courthouse, Cornwallis surrendered to the Americans under General George Washington.

Today there's quite a bit to see in and around the courthouse. The thirty-minute movie explains the battle in context of the whole Revolutionary War. Soldiers on both sides tell their stories. A black slave explains that he's fighting instead of his master because he's been promised his freedom at the end of the war.

"Britain was my country," says a white North Carolinian farmer and militia member, "but no more."

The Battle Map Program follows the detailed movements

of the troops in battle in another short film. The British, represented by red lines, and Patriots, by blue lines, march, shoot, and retreat. Before the ranger starts the film, he passes around a map of the battle drawn by British engineer officers and submitted with Cornwallis's report to his commander, Sir Henry Clinton. The Brits recorded their actions with care.

Modern houses, churches, and a civilian cemetery flank the road. It's only by walking the trails that you can appreciate the hilly topography and streams that contributed to heavy British losses. The largest statue honors General Nathanael Greene and the soldiers of the Southern Army. Guilford Courthouse connects to Greensboro Country Park and Tannenbaum Historic Park for more walking and history.

Local residents use the park to walk, run, and exercise their dogs. It's a little incongruous to see Baggit stations holding plastic bags for pet waste on the military park road. Many visitors don't realize they're in a national park, where kite flying and sunbathing aren't allowed. If visitors complain, Stewart asks them, "Would you sunbathe at Arlington Cemetery?"

℘✦℃

In the pre-Civil War fervor to commemorate the American Revolution, Greensboro locals created a Greene Monument Association in 1857, but they weren't able to raise enough money, and the war disrupted their plans. Through the years, the abandoned battle site had turned into a mess of old fields and tangled vegetation. Almost thirty years later, David Schenck, a nineteenth-century lawyer and Revolutionary War enthusiast, decided to save the battleground from oblivion. Schenck created the Guilford Battleground Company (GBC) and started buying land.

Prominent citizens raised money for land, monuments, and roads. In the custom of the day, they created a Battleground Museum filled with artifacts found on the field and items purchased and donated. Schenck added a picnic pavilion, a restaurant, a baseball field, and even a lake. When the National Park Service took over the battlefield in 1933, they took out all the pleasure park features and returned the area to what it looked like at the time of the battle.

On one side of the visitor center, a row of monuments put up by the GBC was intent on "ornamenting the field," as the information plaque states. Still, the No North, No South Memorial, erected in 1903 in the spirit of American nationalism, was an attempt to heal the wounds of the Civil War. During the Revolutionary War, Americans had set aside their sectional differences. George Washington, a southerner, led mostly northern troops. Nathanael Greene, a northerner from Rhode Island, headed southern troops.

You won't find a statue of David Schenck on the loop road, just a memorial plaque. According to Nancy Stewart, "Schenck asked that a statue of him not be put up."

By 1915, the GBC decided that the site would be better protected by the federal government. At this time, several national military parks had already been established for battlefields of the American Civil War. In March 1917, the United States Congress established Guilford Courthouse National Military Park as the first national park to preserve a Revolutionary War battlefield. The Guilford Battleground Company still operates as a Friends Group for the Military Park, offering financial support and help in interpretation.

6

YOUNG AMERICA

The United States didn't go directly from the Revolutionary War to the Civil War, though it sure seems that way to children learning history. What happened between the two wars? OK, so we had the War of 1812. Then we glided right into the antebellum period.

Antebellum technically means before the war—any war. We usually think of the antebellum period as the years just before the Civil War, though it's difficult to agree on a specific time frame. Some will define it as after the War of 1812 and before the Civil War. Historians usually denote the period between the Revolution and the early nineteenth century, potentially all the way up to Jackson's presidency, as the Early Republic. In this chapter, I've gathered national park units that preserve historic sites between the adoption of the Constitution in 1789 and the Civil War, but aren't connected with wars.

Charles Pinckney fought in the American Revolution with the South Carolina militia. He then moved up the ladder in the South Carolina legislature and ended up as governor. Today, he would be called part of the privileged class. His summer home is now preserved as a national historic site. Contrast that with Cane River Creole National Historic Park, which interprets Creole life in upstate Louisiana. Creole culture, a mixture of French, Spanish, African-American, and Native American cultures, is quintessential Louisiana. The site shows all aspects of plantation life, including slave outbuildings.

Natchez, Mississippi, displays a different kind of antebellum life. Natchez National Historical Park shows the archetypal plantation life. Practically the whole town is a historic site. The city calls itself the bed & breakfast capital of the South, but I stayed in a private house owned by a Natchez native.

Cumberland Island and Cumberland Gap are two different experiences. Cumberland Island interprets the lavish life of the Nathanael Greenes, and later the Carnegies. Pioneers, including Daniel Boone, crossed Cumberland Gap to find a new life in the west, now Kentucky.

ᴄ✦ Charles Pinckney National Historic Site
A life of privilege
South Carolina

Some people discover national park sites that even the natives don't know about. When I tell Charleston locals that we're visiting national parks around the city, I get a blank look. "Fort

Sumter and Fort Moultrie," I say. They recognized those. But the Charles Pinckney National Historic Site? Where is that?

Charles Pinckney National Historic Site is about six miles northeast of Charleston in Mount Pleasant. In 1754, Charles's father bought the 715-acre estate. Charles Pinckney (1757–1824), a fourth-generation Pinckney, enlisted in the South Carolina militia during the Revolutionary War. When Charleston fell to the British in 1780, he was captured and held prisoner. Generals William Moultrie and Charles Cotesworth Pinckney, our Charles's cousin, were also captured during the war and paroled at Snee Farm.

Later, Charles Pinckney became a South Carolina delegate at the Constitutional Convention. Nicknamed Constitution Charlie, he helped shape the Constitution, though exactly how much is still being debated by historians. He was the governor of South Carolina four times. In between his separate stints as governor, he was the ambassador to Spain. He worked for ratification of the Constitution in South Carolina, which occurred in 1788.

Almost thirty years after his father purchased Snee Farm, Charles inherited the property along with its forty slaves, who tended to fields of indigo and rice. Subsequent owners added cotton as the principal cash crop. But Pinckney was too busy to give Snee Farm the attention it deserved. In 1817, he had to sell the farm to pay off his debts. However, he wasn't homeless since he owned an elegant townhouse in Charleston where he spent most of his time.

The Pinckney farmhouse was torn down around 1828, when the new owners built the current house. Today, Snee Farm, Charles Pinckney's summer home, sits on twenty-eight acres. Archaeologists worked for years to find where Pinckney's original house stood. In the process, they found pieces of pottery from China and even a homemade toothbrush. Farther back, on a short trail, the outlines of slave quarters are squared off in brick.

On the ground floor of the house, the walls are covered with posters on Pinckney, slavery, and life in South Carolina during the early days of the republic. Rangers and volunteers are quick to answer questions and engage in lively discussion. It's a quiet historic site and the staff is responsive. A half-mile trail winds its way through red cedars, live oaks, and palmettos, creating a classic lowcountry scene. The walk ends at a platform within sight of private homes in a residential neighborhood.

"So how did Pinckney's estate become a national park unit?" I ask. Over time, most of the original land was sold for residential development and a golf course. In 1987, Friends of Historic Snee Farm raised more than $2 million to buy what was left of the land-holdings. The next year, the site was turned over to the National Park Service. Fortunately, the main house and many outbuildings are clustered in the small area that was preserved. Archaeologists continue to unearth records of the property's history.

More than fifty-three thousand people visited the Pinckney site in 2014. Rangers estimate that you should take about an hour to go through the historic site, but we spent almost two hours here. Lenny, a Revolutionary War buff, says, "It's one of the most interesting national park units."

Should Charles Pinckney National Historic Site even be a national park unit? When I mention that I visited the Charles Pinckney site, a couple of national park enthusiasts roll their eyes.

"It shouldn't be part of the National Park Service," some say.

The major complaint is that the house currently here is not the house that Charles Pinckney lived in. And there are no standing Pinckney-era structures in existence at Snee Farm. But I think that the site could use much more promotion.

Boone Hall, a privately owned plantation, is almost opposite the Charles Pinckney site. It claims to be one of America's oldest working and living plantations. It offers tours, sells wine and cheese, and has a café. National park units can't advertise or sell refreshments directly, but Boone Hall promotes itself heavily as one of the must-see Charleston attractions.

As the national park pamphlet says about the Pinckney House, "the present house built of native cypress and pine in the 1820s is a fine example of a tidewater cottage once common throughout the coastal areas of the Carolinas."

So maybe it doesn't matter whether Charles Pinckney lived in the current house. More than 150,000 artifacts have been found on the property. Friends of Historic Snee Farm preserved and protected an archaeological treasure trove for future generations. And that's what the National Park Service is supposed to do— preserve and protect.

For me, the more park units, the better.

ᥰ Cumberland Island National Seashore
Summer home of the rich
Georgia

Is Cumberland Island National Seashore harboring a secret, or is it merely the victim of bad karma? Is it just coincidence that three powerful men connected with the island died in their prime? What about the three structures, each named Dungeness, that burned under mysterious circumstances? Ranger Ginger Cox, who's giving the Footsteps Tour in the Historic Dungeness District on the southern tip of the island, poses these questions with a twinkle in her eyes. Nothing tops a walking tour with an enthusiastic park ranger.

Cumberland Island, one of the Golden Isles in southeastern Georgia, almost on the Florida border, offers eighteen miles of deserted beach on the Atlantic Ocean. Together these barrier island ecosystems form the first line of defense for the mainland against storms. Barrier islands are dynamic systems, constantly in motion. They react to ocean fluctuations and changing weather patterns while protecting the mainland behind them. Horseshoe crabs look like unexploded bombs. Sandpipers scurry in and out of the crashing waves, searching for crustaceans and insects. Sweeps of marsh grasses that filter the water separate the mainland from the island.

Timucua Indians were the earliest inhabitants on the island, living well on shellfish, game, and plants. A Spanish mission prospered here in the sixteenth century. But the English took possession of the island when General James Oglethorpe erected two forts, one at each end of the island, in the 1740s. He also built a hunting camp at the southern end and called it Dungeness, after a headland back home in England. The Oglethorpe structure probably burned; no trace of it remains.

After the American Revolution, Nathanael Greene, a hero in the southern military campaign, purchased land on Cumberland Island. Greene didn't have much time to enjoy his property; he died of heat stroke when he was forty-four years old. Catharine, Greene's widow, married Phineas Miller, who had worked for the family, first as tutor to her children, then as manager of her Savannah plantation. Together in 1803, they built a mansion on the same southern headland as the other structure and called it Dungeness.

They created a plantation with timber, olives, oranges, mangoes, and other fruit. Cotton thrived with the help of hundreds of slaves. But their island life together ended when Phineas died before his fortieth birthday. Catharine's daughter, Louisa Greene Shaw, continued to enhance the plantation. The second Dungeness structure burned down in the middle of the nineteenth century.

In the 1880s, Thomas Carnegie, brother of the more famous

Andrew, bought the Greene-Miller plantation for his wife, Lucy, as a winter resort. Lucy Carnegie built an estate, which she called a cottage, on the same Dungeness site.

At the height of the gilded age, guests of the Carnegies came to Cumberland Island for weeks of leisure and amusement. The ruins of the recreation area are now fenced off, but we can imagine the lavish lifestyle with its swimming pool, dance hall, barbershop, hair salons, and doctor's quarters.

"The big question each morning would be 'What shall we do today?' And if you were a woman, a second question was 'What shall I wear?' " Ranger Cox explains with great drama.

Thomas Carnegie also died in his prime, at age forty-three, becoming the third casualty of Dungeness, and leaving Lucy to cope with nine children. Her plan was to build a house on the island for each child, but Lucy died in 1916. In 1959, the third Dungeness residence burned mysteriously. The National Park Service has reinforced the remaining structure, but visitors can only marvel at the ruins from the outside.

According to Lucy Carnegie's will, no one could sell the island until her last child had died. Once that happened, two grandchildren tried to sell the island to developers. At around the same time, titanium was found on the property. Turning this idyllic island into a development of second homes would be bad enough, but mining was now considered. In 1972, Congress authorized Cumberland Island National Seashore. Its first acquisition was the Plum Orchard mansion on the northern part of the island, a home built by Lucy Carnegie for her son George. Lucy Carnegie built Greyfield for her daughter Margaret in 1900. In 1962, her descendants converted the mansion into an upscale hotel that is still operated by the family.

Most of the island is managed as a wilderness area, though over twenty families live here. Rangers offer some assistance to residents, including serving as EMTs. Ranger Cox says, "A number of elderly residents have 'do not resuscitate' orders because they want to die on the island."

All this human habitation has left many nonnative species including hogs, cows, and horses. The park sought public comments about what should be done with these animals. The general feedback was: "Shoot the hogs, contain the cows, but keep the horses."

Today about two hundred horses, descendants of those left by the Carnegies, roam the island. Though not indigenous, the horses are historically important. The park doesn't manage the horses nor provide them with veterinary care. They're free to roam and are easy to see on your walk. Other animals have migrated to Cumberland Island. Coyotes managed to swim to the island, taking advantage of land that surfaces at low tide. Armadillos, another new resident, are not that difficult to see.

Visiting Cumberland Island takes some planning. It's not just a matter of driving up to the parking lot. You need to make ferry reservations early and plan for an all-day expedition. Bring your binoculars, and ask for a bird list at the visitor center. The island boasts more than 335 species of birds. On a late fall day, I identify white ibis, laughing gulls, and tri-colored herons from the ferry. Pied-billed grebes, turkey vultures, eastern meadowlarks, tree swallows, and sandpipers are easy to spot on the island. While we're taking the ranger tour, a bald eagle chases an osprey overhead.

SO◆CR

On the next visit on Cumberland Island, Lenny and I have joined the Lands and Legacies Tour. The park started these day trips a few years ago so that visitors could see the north end of the island without either backpacking or traveling on a private boat. Ten visitors climb into a van, driven by Ranger Ron Crawford. We head north on the main road. Ranger Crawford explains that much of the northern end became a federally designated Wilderness Area in 1982, but the road was excluded so that residents could drive to the ferry. If the road had stayed part of the Wilderness, the park couldn't offer these tours.

The ride to the top of the island is slow because the road is minimally maintained. The public hasn't yet caught on that these tours are available. The park also makes the tour sound very rigorous, which scares many visitors away. According to national parks management policies, parks can't pay to advertise in the traditional manner. Therefore, they depend on their websites and word of mouth.

On the road, we find a lost guest. She's looking for the private ferry from the Greyfield Inn and is walking the wrong way. Ranger Crawford stops the van and invites her in. He drives her back to the inn so she can get to her ferry.

"I usually don't do this," Crawford says several times. "It's private land."

We spend the most time in and around Plum Orchard Manor. Ranger Crawford leads the group up and down and all around the enormous house. The manor has the feel of a poor man's Biltmore Estate in Asheville. I need to remember that the Carnegies and others lived on Cumberland Island maybe four months out of the year. Now in January, the temperature is in the seventies and very comfortable, but summers are hot and buggy. Spreading live oak trees shade the house a little, since there was no air conditioning when the house was built. The basement houses its own electric generators.

Our last stop is the Settlement at the north end of the island. Slaves who had worked on the plantations came back as freemen after the Civil War and built the First African Baptist Church in 1893. The church, rebuilt in the 1930s, was the site of the 1996 wedding of the late John F. Kennedy Jr. and Carolyn Bessette. The famous couple chose the church for its privacy and remote location.

Now almost all the residents live on the island under lifetime leases. When they die, the land will revert to government ownership. Eventually, the park service will own 90 percent of the island. Only the Greyfield Inn and an estate owned by the Candler family, the heirs to the Coca-Cola empire, will stay private, until they're ready to sell.

Cumberland Island inspires engrossing books. On my first visit, I picked up *Endangered Species* by Nevada Barr. I'll read a Nevada Barr mystery about any national park, but it's more memorable when I've just visited a site. It turns out that the fictional perp in the book is similar to Carol Ruckdeschel, a turtle biologist who's been living on Cumberland Island for years. Ruckdeschel was so upset by the depiction that she sued Barr. They settled out of court. In the paperback version, Barr changed the criminal to a young man with different traits.

Just before my visit on the Lands and Legacies tour, I finished *Untamed* by Will Harlan, the book of the hour about Cumberland and Carol Ruckdeschel. Harlan, a magazine editor, was a seasonal ranger at Cumberland twenty years ago and worked on this book for many years. He presents a positive image of Carol Ruckdeschel, the only person who lives on the island full-time. For years, Ruckdeschel has fought to keep the island wild and turtles safe from boats. She's tangled with the Carnegies on the island, politicians, and the National Park Service. Harlan wrote a wonderful book.

On the last stop of the Lands and Legacies tour, next to the African-American church, a barbed-wire fence surrounds a wooden house and garden with a Private Residence sign.

WildCumberland.org is printed on a huge banner attached to the barn. Pipes, rope, and lumber lie around the property, indicating that the owner is definitely a do-it-yourselfer. This is where Carol Ruckdeschel lives.

Cumberland Island National Seashore may be the only Southeastern national park that interprets the gilded age. The South was so devastated by the Civil War that the only surviving gilded age homes were owned by Northerners. Altogether, a fascinating place.

So many places in the East seem to be named Cumberland, after Prince William, Duke of Cumberland (1721–1765). However, rich Northerners weren't looking for an idyllic retreat in Cumberland Gap.

⚜ Cumberland Gap National Historical Park
Walking into Kentucky
Kentucky, Tennessee, Virginia

Why haven't I been to Cumberland Gap National Historical Park (CUGA) before? The visitor center in Middlesboro, Kentucky, is only two and a half hours from Asheville. The first sign for CUGA is over fifty-five miles away as I get off I-81 and onto US 25E. Here the local road name is Davy Crockett Parkway, when I'm all psyched about going into Daniel Boone Country. However, Crockett was born in east Tennessee, while Boone was just passing through. Boone, born in Pennsylvania, moved to the Yadkin River Valley in North Carolina when he was sixteen years old.

I expected to learn about Daniel Boone and the gap, but the park is so much more. I drive to the Thomas Walker Parking Area and walk the Object Lesson Road, an ominous name. The federal government funded the gravel road in 1907 to convince voters of the convenience of good roads. I walk to Cumberland Gap from the Kentucky side. The gap isn't large or ostentatious, but it has a sweet sign that says:

> *Salt seeking buffalo*
> *Moccasin clad warrior*
> *Dreaming pioneer*
> *Battling Civil War soldier*
> *Each was here in the Cumberland Gap and now so are you.*

The words on this plaque pretty much encapsulate the history of Cumberland Gap. At 1,600 feet elevation, the gap was the lowest point where people in the southern states could cross the Appalachian Mountains. To put it in perspective, Newfound Gap on the boundary between Tennessee and North Carolina in Great Smoky Mountains National Park is over five thousand feet.

Dr. Thomas Walker was the first white man to explore and write about the gap in 1750. He's credited with discovering the gap, a place that the Indians had known for centuries. American Indians created a Warrior Path while hunting bison. But Walker gets the credit because he wrote about the gap, which again shows the power of documentation.

Daniel Boone first came through the gap in 1769. Land speculator Richard Henderson commissioned Boone to lead a group of axmen to blaze a trail, which became known as the Wilderness Road, through the gap into Kentucky. When I say "blaze" in this case, I don't mean that they painted white blazes on trees like on the Appalachian Trail. They cut a path with axes, literally opening up Kentucky to settlers. That encouraged two hundred thousand to three hundred thousand settlers to cross Cumberland Gap by the early 1820s, each looking for their own piece of land.

Meriwether Lewis and William Clark walked through the gap,

separately, in 1806 when they returned from their western expedition. A side trail veers off to Tri-State Peak, where you can stand in three states: Virginia, Kentucky, and Tennessee. Each state has a plaque with its vital statistics, straight out of an encyclopedia—capital, state bird, state flower, number of counties.

I continue down the Wilderness Road, stopping at the Iron Furnace and the entrance to Gap Cave. I want to retrace my steps and climb back to the gap into Kentucky the way settlers did it. At the gap, I take the Wilderness Road Trail, which is part of the original Boone trail, dated 1780 to 1810. The Daughters of the American Revolution have placed a massive four-sided rock structure to commemorate the Daniel Boone Trail. The DARs from Kentucky, Tennessee, Virginia, and North Carolina—Boone did live in North Carolina—each put up a plaque for their state. They all include the words "From North Carolina to Kentucky." The influence of the DAR is everywhere in historic parks.

Throughout my whole stay at Cumberland Gap, I keep recircling back to the visitor center and checking in with Ranger Brittony Beason with more questions. She explains that the trail through the gap was the old US 25E, a two-lane road, but I find it hard to envision over eighteen thousand motorists crossing the mountain every day. The highway became known as Massacre Mountain Road because of the high number of fatalities. In 1996, US 25E was rerouted by building a tunnel through Cumberland Mountain from Tennessee to Kentucky. Later, Congress appropriated funds to restore the gap to its historic condition. In 2001, the Park Service removed the concrete and reshaped the contour of the land to what it looked like during Daniel Boone's time. I walk to the gap on the southbound lane of the old road and I can't see any sign of a highway, which means that the reroute was a success.

ఴ✦ఴ

This park isn't just about Daniel Boone in the eighteenth century. The next day, again with Ranger Beason's instructions, I visit the Hensley Settlement, an example of modern homesteaders. Sherman Hensley brought his wife and growing family to the top of Brush Mountain in 1903. They were going back in time, living as pioneers—they certainly never had electricity. A few trails connected them to the outside world, but a paved road didn't exist while the settlement was active. Several other related families settled on this high plateau. They were successful in that, at its zenith, the community had fifty to a hundred people and forty structures, including houses, barns, corn mill, and blacksmith shop. The park signs say that the Hensley settlers used the same frontier skills that their great-great-grandfathers used in the mountain hollows in the 1800s.

But why go back to pioneer ways? The park information doesn't really explain but leads you to believe that the male leaders wanted to live a self-sufficient life on their own land. After a chat with rangers and a little searching around, I've come to a more believable answer. The Hensley Settlement was an easy place to make moonshine, on a mountaintop so remote that no one was going to bother them.

William E. Cox, who wrote *The Hensley Settlement*, quotes a resident who said, "He could not remember anyone on the mountain having to serve in the military." The community was off the grid and off the government's radar. The last person left in 1951. By then, most men had gotten better jobs in factories.

You can visit the Hensley Settlement on a ranger-led tour in season, but the road is closed the rest of the time. Today, I walk up the Shillalah Creek Road over ten miles round trip. It's a sunny spring day. Dwarf-crested irises and other spring flowers line the trail, keeping me distracted as I plod up to Brush Mountain.

The park preserved sixty-seven acres and restored many buildings and fences. I peek into the neat schoolhouse with glass windows, but the building is locked. Most children went to school until they were nine years old. Then they were put to work on the farm. Men went into town every week to sell their goods, but women only went once every several weeks. Children didn't get off the mountain until they became adults.

Old man Hensley had twenty-three children, all apparently with the same woman. You can understand the status of women in the settlement by reading the gravestones. Sherman and his wife share one of only two double graves with elegant headstones. Sherman lived to be ninety-eight years old but his wife, Nicy Ann, died when she was fifty-three. Or was it Nicey, as it says on the footstone, along with a different birth date? The descendants couldn't even get her personal details right. The women who lived in the coal mining camp at Big South Fork were positively liberated compared to this settlement.

I meet a father and daughter who came up by horseback, and we discuss the bleak status of women in this isolated community. In contrast, some bloggers, after visiting the settlement with rangers, wax poetic about the birds chirping and the simple life away from phones and email. I don't want to give the impression that I didn't like my visit to the settlement, but I question the picture of the idyllic lifestyle.

I try not to confuse the park with the resource it's trying to interpret. The Hensley Settlement must have been a miserable place to be trapped. However, the park has done an admirable job of preserving and interpreting the era. Visiting Brush Mountain was fascinating, but living in Hensley must have been brutal.

ᕮ Cane River Creole National Historical Park
Plantation life
Louisiana

This morning, I drop Lenny off at the New Orleans airport and start a five-hour drive to Cane River Creole National Historical Park in Northwest Louisiana, a different look at American life after the Revolutionary War. I love driving back roads, but here I'm on interstates almost the whole way. The highways are empty and I can listen to NPR without the constant drone of eighteen-wheelers.

I'm going to stay in Natchitoches. I practice how to say the name of the town in the car all morning, but I'm wrong. Locals pronounce it *Nakatish*, which means place of paw paw. The Natchitoches Indians have vanished as a people.

My first stop is Magnolia Plantation, which was active until the 1970s, when mechanization changed the nature of cotton growing. The site is fenced off to separate it from the original private land where descendants of the LeComte family still raise cotton on both sides of the road for as far as the eye can see. If you're familiar with Mount Le Conte in Great Smoky Mountains National Park, note that this family name is with an *m*.

When I park at Magnolia Plantation, I meet a young woman in a black dress and heels, carrying a notebook and a camera, walking across the field. She's a reporter, here for the soft opening of a two-room cabin furnished as 1950s quarters for a tenant farmer and his family. In the cabin, Ranger Dusty Fuqua is still rearranging the rug and chairs in the bedroom. The park will be working on furnishing another cabin to represent the antebellum period. This plantation focuses on the slave and tenant farming experience instead of the owners in the big house. Eight cabins remain at the back of the property. The

142

plantation home is still in private hands.

"I'm a Creole," Ranger Fuqua says. "My family came over from France in the 1700s. Creole used to mean born in the new world of old stock." It historically referred to those born in Louisiana during the French and Spanish periods, regardless of ethnicity. The National Park Service defines Creole as a culture nurtured by French and Spanish colonial ways, steeped in Africanisms, and enriched by American Indians. A real mélange. Creole is much more inclusive than Cajun.

"Technically, to be a Cajun you must be a descendant from the five hundred people or so who emigrated from France to Nova Scotia and then moved to Louisiana after the French and Indian War," Fuqua says. If you want to differentiate the cultures based on food, Creole is French-inspired city food while traditional Cajun food focuses on country one-pot dishes, most of it too spicy for my taste.

The plantation became part of the Cane River site in 1994 after the LeComte and Hertzog families sold eighteen acres to the National Park Service. Some of the park literature is in French. I wonder how many French speakers visit here, but it's a nice touch.

Oakland Plantation, about ten miles north, is considered the main site. Jean Pierre Emmanuel Prud'homme began raising cotton, tobacco, and later, indigo in the late eighteenth century on a land grant from the Spanish government. By 1815, families concentrated on cotton, and Oakland became the most successful plantation west of the Mississippi. The family completed the main house in 1821. The next year, they went to France to buy furniture. Before the Civil War, the family owned three thousand acres. The daughter of the Magnolia Plantation married a Prud'homme and moved to Oakland Plantation. Families from the area intermarried throughout the centuries, and some still live in the area.

The plantation owners ran the post office until it closed in 1967.

The general store stayed open to the public for another fifteen years. In rural areas, the store was the center of life and more than just where you bought your groceries. It was also the banking and credit source, recreation center, public forum, and a place to exchange news. In front of the big house, two old gas pumps are rusting away.

Don, a volunteer, gives a tour of the main house. He and his wife have traveled from Arkansas for the past three years to work at Cane River. They stay in a trailer just outside the park for three months. "I'm Cajun French," Don says. "That's what drew me to this place. All the buildings on this plantation are original and haven't been moved."

When the last resident moved out of the house in the late 1990s, the family took the furnishings and pictures they wanted and the Park Service kept the rest. The family sold forty acres to the Park Service, including the main house, store, cook's house, and pigeonnier, a structure to keep pigeons so that the family could have fresh squab. Toward the end of their stay on the plantation, it was obvious that the family was hurting financially. Several families lived here at the same time, with a large kitchen dating from the 1950s, complete with a pink stove. I certainly wouldn't want to have to cook in a 1950s kitchen.

⚐ Natchez National Historical Park
Two different lives in the same city
Mississippi

Cane River Creole depended on slave labor. Here in Natchez, the National Park Service preserves the house of a former slave.

"William Johnson was a man caught between two worlds," Ranger Barney Schoby says of the nineteenth-century free black man. Though Schoby is working at the Melrose Visitor Center today, he gives me more insight on the man than I'm able to get from visiting the Johnson house in the center of Natchez.

Natchez prides itself on showing tourists the antebellum experience. Natchez National Historical Park interprets two distinctive houses, one belonging to a free black entrepreneur, and one owned by an affluent white family, the one percenters of the day.

I arrive in front of the William Johnson House, on State Street, a little after nine a.m., but the house is dark. This is unusual for a national park site. Visitor centers always open exactly on time, so I'm apt to notice the few times they're late. After fifteen minutes, Anna Tong, a volunteer, opens the door to the brick home. Tong apologizes and explains that the rangers and volunteers were tied up at a staff meeting.

Johnson was born in 1809 of a mulatto slave woman and white father. His owner-father freed him in 1820, but it wasn't as simple as just letting him go. The white father had to petition the Mississippi General Assembly to allow his son to be free. Johnson grew up to be a barber, entrepreneur, and slave owner himself. After building this house in 1841, he moved his large family upstairs while he reserved the downstairs for his barbershop and other commercial ventures.

Johnson kept a diary, first to record his financial dealings, a kind of ledger book. The laws at the time banned black people from congregating, so he couldn't talk about the issues of the day that were circulating in his barbershop. The diary also allowed Johnson to unburden himself on paper since he was isolated at the top of his social class. He left his heirs $30,000, which might be $750,000 today, an incredible sum for a black man in those times. The Johnson descendants owned the house until 1976, when they sold it to the Preservation Society. Eventually, the city of Natchez donated the site to the National Park Service.

Today, the living quarters on the second floor of the house are closed for renovations, so all I can do is to study the exhibits on Johnson. I find Tong, the temporary volunteer staffing the desk, more interesting. A retired medical technician from Texas, she travels the country in an RV, volunteering for the Park Service full-time. She chooses a park based on location and recommendations from other volunteers, and focuses on historic parks. To learn a new park, Tong goes with seasoned guides and reads written accounts of their tours. She also did a stint at Cane River Creole.

A few miles from downtown Natchez, Melrose, a 1800s Greek revival–style mansion, represented the height of Southern prosperity and the Cotton Kingdom before the Civil War. The house is part of an eighty-acre estate, named after a small Scottish town. The property is an estate or town house, not a plantation, so I can't compare it to Cane River Creole, but it's certainly much more luxurious. The National Park Service brought the furnishings and effects back to the 1840s.

Ranger Don Stephen gives a lively tour of the house. The family bought their furniture from Philadelphia and Boston and china from London. The house survived the Civil War because Natchez didn't provide any opposition to the Union army. When 1,600 soldiers came into town after their victory at Vicksburg, they turned Natchez into a supply depot. Nobody much cared that Grant was a Yankee.

"Natchez thought the war was bad for business," Stephen says.

After the tour, I circle back to the visitor center. Ranger Barney Schoby is behind the desk and I happened to mention that I had seen the Johnson house first thing in the morning. Schoby, who had studied Johnson's life extensively, gives me a short lecture.

Johnson married a mulatto and didn't really belong to either the black or the white world. "He only cut white men's hair and lent money to white men," Schoby says. "Free blacks needed to carry papers all the time to show that they were free. Even so, some white man could grab the papers and tear them up."

Johnson wasn't a religious man, but his ten children were all baptized in the St. Louis Cathedral in New Orleans. "Now why do you think he did that?" the ranger asks me.

Free blacks tended toward Catholicism because the Catholic Church records baptisms. The church would also record their free status, be able to vouch that the person was known and in fact, free. Of course, blacks were always second-class citizens in the church.

"In modern times, Catholic schools were the first to accept black kids," Ranger Schoby points out.

Somehow, the topic got onto the Jews in Natchez. "In 1830, the Jews were pushing a cart to sell their goods," Schoby says. "By 1880, they owned every single store in Natchez." My parents would have called his comment an anti-Semitic stereotypic remark, but I laugh all the way back to my car.

I feel I never have enough time to visit the surrounding town since I spend so much time in the parks. But I'll be back in Natchez when the National Park Service plans to open Fort Rosalie in 2016 to celebrate the 300th anniversary of the French coming into the area.

7

THE WAR OF 1812: LAND OF THE FREE AND HOME OF THE BRAVE

The War of 1812 has been called America's forgotten war or the second American Revolution. You may remember it as the war that produced the American national anthem. Although I haven't yet found a *War of 1812 for Dummies* book, the war had consequences beyond "The Star-Spangled Banner." The Canadians haven't forgotten the war. As a colony of Great Britain, Canada was invaded a number of times by the Americans.

Loyalists didn't believe that the British Empire had permanently lost the fight to keep its colonies. America went to war because the British Navy impressed our sailors. Armed gangs would board

American merchant ships, grab sailors, and force them to work for the Brits. We wanted to annex Canada and debilitate American Indians, who seemed to have sided with Great Britain. America declared war on Great Britain in June 1812, but for a long time, most of the fighting occurred in the north. In 1814, the British invaded Washington, DC, and burned the White House and most of the city. We didn't conquer Canada nor get rid of the British north of us, but the war ensured our existence as a country.

Though Americans and Brits didn't lose territory, American Indians did. The War of 1812 was the prelude to the policy of Indian Removal that Andrew Jackson, as president, would impose on the southern tribes in the 1830s.

After the war, Europe knew that the United States was going to last. We weren't going to revert to colonial status. The website for the Chalmette Battlefield, location of the Battle of New Orleans, summarizes the effects of the war this way: "American democracy triumphed over the old European ideas of aristocracy and entitlement."

Yet, as Matthew Dennis, a history professor at the University of Oregon writes in the *Official National Park Service Handbook*, "If the War of 1812 played a more important role in American public memory, it would likely have earned a less generic name." Dennis feels that its accomplishments are meager compared to the American Revolution and the Civil War that bookend it.

And, oh yes, in case you're wondering, the "1812 Overture" written by Tchaikovsky is not connected with the American War of 1812, even if the cannon fire and fanfare at the end sound like war. The music commemorated Russia's defense against Napoleon.

80 ✦ 03

❧ Horseshoe Bend National Military Park
Searching for Junaluska
Alabama

The first time I heard of the Battle of Horseshoe Bend was in the Cherokee, North Carolina, *Unto Those Hills* pageant, which concentrates on the history of the Trail of Tears from a Cherokee perspective. In the play, they mention that Junaluska, a Cherokee, saved Andrew Jackson's life at the Battle of Horseshoe Bend.

According to John Buchanan's *Jackson's Way*:

> *The Battle of Horseshoe Bend was one of the most important, yet least well-known, battles ever fought in North America . . . Custer's defeat in Montana sixty-two years later does not even deserve to be mentioned in the same breath with Horseshoe Bend.*

Horseshoe Bend National Military Park in central Alabama is not easy to find. Visitors aren't going to drop in on the spur of the moment. It's off a small road, away from any town, and you need to want to come here. I stayed in Oxford, Alabama, the night before. Now I'm following my car GPS, phone GPS, and a state map. About five miles from the entrance, I see the familiar brown sign. On a beautiful fall Sunday morning, I'm the only visitor in the park, and I feel that they opened it just for me.

Two Student Conservation Association (SCA) volunteers greet me. There's no ranger on duty today. I watch a film that recounts the complicated history of the Indian-European situation at the time. Here goes:

The Creek Indians, in what is now Alabama, supplied deerskins to Europeans before the American Revolution, but afterward, the United States was more interested in land than skins. The British gave away Creek land to the new country as part of the 1783 Treaty of Paris, which ended the American Revolution. That was nice of the Brits, but it wasn't their land to give away. To make matters worse, the Creek were split on how they should live with the growing European presence. The Lower Creek adopted European ways, such as agriculture, alcohol, and firearms.

Enter Tecumseh, a Shawnee warrior born in Ohio, who preached going back to the traditional ways and driving out the white man from Indian Land. Today, we'd call him an outside agitator. Tecumseh wanted to create a pan-Indian confederacy to unite against the United States, just as the thirteen colonies had united against the British. His message resonated with the Upper Creek Indians, referred to as Red Sticks because they painted their war clubs red.

After several attacks from both sides, General Andrew Jackson felt that "Creek should not threaten the frontier or American expansion." The Red Sticks built Tohopeka Village into the horseshoe bend of the Tallapoosa River. The fortifications were supposed to render the village impenetrable to attacks.

On March 27, 1814, Jackson tried a frontal attack on the fort, but to no avail. The Cherokees, who had allied themselves with Jackson, swam 120 yards across the river and attacked the Red Sticks from the rear of the village. After a fierce battle, the Creek were defeated. Jackson recalled, "The carnage was dreadful." The losing Creek ceded twenty-three million acres to the United States, much of it becoming the state of Alabama. This victory got Jackson promoted to Major General.

Armed with this brief history and a park brochure, I walk the 2.8-mile loop trail, which crosses and recrosses the road. Each time the trail enters the woods, it has a sign, warning visitors about "Potentially Hazardous Wildlife," such as ticks, mosquitoes, and poisonous snakes and plants. There are more signs on this trail than I saw in days of hiking in Denali. I don't find snakes or mosquitoes and I hope that a tick hasn't bitten me. Today, the forest is a mixture of oak, pine, and hickory. Several quiet meadows punctuate the site. I don't meet a single hiker and only one group of bikers zooms by on the road.

The state and Alabama Power donated 2,040 acres, and in 1959, Horseshoe Bend was proclaimed a National Military Park. However, before it became part of the National Park Service, Congress erected a large monument on Gun Hill to commemorate the battle, but with the wrong date, March 29, 1814.

The US Daughters of the War of 1812 placed a plaque showing the terminus of Jackson's route through the wilderness. Daughters of the American Revolution, the Confederacy, and Union Veterans of the Civil War still exist, so why not the War of 1812? It seems that almost every American war has a Daughters group.

This battle was called one of the great American victories of the War of 1812. The logic is that it destroyed Creek military power before the British could intervene. As for Andrew Jackson, he moved on to Louisiana for the Battle of New Orleans.

However, what happened to Junaluska? Why is he not mentioned anywhere on the Horseshoe Bend site or website? I emailed Ranger Heather Tassin and asked about Junaluska. Here's what she said:

> *We have no records that Junaluska was present at the Battle of Horseshoe Bend since he is not listed in the muster rolls. I have heard this same story, but it is probably more in reference to the Cherokees' participation in the battle than literally saving Jackson's life. The Cherokee warrior Whale swam across the river, stole canoes to shuttle people across, and attacked the village of Tohopeka, which changed the course of the battle and ultimately resulted in Jackson's victory.*

Later, Jackson would order the removal of Cherokees and other eastern Indians to the Indian Territory, now in the state of Oklahoma. Junaluska is said to have declared that had he known Jackson would drive the Cherokees from the Smoky Mountains, he would have killed the general himself. Maybe this is how you reconcile the Cherokee story and the National Park Service story.

Natchez Trace Parkway and Natchez Trace National Scenic Trail
A walking corridor
Alabama, Mississippi, Tennessee

If you need to go from Natchez to Nashville today, the Natchez Trace Parkway isn't the way to go. Even at its top speed limit, 50 miles per hour, it will take you about ten hours with comfort stops. You're meant to take the 444-mile road slowly, savor it, and stop often for historic sites.

The Trace starts in Natchez at milepost 0 and cuts a diagonal through the state of Mississippi. It continues through a small corner of Northwest Alabama and up into Tennessee, ending a little south of Nashville. I could have stopped every couple of miles to check out a diversion or an information placard.

At milepost 15.5, Sharon Foster and her husband are long-term volunteers, working as hosts at Mount Locust. Like other volunteers that I've met, they come in an RV, park it somewhere close to their work site, and show up every day in a VIP uniform. They keep returning because they now know the Mount Locust story. "Also, we like the supervisory ranger," Foster says.

Today, Sharon Foster is at the information center, greeting visitors, handing out pamphlets, and answering questions. Her husband is up at the inn, showing the property as if he owned it. The table is set and ready for a family meal—this

was considered a wealthy home.

Mount Locust was an inn and plantation that adapted to the challenges of the times. In 1784, William and Paulina Ferguson purchased Mount Locust from his business partner and expanded the plantation. After William died, Paulina married her overseer, James Chamberlain. He was probably the best man to marry if Paulina wanted to continue the family business.

Then the boatmen started coming down from the Ohio Valley. The men were called Kaintucks, from a pronunciation of Kentucky, regardless of where they came from. They floated their goods, cash crops, and livestock down the Mississippi River on wooden flatboats and sold them in Natchez or New Orleans. After they disposed of their goods, they dismantled their boats and sold the lumber as well. They probably spent a lot of their hard-earned money on liquor and women before they started the long trip back home.

The Kaintucks walked or rode back on the Natchez Trace, creating the sunken road. This system was only in place from about 1785 to the mid-1820s. When paddle wheelers first came on the scene, they were not only expensive but were liable to blow up. During the height of the Natchez Trace, stands, or inns, popped up about every fifteen miles because they figured that a man could walk that distance in a day. The journey on foot took about thirty-five days, if they didn't take any rest days. They weren't expected to camp out, though they probably carried a bedroll. Mount Locust, 15.5 miles north of Natchez, was the first inn.

Paulina offered a place to sleep and an evening meal of corn mush and milk for twenty-five cents. Later they built Sleepy Hollow, a bunkhouse for the growing number of travelers. It couldn't have been named for Washington Irving's "The Legend of Sleepy Hollow" since the story wasn't published until 1820. Paulina was an ingenious businessperson, not to mention indefatigable. After her second husband left her, she raised eleven

children along with running the successful inn.

When steamboat travel became safe and affordable, Kaintucks stopped walking the Trace. Paulina, who's remembered as Grandma Polly to her descendants, attracted Natchez residents looking for quiet and cooler temperatures than the city. Later, visitors came to escape the yellow fever epidemic. By 1842, Mount Locust was no longer an inn but still a thriving plantation. After the Civil War, the plantation system was over and Mount Locust started to deteriorate. The National Park Service bought the property, but the Chamberlain family stayed here until 1944. The owners never modernized the home with running water or electricity.

Today, the property includes a slave cemetery. Ten bodies are buried here, but only one unmarked stone stands. Close by, Paulina and William Ferguson are buried in the family cemetery, which is still being used. Several Chamberlain men worked as rangers on the site.

Mount Locust is only one of dozens of sites on the Trace. Driving the Natchez Trace Parkway, you're reminded that Natchez and Mississippi were not part of the United States for years after the Revolutionary War. The area was considered part of the Old Southwest, an informal name for the southwestern frontier territories. The Natchez, Chickasaw, and Choctaw nations walked up and down a rough trail. In 1798, the government cleared a road between the newly acquired Mississippi Territory and Tennessee.

President Thomas Jefferson designated the Trace a national post road for mail between Nashville and Natchez. The Trace played a role in the War of 1812. General Andrew Jackson, commander of the Tennessee militia in January 1813, brought his men outside Natchez. Three months later, because of political wrangling, Jackson's troops disbanded without ever seeing combat.

Jackson and his men plodded along the Trace through the six-week journey. He offered the only three horses in his battalion to the sick and walked alongside his men. His men gave Jackson

the nickname Old Hickory, meaning he was as strong as a hickory stick. After the Battle of New Orleans in 1815, volunteer soldiers walked back up the Trace. Tennessee became the Volunteer State because of the role the volunteer soldiers played in the War of 1812, particularly the Battle of New Orleans.

The Daughters of the American Revolution became concerned that the history of the Trace was disappearing. In 1905, they started putting commemorative markers in every Mississippi county through which the Old Trace traversed. When they dedicated each monument, they made speeches, which brought the attention of the Trace to politicians and the press. It worked. Mississippi Congressman Thomas Jefferson Busby called for a survey of the "old Indian trail known as the Natchez Trace." He's now considered the father of the Natchez Trace Parkway. The Trace is full of early travel stories and artifacts.

It might be tempting to compare the Natchez Trace Parkway to the Blue Ridge Parkway because both parkways were depression-era projects, but there's a world of difference between them. The Blue Ridge Parkway lies on the crest of the Blue Ridge Mountains, which goes above six thousand feet. Over three hundred miles of the Mountains-to-Sea Trail across North Carolina lie on the Blue Ridge Parkway. In contrast, five small sections of the Natchez Trace National Scenic Trail weave through the Natchez Trace Parkway. Some of the trail is on the original sunken road. And it really has sunk. Swamps and mosquitoes challenged the construction of the Trace, which started in 1937. A year later, Congress passed legislation creating the Natchez Trace Parkway, but it took until 2005 to finish the road.

The era of Kaintucks is over, and now everyone drives the Natchez Trace Parkway. However, Andra Watkins may be the only person alive who recently walked the whole 444 miles. In her engaging memoir, *Not Without My Father,* she recounts her five-week trek on the asphalt. Her father dropped her off each morning and picked her up fifteen miles later every day, hence the title.

☙ Jean Lafitte National Historical Park and Preserve
Named after a pirate
Louisiana

In 1814 we took a little trip
Along with Colonel Jackson down the mighty Mississip
We took a little bacon and we took a little beans
And we caught the bloody British in the town of New Orleans

I have been waiting for years to use these lyrics. This song, "The Battle of New Orleans," performed by Johnny Horton, was the number one song in 1959. I knew the song long before I'd even heard of the War of 1812. When I started visiting Southeastern national parks, I knew that I'd be going to the site of the Battle of New Orleans: Chalmette Battlefield, part of Jean Lafitte National Historical Park and Preserve. The War of 1812 also produced "The Star-Spangled Banner," but the tune isn't as catchy.

The Battle of New Orleans, January 8, 1815, was the last significant battle of the War of 1812. The war was a muddle of partial wins and losses, but the Battle of New Orleans was a clear victory for the Americans. Though the British infantrymen had just defeated Napoleon, they could not match the fervor of American soldiers, including Choctaw warriors. Major General Andrew Jackson became a national hero, which propelled him to the White House.

Today Chalmette Battlefield, which lies east of New Orleans, is a quiet site with a large, well-maintained lawn, surrounded by a driving loop. A group of army captains from Alabama on a Captains Career Course is here to study the battle. They've zipped through the visitor center in five minutes and now gather around the picnic area to wait for the ranger talk.

"Why did you choose to come to this site?" I ask the sole woman captain in the group.

"Mostly it was a chance to come to New Orleans." Yes, it is a lively city.

The ranger introduces the battle. He's running the visitor center by himself today and he gives a ponderous and hesitant talk. He's an anomaly since most rangers are lively and jovial. I lose the thread of his story.

The soldiers listen almost at attention, but no one is taking notes. Two wives, who've accompanied the group, have long lost interest in Jackson's tactics and stare at their cell phones.

"I'd like to see your report from this trip," I say to a couple of captains after the talk.

"Yeah, me too," one laughs.

"How do you think the Battle of New Orleans applies to the work you're doing now?"

"Technology and tactics change, but leadership stays the same." That's the upshot of their trip.

The Chalmette Monument obelisk rises one hundred feet. Its cornerstone was placed in January 1840, a few days after Andrew Jackson visited the field on the twenty-fifth anniversary of the battle. I climb the spiral staircase to the top, where I can look out through the slits. Today, however, wasps have invaded the viewing area, and I shoot back down.

A mile-and-a-half walking or driving loop explains the tactics of both armies. The park has planted a British flag. After all, we're friends now. A side trail leads to the Chalmette Cemetery, where Civil War and other veterans are buried.

How was the battlefield preserved until the National Park Service took it over in 1939? Jean Pierre Fazende, a free man of color, inherited land in the battlefield in 1857. After the Civil War, he divided his property and sold it to freed slaves. The community grew to more than two hundred residents. A small African-American village named Fazendeville, located in the center of the battlefield, was sandwiched between the Chalmette Monument and the national cemetery. The village thrived through the struggle of the Jim Crow laws. By the early 1960s, it had a one-room schoolhouse, three general stores, and several churches.

As the 150th anniversary of the Battle of New Orleans neared, Chalmette Superintendent Lyle K. Linch felt that Fazendeville was an anachronism, making it difficult for visitors to appreciate the historic significance of the site. The National Park Service bought land in 1966 after long and contentious negotiations. Residents moved to New Orleans's Ninth Ward but still keep in contact with each other.

Today, modern life is all around the battlefield site. Several smokestacks from an industrial park spew out cloudy vapor. You can only buffer parks so much from everyday life. The battle only took two hours, but we spend a lot more time at the site. Those lyrics were in my head for days.

We fired our guns and the British kept a-comin'
There wasn't nigh as many as there was a while ago
We fired once more and they begin to runnin'
On down the Mississippi to the Gulf of Mexico

ဆာ♦ᢉᏒ

Chalmette Battlefield is one of six sites belonging to Jean Lafitte National Historical Park and Preserve, the only national park named for a criminal. After Congress banned the importation of slaves in 1808, enslaved labor became more expensive.

Jean Lafitte, a pirate and privateer, smuggled slaves in from the Caribbean islands and ships he hijacked. When it was obvious that the British were going to attack New Orleans, Lafitte offered to help Andrew Jackson against the enemy with the understanding that the government wouldn't prosecute him or his crew for their past crimes. Jackson agreed, though he really had no authority. President Madison took some convincing. Now six sites are part of Jean Lafitte, including Barataria Preserve south of New Orleans. The area has been called Barataria since the days of Lafitte and his pirates, referring to a fictional land in Cervantes' *Don Quixote.*

Lenny and I walk a mile from the Barataria visitor center to Bayou Coquille Trail on the boardwalk, where we meet Ranger Amber Nicholson. *Bayou* means slow-moving water.

The ranger starts her walk introduction with, "Are you afraid of anything?"

"Yeah, one-eyed, one-horned flying purple people eaters . . ."

The one other visitor with us rattles off "snakes, spiders, gators . . ." Ranger Nicholson redeems herself with her knowledge and casual demeanor.

In the mountains, you need a change in elevation over one thousand feet to influence forest types. In Louisiana, we measure elevation in inches. Here, changes of a foot can mean the difference between live oaks and swamp maples, between bald cypress and open marsh.

Dwarf palmetto, bald cypress, and water tupelo live on the high ground of a swamp, which is defined as forested wetlands. Marshes on lower ground are devoid of trees. On our walk, moss, vines, trees, and air plants envelop every surface and take over every vista. Huge swamp marigolds have filled in the canals, creating a yellow-flowered road. We keep our eyes out for animal life and find an alligator and several turtles in the marsh. A golden silk orb weaver, a large banana spider, builds a huge web on the side of the trail.

The National Park Service protected over twenty-three thousand acres of wetlands in 1978. The water should be fresh, but it's brackish now. Before artificial levees were constructed, water full of sediment created natural levees during spring floods. But after the great flood of 1927, the public cried out for the government to do something, anything, to control the Mississippi River. The Army Corps of Engineers built levees almost the whole length of the Mississippi. Levees, dams, weirs, canals, and jetties—all these structures have hemmed in the river. The Mississippi River is now in a straitjacket so high that it won't be able to jump its banks ever again in its present form.

Then the oil and gas industry came in, causing more problems, but at least they brought jobs. Several oil companies still own subsurface rights. In theory, they could do directional drilling into the preserve by going underground and across parkland.

Back at the visitor center, Ranger Aleutia Scott speaks passionately about this land. "Deltas are a conversation between sea and river. Besides all the levees, the sea level is also rising. Our wetlands are being lost. The public should care!"

Ranger Scott echoes almost exactly what Mike Tidwell writes in *Bayou Farewell*. Tidwell learns about the disappearance of the bayou country by hopping on shrimp boats and talking to Cajun shrimpers and their families, those most affected by the changes. The Louisiana coast is losing land equal to the size of Manhattan every ten months. The public and major environmental groups aren't taking up the cause, maybe because the area lacks charismatic megafauna, a term used for cute, wondrous animals that ecotourists want to see. It's easy to love the pelicans and alligators in the Everglades, a region with similar problems.

"So what can we do?" Lenny asks Scott. "At some point, it all comes to using our tax dollars to remedy the situation."

Ranger Scott hesitates. "Lenny," I intervene, "Ranger Scott is in uniform."

She looks relieved. I drop a fiver in the donation box as we leave the visitor center.

⊱ Trail of Tears National Historic Trail
The Cherokee survive
Alabama, Arkansas, Georgia, Illinois, Kentucky,
Missouri, North Carolina, Oklahoma, Tennessee

The Trail of Tears commemorates the forced removal of the Cherokee people from the Southeast to what is now Oklahoma. The Cherokee, along with the Chickasaws, Choctaws, Creeks, and Seminoles, signed many treaties ceding land to the United States. However, that wasn't enough for President Andrew Jackson. He advocated a policy of Indian removal, and Congress passed the Indian Removal Act in 1830. By then, gold had been discovered in North Georgia, near Dahlonega, and whites were eager to dig on Cherokee land.

The Cherokee people were split. Though most opposed removal to a harsh, unknown part of the country, a splinter group of the tribe bought into the plan because they felt that it was the only way to survive as a people. This small minority of Cherokee signed a treaty with the federal government to give up their eastern tribal land and move to a new home in Indian Territory.

Removal itself was brutal. In 1838, Federal and state soldiers rounded up Cherokees and confined them in stockades. Then the Cherokees were forced to walk hundreds of miles west. Many died of overcrowding, poor sanitation, and the struggle of the march itself. The ones who survived eventually rebuilt their nation in present-day Oklahoma. However, a small number of Cherokee were able to escape the roundup by hiding in the rugged Smoky Mountains. Others owned land individually. These people became the Eastern Band of Cherokee Indians. Most live in Cherokee, North Carolina, just outside the Oconaluftee entrance of Great Smoky Mountains National Park.

The current historic trail stretches over five thousand miles, across nine states, along three major land routes and a water route. You can walk it, but it's not a hiking trail. Rather the trail consists of a series of certified sites owned by various agencies, such as museums, state parks, conservation associations, and even private homes.

Benge's Route, the middle trail, starts in the northeastern Alabama town of Fort Payne, where the army built a fort used to intern Cherokees until their relocation to Oklahoma. The town is proud of its historical connections and has done a great job of documenting the historical route. Fort Payne promotes its Trail of Tears sites well, even those on private land.

The Old Cabin site was a major departure point for Cherokees forced to leave their Alabama homes. Located on a side street in downtown Fort Payne, it's easy to find. The cabin, dating from 1825, was seized by the military in 1837 to establish Fort Payne. Today, the cabin is gone and only the chimney and foundation remain.

I try to follow the Original Route signs along with my website instructions to find the Willstown Mission Cemetery. Turning onto Sanders Avenue, I'm in a neighborhood of neat, one-family homes. Where is the cemetery? I park in front of a house and check the street name. I seem to be on the right street and walk up and down, not finding the cemetery. An old gardener is in his front yard and I don't waste any time getting his attention.

"Excuse me," I holler. "Can I ask you something? I'm looking for the Willstown Mission Cemetery." I wave my paper instructions with some authority.

"Oh, yes. It's right here." Bruce Brooks introduces himself and beckons me to come through the back of his neighbor's property. Here the signs for the cemetery are obvious. A large metal sign put up by the Cherokee Chapter of the Colonial Dames reads:

Willstown Mission 1823–1839
Cemetery 1825–1898

Brooks explains what he knows about the cemetery. "I bought the property in 1970 and built my house. Then I found the cemetery and cleared it, but everyone knew that the cemetery had always been here."

A Boston-based group organized to "further education and Christianity among the Cherokee Indians" built a mission school, which operated until Indian Removal. The original mission smokehouse still stands behind Bruce's house. Many of the trees in the cemetery were cut down and only large stumps remain. Over fifty bodies may be here, but most just have a rock to mark their graves. A stone marker designates the site of the mission along with the grave of Ard Hoyt, Superintendent of the Mission for ten years. Members of the Larmore family, whose descendants donated the cemetery to Landmarks of DeKalb County, are also interred here.

The house of Andrew Ross, brother of Principal Chief John Ross, the leader of the Cherokee Nation, is also a certified Trail of Tears site in Fort Payne. Andrew, a Cherokee businessman and judge on the Cherokee Supreme Court, differed with his brother on Indian Removal. As a member of the Ridge Party, Andrew signed the Treaty of New Echota, which gave tribal land to the US Government for $5 million. Andrew Ross and his family voluntarily moved to the Western Territories in 1836, before the Cherokees were rounded up in Fort Payne.

The current house, owned by a dentist, contains whole sections of the original home, built in 1821. The front of the house faces the Cherokee trading route, which can still be seen on parts of the property. Today, the Greek revival house looks palatial. I walk down the private driveway to get a better look at the outside. No one invites me in for a cup of tea.

8

Coastal Defense:
A Late Reaction to the War of 1812

If you want to understand why masonry forts were built from Maine to Louisiana, you need to listen carefully to our national anthem.

> *Whose broad stripes and bright stars thro' the perilous fight,*
> *O'er the ramparts we watch'd were so gallantly streaming?*
> *And the rockets' red glare, the bombs bursting in air,*
> *Gave proof through the night that our flag was still there.*

The British burned Washington, DC, during the War of 1812,

but Fort McHenry in Baltimore Harbor kept the British fleet out. Constant bombardment by the most powerful fleet in the world at the time could not take down our flag, inspiring Francis Scott Key to write "The Star-Spangled Banner." Since Fort McHenry held firm, our military concluded that masonry forts were the answer to homeland security, nineteenth-century style. As a National Park Service flyer explains, before the age of nuclear weapons, homeland security meant harbor defense.

After the War of 1812, Congress created a cohesive system of national defense, protecting the country from a naval invasion. President Madison invited General Simon Bernard, a French military engineer who had worked for Napoleon, to design a system of forts. In those days, Americans seemed to believe that Europeans had all the skills needed for almost anything.

Castle-like forts were built at all major harbors. Between 1816 and 1867, more than thirty forts were built, including Fort Sumter, South Carolina, Fort Pulaski, Georgia, Fort Jefferson in Dry Tortugas National Park, and Fort Pickens in Gulf Islands National Seashore in Florida. Foreign invaders never attacked these forts, though many lasted as part of our defense until World War II. By then, it was obvious that forts built in the 1800s weren't going to offer protection against air and submarine attacks.

The forts played a big part in the Civil War, even though they were built for a different purpose. The National Park Service preserves four forts in the Southeast. Others are state parks. From visiting several forts in the Southeast, I conclude that if it weren't for the War of 1812, we wouldn't have all these national park units.

 හ♦ලි

ᏧᎯ Fort Sumter National Monument
Where the Civil War began
South Carolina

The Civil War started with a bang at Fort Sumter in Charleston. South Carolina seceded in December 1860, after Abraham Lincoln was elected. The state wanted the Federal troops out because they no longer considered themselves part of the United States. Negotiations didn't work, so force was the next step.

On April 12, 1861, the Confederates started shelling the fort. After thirty-four hours, the Union flag was lowered as the Federals surrendered. Union soldiers would spend the next four years bombing the fort to get it back into Federal hands, but the Confederates held on until the war was over. During the siege, the Confederates were able to survive by depending on supply boats that made night runs to Fort Sumter. Union guns generally didn't fire at night.

All this history is well told at the Fort Sumter Visitor Education Center at Liberty Square on the Charleston waterfront. Lenny and I went to the visitor center ahead of time to be prepared for our tour to the fort today. The building sits on the site of Gadsden's Wharf, where hundreds of thousands of enslaved Africans were brought into the United States.

Now we're signed up for the thirty-minute ferry ride with Fort Sumter Tours, the concessionaire. The park limits the number of people on the island at one time to protect resources. Today the line is long with eager visitors.

Before we get on the boat, we're all shepherded in a line to get our picture taken. The tour operator calls this "a trip of a lifetime," a bit of a hyperbole. I guess they mean that most visitors will only go to Fort Sumter once in their life. On the boat, I meet Lance, the

VIP (Volunteers in Parks), and ask if I can take a picture of him.

"I photograph park volunteers in their uniforms," I say. While ranger uniforms are all green and gray, from Maine to California and beyond, VIPs wear a variety of clothing, depending on the climate and what volunteers can provide for themselves. Lance's green polo shirt and green jacket are part of his uniform.

The fort is a five-sided structure built on an artificial island. With no natural springs or wells, all the water comes from rainwater held in a group of cisterns. The Army Corps of Engineers began to build Fort Sumter in 1829 to protect Charleston Harbor from foreign invaders. By 1860, it was 90 percent complete and considered old technology.

Ranger Gary Alexander gives a talk on the harsh conditions that both sides endured between 1861 and 1865, when the Confederates left. A VIP dressed as a Confederate soldier, with a gray jacket and a white satchel at his side, shows how he can reload and shoot three rounds in a minute. He tears off the paper cover from the cartridge with his teeth.

"When you joined the regiment, they checked that you had both top and bottom teeth. If you gummed your food, you weren't going to be able to reload and shoot quickly," Ranger Alexander says.

There was life at Fort Sumter after the Civil War. At the start of the Spanish-American War, the army built Battery Huger as part of a major upgrade of coastal defense. The battery now takes up much of the interior of the original fort. Fort Sumter lasted as a military base until 1947 and became a national monument the next year.

You only have an hour on the island before you need to get back on the boat, and that's not enough time to see the museum properly. I'm not sure what the consequences are of overstaying your visit. Do they make you swim ashore?

ℵ✦ℭ

In the afternoon, we drive to Sullivan's Island to see Fort Moultrie. This visit is more relaxed since there are no tours or timetable. Fort Moultrie dates back to the Revolutionary War. In June 1776, nine British warships attacked the still uncompleted fort, but the enemy was forced to turn back. Charleston was saved—for now. The fort was named for Colonel William Moultrie, the American commander of this victory, who then was promoted to general. Nothing original is left from this era.

A second fort was destroyed by a hurricane in 1804. The third Fort Moultrie survived the longest. When South Carolina seceded from the Union, the Federal garrison abandoned Fort Moultrie for the stronger Sumter. Fort Moultrie continued to be modernized up to World War II. Once submarines and aerial attacks emerged on the military scene, forts like Moultrie became obsolete.

The fort now has been restored to show the major eras from the log forts of 1776 to the World War II control post. The chambers in these forts remind me of a medieval dungeon where they keep the violent brute or the fair damsel. The passageways and rooms are dark and difficult to photograph. Both Fort Sumter and Fort Moultrie are part of the same national monument.

⚜ Fort Pulaski National Monument
End of an era
Georgia

Count Casimir Pulaski, a Polish nobleman, is not a household name, but he may be one of the most commemorated individuals in the United States. From Pulaski, Wisconsin, to the Pulaski Skyway in New Jersey, his name seems to be used by towns, landmarks, and monuments everywhere. Pulaski came to America to help the Patriots in the Revolutionary War. He fought in a battle to retake Savannah from the British in 1779, where he died of his wounds.

Fort Pulaski National Monument, about fifteen miles southeast of Savannah, is a destination, not a place just off the interstate. If you look at pictures of the forts built after the War of 1812, they all look the same with their moats, sally ports, and eight-foot-thick walls. Fort Pulaski, on Cockspur Island, seems formidable. It took eighteen years and twenty-five million bricks to build the massive structure that protected Savannah, presumably from a mighty European sea power. However, no foreigner ever attacked Fort Pulaski. The fort was supposed to be impregnable to the smooth-bore naval cannons, the technology available at the time. After the fort was completed in 1847, General Joseph Totten said, "You might as well bombard the Rocky Mountains as Fort Pulaski."

By the time Georgia seceded from the Union, only two care-takers were watching over the fort; the state of Georgia easily took it over from the federal government. Soon Confederate troops moved in and prepared for a likely Union attack. The Confeder-ates had abandoned Tybee Island, from which the Union could now bombard Fort Pulaski. For two months, the Union moved cannons in silence at night to a spot on Tybee to prepare for a siege. The impregnable fort's undoing was a new rifled cannon with longer range and accuracy. After thirty hours of shelling, the South surrendered on April 11, 1862. The Union took over the fort, ending the era of the original masonry forts.

After surrender, the fort was so badly damaged that it couldn't hold the new Confederate prisoners of war, and they were sent to Governors Island in New York. Over one thousand Federal troops worked to repair the devastation so they could live here for the rest of the war. But you can still see the damage left by the newfan-gled cannons.

The cannons that reduced much of the fort to rubble are displayed prominently on its parade ground. The small exhibits in the rooms present the most questions. Rows and rows of thin-soled leather shoes sit on shelves. Where did the park service get all those shoes? Is there a story behind the shoes? What sizes did the shoes come in? It's doubtful that they provided wide and narrow fit, like today. Blue trousers with buttons instead of modern zippers lie on the next shelves. A row of lanterns is displayed close by. These artifacts show that human beings had to deal with these awful experiences. You can't humanize war, but you can show the human details.

In October 1864, Union troops stationed at Fort Pulaski accepted transfer of a group of imprisoned Confederate officers, who later became known as the Immortal Six Hundred. They were moved from Charleston because of a yellow fever epidemic. Thirteen who died during their confinement, mostly from dysentery, are buried on Cockspur Island.

In 2012, the Georgia Sons of Confederate Veterans erected a granite monument, which is inscribed *Joshua 4:1-7* without any further explanation. The Old Testament passage refers to the Lord telling Joshua, successor to the prophet Moses, to choose twelve men, one from each tribe. Each man should take a stone and place it in the Jordan River. These stones became a memorial for the children of Israel. In other words, we should never forget the Immortal Six Hundred, the six hundred men who were incarcerated here. Specifically, never forget the thirteen Confederate soldiers who died on Cockspur Island, including one man who died during the bombardment.

The next time Lenny and I visit Fort Pulaski, we share it with a group of eighth-graders and their teachers. We're outside in the cold drizzle, watching a musket firing demonstration. The theme for the class trip is simple tools. In one of the rooms inside the fort, two women from the Oat Island Wildlife Center, an outdoor education center, use simple tools to cook corn bread in a Dutch oven over an open fire. After they pull it out of the oven, they cut the round loaf into tiny pieces and drizzle liquid sugar on top. Their sharp looks tell me that this treat is meant for students and teachers, and not for the likes of us.

We drive to Tybee Island and turn into a small parking area outside Battery Row, a gated development. Several NPS plaques assure me that we're on the spot from which the Union shelled the Confederate fort. The sign says that there should be guns and sighting tubes, but I can't find either. I don't need a sighting tube. Past the lighthouse, I see the fort. New trees are blocking a clear view, but during the Civil War, there weren't any trees. The Union had a straight shot.

✺ Fort Pickens in Gulf Islands National Seashore
Oasis in a sea of development
Florida, Mississippi

Pensacola is a navy town. A little farther south, motels, private homes, restaurants, and tourist shops fill the community of Pensacola Beach on Santa Rosa Island. It's also the gateway to an entrance to Gulf Islands National Seashore. Both ends of the long, skinny island are part of the national seashore. Leaving the ice cream vendors and shops selling beach paraphernalia, I drive west into the pristine national seashore, heading for Fort Pickens. Pelicans and gulls now inhabit the beach. Sea oats hold the sand together on the barrier island. Unlike Cape Hatteras National Seashore, you can't drive your vehicles on the sand.

Once in the park but long before reaching Fort Pickens, you can feel that this tip of land was a place of war, or at least national defense. Between the Civil War and World War II, ten batteries were built to protect the coastline along today's six-mile drive. Battery Langdon, hidden behind spreading vegetation, was constructed between 1917 and 1923. During World War II, soil camouflaged the structure to hide it from enemy aircraft. Though foreign enemies never attacked the area, artillerymen suffered through the brunt of firing practice.

"Lots of boys would bleed from the mouth and ears because of the concussions of the guns," a soldier observed during the 1940s. At Battery Worth, completed in 1899, gun crews needed to "stay loose and keep your mouth open." Though soldiers could stuff their ears with cotton, most didn't bother.

Batteries have either a dirt path or stairs to the top. I'm up and down as many staircases as I can find to climb. You don't have to appreciate military defense or understand how these weapons were supposed to work to be awed by the massive casemates, fortified chambers from which guns are fired.

In the middle of all this defense armament lies Chasefield Plantation Cemetery. William H. Chase, who supervised construction of Fort Pickens, lived on the plantation. The headstones of several Chase family members were moved from land now occupied by Pensacola Naval Air Station. After several more batteries, I reach the formal gates of Fort Pickens, the largest of the four forts that protect the Pensacola coastline: Fort Pickens, Fort Massachusetts, Fort Barrancas, and the Advanced Redoubt.

This location was long prized for its defensive posture. In the mid-1700s, the British built the Royal Navy Redoubt on the mainland of today's national seashore near Pensacola. The young United States saw Santa Rosa Island as a better position, and started work on Fort Pickens in 1829. The project took five years and more than twenty-one million bricks. The five-sided brick fort came from the same design as the other forts of the era: the dry moat, sally port, casemates, secret rooms, and numerous tunnels.

I spend the day exploring all the ups and downs and twists

and turns of the fort. One of the rooms shows the fifteen-minute introductory film, the start of any park visit, where the ranger historian takes you on a virtual tour of the fort. Then I wander by the officers' quarters, past the casements, and up onto the Tower Bastion, with sweeping views of the Gulf of Mexico. In the 1880s, the fort held Apache prisoners, including the legendary Geronimo. Indian tribes had been forced off their traditional lands out west. Sixteen Apache men separated from their families worked on the fort and became a tourist attraction for a while.

The fort was modernized several times to keep up with new threats. The day after Fort Sumter surrendered, Fort Pickens was reinforced to prevent Confederates from controlling Pensacola Bay and using the Pensacola Navy Yard. During the Civil War, Fort Pickens stayed in Union hands.

In 1898, a concrete and earth gun battery, named Battery Pensacola, was built in the fort's parade ground. After a disastrous explosion and fire the next year, Fort Pickens was repaired and modernized. But eventually atomic bombs, guided missiles, and long-range destroyers rendered the complete military structure at Santa Rosa Island obsolete. The last soldier left in 1947.

The area became a Florida state park and then part of the national seashore in 1971. Fort Pickens is one of twelve areas comprising Gulf Island National Seashore in Mississippi and Florida. The state of Alabama, in between, chose not to become part of the national seashore. In addition to visiting forts, you can walk flat, sandy trails, sail, camp, and watch birds. More than 80 percent of the seashore is underwater. The park describes itself as an "oasis in a sea of development."

80 ♦ 08

⚘ Fort Jefferson in Dry Tortugas National Park
Dr. Mudd was here
Florida

The masonry fort in Dry Tortugas National Park is only one of several enticements to visit this park. You can go to this tropical paradise for the day to find clear water, gentle waves, and bright sunshine. The snorkeling and birding are phenomenal. And no one is pushing drinks on you.

Yet it may be the most remote and one of the least visited national parks in the East. In 2014, Dry Tortugas counted almost sixty-five thousand visitors, while Everglades National Park, its closest national park neighbor, had over a million. Dry Tortugas, which lies seventy miles west of Key West, consists of open water punctuated by several small islands. Garden Key, where most visitors go, is the only one accessible by commercial ferry, the *Yankee Freedom*. You can go by commercial seaplane, but if you think the boat is expensive, you don't even want to ask about the cost of flying.

The Dry Tortugas has a long human history. Ponce de Leon first named the islands Las Tortugas, the turtles, in 1513. The name quickly changed to the Dry Tortugas on maps to show that there was no fresh water. John Jay Audubon came here in 1832 to study birds and marine life. Fort Jefferson, built between 1846 and 1875 as a late reaction to the War of 1812, takes up most of the land on Garden Key. It was designed to hold 450 cannons and 1,500 men, with walls between eight and eleven feet thick. Its many casemates were meant to hold cannons, but not one shot was ever fired in anger from here. The fort was never finished. A moat surrounds the structure to prevent storm surges from hitting the fort with full force.

Although located at the southern tip of Florida, the fort stayed under Union control during the Civil War. It was used as a prison, mostly for army deserters. The most famous prisoner was Dr. Samuel Mudd, the physician convicted and imprisoned for aiding and conspiring with John Wilkes Booth in the 1865 assassination of President Lincoln. You can see where Mudd was imprisoned by going through an arch that says, "Whoso entereth here leaves all hopes behind."

Dr. Joseph Sim Smith, the army doctor on site, died in 1867 in a yellow fever epidemic. A memorial to the doctor and his son is located on the grounds. When the fort was left without a medical officer, Mudd eagerly volunteered to work with the sick. President Andrew Johnson pardoned Mudd, who left Fort Jefferson on March 11, 1869.

The Everglades Association, the cooperating association that supports the South Florida parks, staffs the visitor center and bookstore located in the fort. Several notebooks filled with historical information on the park lie on a table. Letters between Dr. Richard Mudd, a grandson of Dr. Samuel Mudd, and President Jimmy Carter make fascinating reading. Richard Mudd spent his whole life trying to clear his grandfather's name. Though President Andrew Johnson pardoned Samuel Mudd, a pardon is considered a statement of forgiveness and not innocence. President Jimmy Carter wrote to the grandson that he was persuaded that the conviction was wrong, but said that he couldn't set it aside. At the time of his death in 2002, Richard Mudd was still fighting for his grandfather's reputation. The next year, the Supreme Court refused to hear the case, effectively letting the 138-year-old conviction stand.

After the army abandoned the fort in 1875, the structure deteriorated. It was briefly used during the Spanish-American War, but military presence ended in 1912. Dry Tortugas became a national monument in 1935 and a national park in 1992. Now the fort is sinking into the coral and the park has initiated a major stabilization effort.

ဆာ◆ઇ

If you go for the day, you only get about four hours on the island, arriving at 10:30 a.m., and getting back on the boat by 2:45 p.m. The boat trip takes two and a half hours each way. Lenny and I visited Dry Tortugas the week between Christmas and New Year's. After studying the park website and reading other articles, we realized there was too much to do to fit in a day and decided to camp for a night.

As soon as we get off the ferry, we take the tour offered by a knowledgeable and enthusiastic *Yankee Freedom* employee. Then we walk on the top walls for great views and check out the lighthouse. From the path outside the fort, it's obvious that the structure is crumbling.

The beach slopes gently down to the tropical blue water. Even as a snorkeling newbie, I'm able to see coral and an assortment of fish. *Yankee Freedom* shows an instructional video on the way to the island and lends out snorkeling equipment. Birds are big and recognizable and you can get quite close to them. You don't have to be a knowledgeable birder to enjoy the birds. Magnificent frigatebirds (*Fregata magnificens*—magnificent is part of their name) seem to float overhead with their eighty-five-inch wingspan. Brown pelicans, cormorants, black-bellied plovers, and ruddy turnstones are common most of the year. My favorite is the royal tern with its orange bill and black cap punk hairdo. Dedicated birders know to visit between February and September, when sooty terns gather on Bush Key to lay their eggs. More than two hundred species of birds pass through the area during migration season, peaking in April through mid-May.

You must come with everything for your stay, including food, water, and gear, whether you're here for a few hours or for a few days of camping. You'll also take all your trash when you leave.

Because we were camping, we had to arrive at the terminal at 6:30 a.m. to load our gear on the boat. Day trippers check in an hour later for an eight a.m. departure. *Yankee Freedom* offers a lovely breakfast on the boat and later a buffet lunch, both included in the cost of the ticket.

After the day visitors get off the boat, Ranger Williams meets the campers and explains the rules.

"I'm the emergency medical technician," Ranger Williams says. "If you have a medical emergency in the middle of the night, come and knock on my door." Between ten and fourteen Park Service employees live in apartments built into the fort.

"Also, from time to time, there may be Cuban refugees landing on Garden Key," Ranger Williams continues. "If that happens, come and get me. I call the Coast Guard, who checks them out."

I'm flabbergasted. No one expects to be watching out for Cuban refugees on a camping trip. Though Garden Key is farther away from Cuba than Key West, there are fewer Coast Guard ships patrolling the area around the Dry Tortugas. So Cuban refugees feel they have more of a chance to get one foot on dry land. That's all Cubans need to be on their way to permanent residency and American citizenship. The Cubans come in chugs, which look like large rowboats. One is permanently on exhibit in the fort.

The tour guide explains that the trip from Cuba takes two days. After the refugees are checked out, they're taken to the mainland on the *Yankee Freedom*, a trip that inspires the phrase "come to freedom on the *Yankee Freedom*." So while the rangers are safely tucked away in their air-conditioned apartments in Fort Jefferson, campers are the first line of defense if Cubans make it to Garden Key. It's an exciting prospect, and I have a hard time sleeping. However, no one lands in the middle of the night while we're here.

Camping in Dry Tortugas is like car camping without the car. You need to take all your camping gear such as a tent, sleeping bag, and pad. Though you'll be sleeping on the beach, the ground is solid, so you'll probably want a foam pad or air mattress. Bring all your water because there are no streams on the island to refill your water bottles. "Water, water everywhere but not a drop to drink" really applies here. For two days, we brought one and a half gallons each. I had to rethink my usual camping menu because *Yankee Freedom* doesn't allow most camping fuels on the boat. You can cook with Sterno, charcoal, or just cold camp. It's so warm that cold camping is a misnomer, though I missed my breakfast cup of tea. For one night, we brought Subway sandwiches for dinner.

When boarding the boat, you hand over your camping luggage to the boat staff. Once you dock, you put your camping gear in a handcart and wheel it to the camping area, a couple hundred yards away. A staff member assigns campsites in an orderly manner. Though you can't reserve a specific site, I felt comfortable that we'd have a place to pitch our tent. Each site has a picnic table and a barbecue grill. Composting toilets, reserved for campers, are closed until the day visitors leave. During the day, everyone uses the facilities on the boat.

After the ferry leaves with the day visitors in the afternoon, campers are not the only ones on Garden Key. Seaplanes bring their afternoon clients. Campers on private boats also come ashore, but the island is definitely quieter. We get together to chat on the beach. I walk around with a flashlight, feeling like I'm on a deserted island. A woman reads the Nevada Barr mystery *Flashback*, which intertwines two stories about the fort, one present day, and the other during the Civil War.

Since our taxes aren't funding the national parks adequately, parks use volunteers for many functions. And volunteers love it. The Dry Tortugas can't have people coming over to help out just for the day. Here, volunteers live in the fort for several weeks. I don't think they can get Boy Scout troops for a day to clean up the island. That's where visitors can come in.

Between October 15 and January 15, you can take the half-mile walk around Bush Key, connected to Garden Key by a short land bridge. The next morning when the boat comes with a fresh load of visitors, I ask the *Yankee Freedom* staff for large trash bags.

"We're going to pick up garbage on Bush Key."

The staff is amused and bemused but say, "Yeah. Go for it."

We find Styrofoam buoys, plastic bottles, and a propane can, mostly junk from boaters. Walkers who notice us probably think that we're wards of the court. They surely don't pitch in to help.

9

THE CIVIL WAR

What I remember from school about the Civil War is pretty murky. I went to high school in Brooklyn in the early 1960s. The Civil War history unit mostly consisted of the evils of slavery and the demonizing of the South. But I'm a southerner now, or working on it. Many friends here can trace their lineage back to ancestors who fought on the Confederate side.

After I finished school and didn't have to write history essays anymore, I didn't really think about the Civil War or any war. Sure, I'd been to Gettysburg and Antietam and walked those huge battlefields. I listened as the ranger talked about Union troops in blue going one way and Confederates in gray going another way, battle tactics that made my head swim. Most visitors want side-by-side comparisons of tactics and troop movement. But to me, concentrating on where each side stood on the battlefield is a way of avoiding the bigger questions of causes and effects, then and even now.

When I started visiting national parks in a deliberate way, it became obvious that there's a lot more about the Civil War than battlefields. Civil War sites spread from Gettysburg, Pennsylvania, in the north, to Arkansas and Missouri on the western end, to the Dry Tortugas, west of Key West. The Civil War took advantage of the new technology of the day, such as photography, telegraphy, railroad, and mass production of weapons.

In *The Golden Age of Battlefield Preservation*, Timothy B. Smith, a lecturer at the University of Tennessee, Martin Campus, recounts how Civil War veterans created five Civil War battlefields. The southeast parks, Chickamauga and Chattanooga, Shiloh, and Vicksburg were preserved by 1899. At the time, veterans dominated both federal and state legislatures. By including both sides of the conflict in planning and marking the battlefields, there was some hope that the country would reconcile and reunite. Veterans wanted to preserve the sites in their original configuration. They were adamant that they didn't want their battlefields turned into pleasure parks with amusements and boating on artificial ponds.

The Civil War Remembered, a series of essays published by Eastern National for the National Park Service, doesn't mince words. The book clearly states that the Civil War was about slavery. Yet a volunteer behind the desk at Chickamauga whispers to me, "Some visitors will still argue that the war was not about slavery but about states' rights."

಄♦ಞ

ᘓ Underground Railroad Network
Searching for safe haven
North Carolina

If you can cross the creek to Roanoke Island,
you will find safe haven.

These words are now inscribed on the First Light of Freedom Monument at Fort Raleigh National Historic Site in eastern North Carolina. With this encouragement, hundreds of slaves streamed into Roanoke Island in eastern North Carolina, looking for freedom. Now this site, along with hundreds of others, is part of the Underground Railroad Network to Freedom program. No one place can tell the complete story of the Underground Railroad movement.

The Underground Railroad wasn't physically underground and wasn't a system of railroad tracks. Rather, it consisted of a network of people, routes, and safe houses used by enslaved people to escape to freedom in the North and Canada. The conventional scene of the Underground Railroad movement is that of African-Americans fleeing Kentucky to find freedom and refuge in Ohio. Yet, traveling to eastern North Carolina, I found several Network to Freedom sites.

Long before the Civil War, slaves escaped into the Dismal Swamp, located in northeastern North Carolina and southeastern Virginia. Between 1793 and 1804, black labor was used to dig the Dismal Swamp Canal completely by hand. As a result, slaves were so familiar with the swamp that the area became a haven for runaways. The rugged route was full of insects, snakes, black bears, and bobcats. Not a place you'd want to be alone without knowing your way around.

The Dismal Swamp Canal, the oldest continually operating

constructed waterway in the United States, is still used by pleasure boats. Today, you can walk in Dismal Swamp State Park to understand how rough it would be to find your way in the swamp. If you take the wide, flat Canal Road, a walking and biking trail from the visitor center, you'll feel the brambles, trees, and bushes closing in. Walking the Supple-Jack Trail, I can hardly see the sky for all the vines entangled through trees and bushes. The sides of the trail look impassable and threatening. The Dismal Swamp may have harbored the country's largest maroon colony, a community of runaway slaves who lived deep in the swamp. Others used the Dismal, as it's called, as a resting place before moving farther north.

A copy of the certificate that designates the Dismal Swamp as an Underground Railroad Network Site states in part that "the Dismal Swamp makes a significant contribution to the understanding of the Underground Railroad history." A little farther south, the Elizabeth City waterfront has a large plaque proclaiming its inclusion in the Underground Railroad Network. The Pasquotank River in the city is the first river to receive this designation. Once slaves reached Elizabeth City, they escaped on ships heading north or south to the West Indies. Some runaways were able to go as far as Hawaii.

Although the Outer Banks is less than one hundred miles away by road from the Dismal Swamp, the two areas are as similar as chalk and cheese. Most of the Outer Banks is now part of Cape Hatteras National Seashore. During the Civil War, Federal forces seized Hatteras Island in August 1861. Almost immediately, slaves from eastern North Carolina found their way to the Outer Banks. They helped Union troops build fortifications during the rest of the war in exchange for food and lodging.

So many runaway slaves fled to the army that the *New York Times* of January 29, 1862, reported that a "Capt. Clark has erected a very commodious wooden house on the beach for the use of fugitives who have recently arrived from Roanoke Island. It's christened 'Hotel De Afrique.' " Just like today, a French name gave the place a certain prestige, even if meant to be ironic. An image in *Harper's Weekly* shows two wooden buildings, one flying the American flag. The original site had twelve buildings.

Today, the area, which has been washed over by repeated storms and hurricanes, is overgrown with brush. Nothing is left of the hotel. The only reminder is the *New York Times* quote, engraved on a large plaque, standing in front of the Graveyard of the Atlantic museum.

Roanoke Island, located between the Outer Banks and the eastern North Carolina mainland, fell to Union forces during a Civil War battle on February 7–8, 1862. Word of safe haven spread throughout the state. So many escaped slaves arrived on the island that the federal government needed to establish some organization and order. The Freedmen's Colony, as it was called, became a formal settlement offering training and education to its members. They established schools and churches. At the end of the war, the land reverted to the previous owners and most freed blacks moved back to the mainland.

The Freedmen's Colony exhibit is within Fort Raleigh National Historic Site. Though the site is primarily concerned with the first New World settlement and Virginia Dare, the beautiful visitor center also devotes space to the Civil War and its aftermath. A large memorial outside the visitor center commemorates the Freedmen's Colony.

The Underground Railroad Program recognizes hundreds of historical places, museums, and interpretive programs throughout the country. The website has a database organized by state and facility. Most sites are not national park units, but members of the program that provide their own interpretation.

If there's one commonality among the several sites in eastern

North Carolina, it's that there are no artifacts left of the Underground Railroad. Stories and memorials are all that a visitor can experience of this heritage. That's why I found walking the Dismal Swamp so fascinating. Here, I could understand how slaves were able to find safe haven.

᪥Fort Donelson National Battlefield
First significant Union victory
Tennessee

The temperature is almost down to freezing when I start out this morning for Fort Donelson in Northwest Tennessee. I haven't yet put my ice scraper away, and it's a lucky thing too since my car windows need a good working over.

After the state of Tennessee seceded from the Union, the Confederates built Fort Henry on the Tennessee River and Fort Donelson on the Cumberland River outside of Dover to prevent a Union invasion of Tennessee. Fort Donelson, named after Confederate general and politician Daniel S. Donelson, was meant to control the river leading to the heart of Tennessee. The capture of Fort Donelson was the first significant Union victory. It not only opened the heartland of the Confederacy to Federal forces, but it propelled Ulysses S. Grant to hero status. Brigadier General Simon B. Buckner, who was left to negotiate a surrender with Grant, didn't do too badly either, as he became governor of Kentucky after the Civil War.

The visitor center film features more than just the battles. Buckner and Grant were friends at West Point, and Buckner even lent Grant some money. In 1885, Buckner visited Grant on his deathbed, as an act of reconciliation. I always wonder about the small things I learn at a visitor center. A display explains that war was 99 percent boredom and 1 percent terror. What did soldiers do to entertain themselves when they weren't fighting or attending to personal chores? They wrote letters, played cards, gambled, whittled, and participated in cock fighting. Cock fighting?

"Where did they get the roosters?" I ask the ranger on duty.

"Well, it's illegal now," she says, "but probably from local farms."

In some national parks, I feel like I'm the only visitor on the site and that they've opened up just for me. However, I'm never alone in a Civil War park site. Today, in addition to a couple of Civil War enthusiasts, two busloads of high school ROTC students from Dickson County, an hour away, pour into the visitor center.

I start the drive through the battlefield. I forgot to ask how long the auto tour is and whether it's reasonable to walk it. The United Daughters of the Confederacy erected a Confederate monument in 1933 to remember the Confederate soldiers who fought and died here. Though there's a national cemetery at Fort Donelson, Confederate soldiers couldn't be buried here because they had fought against the United States. The monument depicts a soldier holding a rifle on a tall spire, with a stone confederate flag flying above him. An inscription reads, "There is no holier spot of ground than where defeated valor lies."

I expected to see a brick and mortar fort like the old masonry forts, but this structure is built of earthworks. I must have read right over the word "earthworks." Soldiers and slaves built the fort with walls made of logs and earth that could be put up faster than structures that are more substantial. But today, the earthworks look so inconsequential. I catch up with the school buses here. Ranger D. J. Richardson explains that this was the first major winter confrontation, February 12 through 16, 1862, with the big battle on Valentine's Day. I still can't picture the protection of an earthworks fort.

"Do the earthworks form a closed loop?" I ask the ranger.

"Yes. It's a challenge to preserve earthworks. In addition, the army planted oak trees in the 1920s and the trees are coming to the end of their lives." Some have toppled over. At the time, the earthworks would have been much higher, but they've sunk over the years.

A bald eagle flying above us interrupts Richardson's talk about cannons on the riverbanks. The girls in the group, who looked so bored until now, perk up.

"Did you name the birds?" a female student asks.

"No," Ranger Richardson says. "But I understand that at Shiloh, they've named a pair Hiram and Julia."

Hiram was Ulysses S. Grant's original first name, which was changed when he entered the army. Julia was his wife. The ranger confesses that General Grant fascinates him.

Several high school students are wearing just a T-shirt and must be freezing, standing still while the ranger speaks. Today, the cold and rainy weather is similar to what soldiers had in February of 1862, while they camped here. I'm glad I'm not camping. After I return to the visitor center, I walk the Donelson Trail through the woods, but a sleety downpour makes me turn around.

Some claim that the rebel yell, a battle cry used to intimidate the enemy, originated here when a Confederate cannon hit a gunboat. But the feeling of success was short-lived. The Confederates were so busy strengthening their position they didn't notice that Grant's army was marching to encircle the fort's earthworks. After more fighting and confusion on the part of Confederate commanders, the Union surrounded the fort.

I drive to the Dover Hotel, built between 1851 and 1853, in downtown Dover. It stands on the banks of the Cumberland River, an attractive stop for riverboat travelers. During the battle, the hotel became General Buckner's headquarters, where he met Grant to discuss surrender terms on February 16, 1862. The top Confederate commanders, Floyd and Pillow, had escaped to Nashville before they could be taken prisoner. They left the command to General Buckner, who wasn't about to desert his men.

A humorous film at the Dover Hotel reenacts this decision. Buckner decided to surrender and asked Grant for the terms. "No terms except an unconditional and immediate surrender can be accepted." The U. S. in U. S. Grant, some said, stood for Unconditional Surrender.

The Dover Hotel reopened after the war and stayed in business until the 1930s. My drive takes me through Dover, the home of the fort, a small sad town that may still be feeling the effects of the Civil War.

⚜ Shiloh National Military Park
Bloody Shiloh
Tennessee

Who is this woman showing her breast, her nipple no less, in a national park? Even on my hike through France, where every tiny village had a World War I memorial, I never saw a statue of a woman so exposed. Now that I have your attention . . .

I take a picture of the seventy-five-foot Iowa Memorial, one of the tallest in the park. *Fame*, as the statue is called, is writing the names of Iowans who died here. The state of Iowa suffered 2,409 casualties, including killed, wounded, and missing, the largest loss of Iowans in any battle in any war. Shiloh was the first really bloody battle of the Civil War. In just two days, April 6 and 7, 1862, there were 23,746 casualties. The first day didn't look too good for General Ulysses S. Grant's forces as the Confederates pushed the Union troops back toward the river. That night, fresh Union reinforcements arrived and attacked the second day.

The forty-five-minute movie at the visitor center goes through every movement of both sides. I understand the chaos of the bloody battle, but the detailed tactics are lost on me. I note that Shiloh was one of the first battlefields to use tent field hospitals. This way, injured soldiers could be treated quicker without moving an unstable patient. But I can't picture how a surgeon could work as bullets whizzed by. The poet Walt Whitman, who worked as a nurse, captures the hospital scene in *Leaves of Grass*, independent of any actual battle.

> *Surgeons operating, attendants holding lights, the smell of*
> *ether, the odor of blood;*
> *The crowd, O the crowd of the bloody forms of soldiers—*
> *the yard outside also fill'd;*
> *Some on the bare ground, some on planks or stretchers,*
> *some in the death-spasm sweating;*
> *An occasional scream or cry, the doctor's shouted orders or*
> *calls;*

Shiloh was protected in 1894, the second military park placed under the Department of the Army. Over six thousand acres were set aside as one of five battlefields for the five Union armies. Veterans pushed for protection of these battlefields. In particular, the Speaker of the House in the 1890s was a Civil War veteran, whose brother was killed at Shiloh.

At the time, the army was focused on preservation and commemoration. They wanted to make sure that all battlefields were maintained the same way. A ranger points out that the army had two or three plans for the superintendent's house, which all the battlefield parks had to follow. You can't get details like that from the web. You have to be lucky and interested enough to engage a ranger in conversation.

On the driving tour through the battlefield, I stop at the Shiloh Church, which gave the battle its name. Southern Methodists built the original Shiloh Meeting House, a one-room log structure, around 1853, nine years after the church had split over the slavery issue. The original church, destroyed in the battle, was recently reconstructed. A modern church on the same private inholding is still active.

This evening, I reread what Tony Horwitz has to say about Shiloh in his best seller *Confederates in the Attic* to see if I missed anything. Horwitz writes, "Park rangers later confided to me that *Fame* nurtured Boy Scouts these days, who snapped pictures of each other sucking on the monument's marble nipple." No one told me that!

⟡ Stones River National Battlefield
First Civil War memorial
Tennessee

Just outside Murfreesboro, Tennessee, a seven-hundred-acre site commemorates a three-day Civil War battle from December 31, 1862, to January 2, 1863. As the museum says, soldiers joined up for adventure, to defend their nation, protect their homes, maintain or end slavery, or earn money. Soldiers were hungry and bored most of the time. Occasionally, a raging battle terrified and exhilarated them.

After the first day of conflict at Stones River, the Union and Confederates were too exhausted to fight. They spent New Year's Day collecting and burying their dead. Resuming the battle the next day, they turned Stones River into one of the bloodiest battles of the war with an over 30 percent casualty rate. Names like the Slaughter Pen and Hell's Half Acre give you an idea of how brutal the fighting was. Tactically, the outcome of the battle was a draw, but strategically, it was a victory for the Union. General Braxton Bragg, the Confederate commander, retreated just as the Southern side did at Shiloh.

The Union forces, led by William Rosecrans, then marched into Murfreesboro and declared victory. On January 1, 1863, President Lincoln freed the slaves, and this immediate victory added muscle to the Emancipation Proclamation. Stones River Battlefield was preserved in 1927.

I start at the new visitor center with a museum, which discusses conditions before, during, and after the battle. A small theater shows a short movie. However, the best interpretation is on a 2.2-mile walk through fields and the rocky Slaughter Pen. Battlefield parks offer easy walking compared to the mountains. We meet up with a spirited ranger who ends his talk with, "The South wasn't going to win the war, no matter how brutal or bloody the battles." That's like giving the conclusion of the story two and a half years before the end of the war.

We walk across the street to the national cemetery, where over six thousand Union soldiers are buried. The Confederates are interred in another cemetery.

A little farther on, the Hazen Brigade Monument commemorates the Colonel Hazen Brigade, the only Union soldiers to hold on to their position after the first day of fighting. The most amazing part was that the survivors of this battle built the monument in 1863, while the Civil War was still raging.

Vicksburg National Military Park
Art Park
Mississippi

"Vicksburg is the key," said President Lincoln. "The war can never be brought to a close until that key is in our pocket."

Jefferson Davis shared the same thoughts about the importance of Vicksburg. "Vicksburg is the nailhead that holds the South's two halves together."

Every Civil War national battlefield I've visited claims to be the turning point of the war, except maybe the one-acre parks in Tupelo. However, Vicksburg on the Mississippi River was a major factor in the Union victory. The Mississippi River fed the Confederacy. If the Union was able to take the river, it would split the enemy. The Vicksburg campaign was complicated. Whereas many Civil War battles lasted a day or two, Vicksburg was a long engagement, from March 29 to July 4, 1863. This conflict can't just be described as the Blue (Union) coming in from one side and the Gray (Confederates) from the opposite side.

Before the Civil War, Mississippi was one of the wealthiest states in the Union. Vicksburg's merchant class created a cosmopolitan city and elected pro-Union legislators, but the state seceded in January 1861. Vicksburg was considered as strong as Gibraltar. The Confederates had armed the bluffs above the Mississippi and thought the city was impregnable. The Union tried many tactics to penetrate Vicksburg. General Grant ordered his men to dig a canal to bypass the enemies' batteries. He even hoped to change the course of the Mississippi River and cut off Vicksburg's water. It might have been a great idea, but the canal collapsed.

After several setbacks, navy gunboats ran the gauntlet past the Confederate canons on the hills. This daring move allowed Union boats to transport soldiers and supplies across the Mississippi. Now Grant could attack, but he still couldn't bring down Vicksburg and control the river. Grant switched tactics and instituted a siege. Diaries tell of the constant boom of cannons and the cries of the wounded. During the siege, civilians lived in caves to get away from the fighting. The Confederates hoped that help would come from Jackson, the capital of Mississippi, over forty miles away, but aid never came.

Forty-seven days later, Vicksburg surrendered on July 4, an

auspicious day. Now the Union controlled the Mississippi River and split the enemy. The day before, General Lee had been defeated at Gettysburg. The combined victories turned the war around, even if peace didn't come for another year and a half.

Vicksburg became the fifth national military park in 1899. After the Civil War, veterans groups organized to lobby Congress and save the battlefield. The veterans showed historians where the battle lines were, making Vicksburg one of the most accurately laid-out battlefields. Confederate positions are identified by red tablets, and the Union by blue, colors used to illustrate military units on historical maps and other battlefields. The practice stems from the Revolutionary War, when Americans wore blue and the British wore red.

Today, the visitor center at Vicksburg National Military Park is busy. About thirty high school ROTC students from nearby Rolling Fork, Mississippi, file in to watch a fiber optics map showing the progress of the two advancing armies. Blue and red lights march across a large wall.

ဆ◆ఴ

For me, the highlight of the visit is the sixteen-mile auto tour. A Civil War veteran put it best: "Vicksburg is the art park of the world!"

Renowned American sculptors of the day created this collection of stone and bronze work. Though the sculptors had to focus on commemoration, each major piece is different and original. Vicksburg may have the most monuments of all the Civil War battlefields. Depending on what National Park Service pamphlet or web page you read, it may have more than 1,328 monuments and markers, or more than 1,350, or even over 1,700. Since park boundaries have shifted, some monuments are now outside the park. Many large structures were built with huge, imposing steps, probably without considering disabled Civil War veterans who might want to see their old battlefields.

Compared to the crowds in the visitor center, few people are on the one-way road. Fewer still get out of their cars to study the monuments. When I first start the drive, I stop at every monument, but I realize that checking out each stone would take days. Still I'm like a jack-in-the box, popping out of the car frequently.

Most memorials were commissioned by the twenty-nine states that fought for control of Vicksburg, but few monuments have dates. Massachusetts dedicated the first memorial in 1903, but the symbol of Vicksburg is the Illinois Memorial erected three years later. The imposing round-domed building with columns in front is modeled after the Roman Pantheon. Bronze tablets list all 36,325 Illinois soldiers who participated in the campaign. The forty-seven steps up to the building, referred to as the temple, represent the forty-seven days of the siege. It cost approximately $190,000 to construct the memorial in 1906. According to an information sign, that translates to over $4.6 million to build a similar structure today.

It took decades for many Southern states to have the resources to put up their memorials. Maybe it seemed at the time that the North was showing off its wealth by coming down to Mississippi and erecting huge structures. The Mississippi State Memorial, dedicated in 1909, wasn't finished until 1912. Mississippi placed a second memorial in 2004 to commemorate contributions of African-Americans on both sides of the conflict. Three African-Americans on a large pedestal commemorate the "Service of the 1st and 3rd Mississippi Infantry of African Descent and All Mississippians of African Descent Who Participated in the Vicksburg Campaign."

In 1917, Missouri dedicated *The Spirit of the Republic*, with a winged angel of peace in the center. Bronze reliefs depicting Union and Confederate soldiers memorialize the dead on each side of the conflict. You always hear about "brother fighting brother," but here it is literally carved in stone and bronze. The monument, erected on the spot where two opposing Missouri regiments fought each other, stands forty-two feet tall. Forty-two Missouri units, twenty-seven Union and fifteen Confederate, fought at Vicksburg. Kentucky is the only other state to have a memorial to both armies. Bronze statues of United States President Abraham Lincoln and Confederate President Jefferson Davis, both native Kentuckians, face each other, but certainly don't shake hands.

On the drive, I reach Vicksburg National Cemetery, created in 1866 to bury about seventeen thousand Union dead that lay in small cemeteries and sites far from Vicksburg. As a result, 75 percent of the remains are of unknown soldiers. Only two Confederate soldiers are buried here. When the National Cemetery System was enacted in 1862, it stated that only "the soldiers who shall die in the service of this country" could be buried in a Federal facility. At the time, this meant just those in the Union Army. Over five thousand Confederate soldiers are buried in the Vicksburg City Cemetery.

There would have been more plaques and markers but for the metal drive during World War II. Because the demand for metal was so high, the war effort enlisted the National Park Service. Nearly 145 of the largest and heaviest cast-iron tablets were melted down. It seems like just a token gesture for the war effort, but it was significant to the individual parks involved. Since then, only a few tablets have been replaced.

According to Ranger Rick Martin, the metal drive involved military parks all across the country. Cannons also contributed to the war effort.

"Certain plaques weren't necessary to tell the story at this time, so they were melted," Ranger Martin explains.

It sounds like he's trying to justify the park's wrong answers. Now the Friends of Vicksburg National Military Park are raising money to replace these memorials. Would the Park Service allow this meltdown of our heritage now?

Vicksburg National Military Park, established in 1899, was the last of the battlefields preserved during the golden age of battlefield preservation. Veterans led in the efforts of protecting and marking it accurately. By the time the next Civil War battlefield was created, Civil War veterans no longer dominated the legislatures, and almost all were gone.

☜ Abraham Lincoln Birthplace National Historical Park
One of many Lincoln sites
Kentucky

At Abraham Lincoln Birthplace National Historical Park, outside of Hodgenville, Kentucky, I get the conventional view of our sixteenth president. It's the story of the American dream, the ability to rise from simple beginnings to one's highest potential. Eloquence and common sense marked Lincoln's speeches. The 266-word Gettysburg Address at the dedication of Gettysburg National Cemetery stirred the nation.

However, I also find an unconventional look at Lincoln in an enlightening visitor center film. Abe Lincoln's father, Thomas, a successful carpenter, was able to buy Sinking Spring Farm for $200 cash in 1808. Abe Lincoln was born in a middle-class family, perhaps upper-middle, in a frontier town. Abe's grandfather was the true pioneer, having come through Cumberland Gap, maybe with Daniel Boone himself.

Abe was born in a log cabin on February 12, 1809, a year after the family settled on the Kentucky farm, but he spent only two years here. The family was forced off the farm because of a land deed dispute. They moved to what is now preserved as his Boyhood Home at Knob Creek. Unfortunately, the Boyhood Home is closed to the public for construction when I plan to visit.

The highlight of the Abraham Lincoln Birthplace is the Lincoln Birthplace Memorial. Before the Lincoln Memorial in Washington opened in 1922, the memorial here was dedicated in 1911. Its fifty-six steps symbolize the fifty-six years of Lincoln's life. The steps lead to a building with columns inspired by the Parthenon in Greece. The Lincoln Farm Association, composed of prominent men of the times including Samuel Clemens (Mark Twain), bought the site in 1905 and built this Lincoln Memorial. President Theodore Roosevelt laid the cornerstone on the 100th anniversary of Lincoln's birth. In 1916, the site became a national park, overseen by the War Department until 1933.

A one-room cabin, which for a long time was thought to be Lincoln's original home, sits in the building. After a great deal of research and testing, the National Park Service concluded that the logs were of a later era. The log cabin remains on the original site as a symbolic cabin. The Sinking Spring is below, now fenced off so that visitors don't drink from the same water source that Lincoln did.

In 1816, the family was involved in another land dispute and had to leave Knob Creek. That was the last straw, and they headed for Indiana.

80◆CR

ᵥ❧ Chickamauga and Chattanooga National Military Park
First military park
Tennessee, Georgia

Do you know there's an International Towing and Recovery Museum in Chattanooga? I'm trying to find Lookout Mountain in Chickamauga and Chattanooga National Military Park— ChickChatt, as they call it. While I search for the battlefield, I see more brown signs for the towing museum than for Lookout Mountain, along with plenty of signs for Point Park, Ruby Falls, and Rock City. My car GPS is confused as well. It turns out that all those black Point Park signs go up to Lookout Mountain.

At the Chattanooga Visitor Center, a disinterested ranger hands me the park brochure. However, at ten a.m. sharp, a volunteer shows up behind the desk, eager to talk to visitors. Here's a little history of the Battle of Chattanooga.

After Union troops were defeated in Chickamauga (Chick), they retreated to Chattanooga (Chatt), fifteen miles northwest. Confederates then blocked the roads and rail lines, preventing Federal supplies from entering Chattanooga. With reinforcements, Federal troops were able to open a shorter supply line, which they called the Cracker Line, because they brought hard tack, a cracker that could break whatever teeth soldiers still had. But, hey, it was food. This reinvigorated the Union Army, which pushed the Confederates out of their defenses, on hills above Chatt; this was known as the Battle Above the Clouds.

Chattanooga, the gateway to the Deep South, was now in Union hands. It was a very strategic victory because the area had roads and railroads in every direction, in addition to the Tennessee River. Chatt became the base for Sherman's drive to Atlanta and the sea.

The visitor center shows the obligatory film and displays, but it also has a huge painting by James Walker titled *The Battle Above the Clouds*. From the web and as described at the visitor center:

> *In 1864 artist James Walker completed a painting commissioned by the federal government of the action of November 24, 1863, which he called "The Battle of Lookout Mountain." In 1870 General Joseph Hooker commissioned Walker to paint a much larger version (13 feet by 30 feet) of his original painting for $20,000. Walker returned to Chattanooga and studied the landscape. He paid a photographer to take pictures as well. After Walker presented the painting to Hooker it toured the United States and remained in Hooker's family until 1970, when it was donated to the National Park Service. Today the painting hangs in the Visitors Center near the entrance to Point Park.*

But enough history. I leave the visitor center and walk the trail on top of Lookout Mountain. A memorial from New York State overwhelms the area. The Tennessee River and city of Chattanooga are spread out below. No place to go but down into a network of rocky trails, beneath cliff towers. I walk down to Sunset Rock past rock climbers and a man reading in a hammock. The trails are lush with late summer flowers, kudzu, and poison ivy. I could have spent a couple of days exploring the trails, but I'm eager to move on to Chickamauga and check it out tomorrow. Most visitors would go to both areas in one day, and maybe do even more, but I can't absorb more than one site a day.

ଚ୨◆୦ଃ

Chickamauga Battlefield in Fort Oglethorpe, Georgia, with a

large, modern visitor center, is much bigger than Chattanooga.

I start by driving the seven-mile loop road. I stop, get out of the car, walk a few steps, read the plaques, and get back in the car. I always find this exhausting but I feel that I'll get the typical visitor experience this way.

One stop shows the boundary line between the Union and Confederates. You don't have such clear-cut lines separating the two sides in modern wars. A busy road bisects the park. Numerous monuments commemorate both sides of the conflict.

The Wilder Brigade Monument stands out among all the others, with a White-Castle-restaurant-type tower. The monument honors Illinois and Indiana troops, including Captain Eli Lilly of the 18th Indiana Battalion, who went on to found one of the largest pharmaceutical companies in the world. Visitors can climb the steep circular staircase to the top of the tower and get a great view of the whole battlefield. On my way up, I meet a couple with a dog, thankfully on a leash. They're trying to encourage this poor animal to walk down the narrow, tight stairs. The dog should have stayed in the car.

The park has about fifty miles of trail. I walk a seven-mile loop through the military park, past more memorials. The Snodgrass House, used as a makeshift hospital during the battle, still stands. Only two hikers are on the trail, along with four women doing a day of service by cleaning memorials with a spray of water.

"But where is the fort in Fort Oglethorpe?" I ask the ranger.

Soldiers trained here for the Spanish-American War, World War I, and World War II, living in barracks behind the park, now on private property. After World War II, the military decided that the post was just too small and declared it surplus land. The modern city of Fort Oglethorpe grew on the old site.

ChickChatt was the first national military park, created in 1890. Veterans from both sides recognized that preserving portions of battlefields to commemorate the deeds of their comrades and honor the men who had fallen would benefit the reunited nation.

"The project," wrote a veteran, "is based upon the belief that the time has fully come when the participants in the great battles of our civil war can, while retaining and freely expressing their own views of all questions connected with the war, still study its notable battles purely as military movements."

In addition to its historic and educational values, the National Military Park was created as part of the healing process for a nation that had been torn apart by war. Veterans on both sides could discuss military tactics, a safe topic that would eventually lead to reconciliation. Maybe it's like sports banter for men nowadays. When Lenny talks to male acquaintances, he can talk sports like the best of them. I wonder where he gets his information.

The wall exhibits in the visitor center explains this position. Most historians would say that it's more complicated than that, but I'm a history user. This also explains why the military parks concentrate on maneuvers and tactics so much—the blue stood here, the gray stood there—instead of bigger questions of causes and effects of the Civil War.

ᑫ Andersonville National Historic Site
The saddest place in the South
Georgia

Sometimes I have difficulty separating a national park unit from the history that makes the area worth preserving. I thought about this when I wandered around the Hensley Settlement at Cumberland Gap, but the feeling of confusion is magnified here at Andersonville.

Camp Sumter at Andersonville, site of the largest Confederate military prison during the Civil War, was a sad, depressing, horrible place. Nearly a third of the Union soldiers confined here died. Set in central Georgia among working cotton fields, the park unit reminds us of man's inhumanity to man—literally. The national historic site is so evocative of the horror that occurred here and so well interpreted that it's been called the South's Holocaust Museum.

At the beginning of the Civil War, captured men on both sides were released on the condition that they wouldn't return to battle. Though it seemed to be the easiest way to deal with prisoners of war (POWs), this system didn't last long. In 1863, there was a breakdown of the prisoner exchange system, partly because the South treated African-American prisoners of war differently from white POWs. Some black soldiers were either shot or pressed into slavery.

The Confederates kept Union prisoners in old warehouses, but soon they needed to build camps. In 1864, the Andersonville prison, officially known as Camp Sumter, was erected, mostly by African-American slaves. The first prisoners were brought here in February 1864, and the prison was active for only fourteen months. The prison stockade in Andersonville was described as hell on earth, with four hundred men arriving each day. About forty-five thousand men passed through, and almost thirteen thousand died here during the prison's short existence. A few captured women were put under house arrest in the community, but not placed in the stockade. They spent their time nursing soldiers.

The prison didn't provide any protection from the weather. Men bought wooden poles and gathered blankets and pieces of canvas to make tents. Three men, spooned, slept inside the makeshift shelter. Georgia is in the South, but winters are cold here. If a man came to Andersonville in the summer, he had no protection but the clothes on his back. Little food was available. The water was contaminated, causing dysentery and diarrhea.

"This little creek was our only water supply, and when we would go after water we would often sink to our hips in the mire, and men would often have to be dragged by their comrades," wrote Charles C. Fosdick, 5th Iowa Infantry.

The wooden stockade surrounding the first 16.5 acres was well-designed. The stockades added six months later show the signs of hasty construction, with gaps in the walls. Guards stood watch in wooden towers set every ninety feet. Even so, prison discipline broke down. In the stockade, men known as Raiders terrorized fellow prisoners. The Confederates allowed Union prisoners to deal with these criminals and try them. The six ringleaders were hung.

Since seasoned troops had been sent to fight on the front lines for the Confederate Army, old men and young boys took over as watch guards, but they weren't much better off than the POWs. Food and facilities were awful for them as well. Captain Henry Wirz was assigned to manage the prison, but he wasn't really in charge.

When confronted by prisoners about the conditions, he said, "I am doing the best I can." He didn't have control over supplies or guards. Still, at the end of the war, the North was angry and wanted retribution. A military tribunal tried Wirz and found him guilty of war crimes, specifically murder and conspiracy.

"I know what my orders are, Major. And I am being hanged for obeying them," Wirz said.

He was executed in Washington, DC, in November 1865. Captain Wirz wasn't forgotten. Though he "wasn't from around here," having been born in Switzerland, Southerners honored him. The United Daughters of the Confederacy dedicated an obelisk to him in 1909 in the community of Andersonville; it stands opposite the entrance to the national park unit.

If you think that this piece of history would inspire good fiction, you're right. MacKinlay Kantor won the Pulitzer Prize in 1956 for his novel *Andersonville*. At least two TV movies were made on the subject: *Andersonville*, in 1996, about the conditions of the Andersonville stockade, and *The Andersonville Trial*, a 1970 courtroom drama about the trial of Captain Wirz.

The large, modern visitor center building encompasses exhibits about Andersonville and the National Prisoner of War Museum and shows two films. A twenty-eight-minute film describes the nightmare of trying to survive Andersonville Prison. Young, thin actors speak of the dreadful conditions, their dialogue based on prisoners' memoirs. Old paunchy reenactors are used in background shots of the prison.

The Civil War was the first major American conflict where photography was available, so the horrors were more visible. A. J. Riddle, a photographer working for the Confederate Government, made several plates showing the overcrowded conditions of the camp. Photographs of naked, emaciated men, taken after the war, are heartbreaking.

In the visitor center, the central hallway focuses on Andersonville. The National Prisoner of War Museum, which honors POWs from all wars, takes up the walls and side rooms. You really need to read the fine print to understand which war is being described. In the commemorative courtyard, a wall sculpture and plaques honor various POW groups.

Who is a POW? The display puts Andersonville in context from ancient times until the present. Nathan Hale, a soldier for the Continental Army during the Revolutionary War, was a spy and therefore not protected as a POW; the British hung him. Were African-Americans fighting for the Union side POWs or runaway slaves? Visitors walk through the galleries as if they were POWs. Rifles stick out of the wall and point at the passersby. Videos show POWs recalling their experiences. Metal sculptures outlining bodies stand together, and handwritten letters decorate the walls.

You can explore the historic site with a one-hour audio driving tour, but I get impatient with audio tours and just walk across the grounds. Two parallel lines of white posts surround the whole stockade area. The outer posts outline the stockade itself. The inner posts show the deadline, a no-man's land that prisoners were forbidden to cross upon threat of death. Let's think about these consequences when we miss a deadline at work or school. The top of the stockade area now displays huge monuments from several northern states, including Massachusetts, Michigan, and a large obelisk from Ohio. A smaller stone memorial commemorates the 1,284 Union soldiers imprisoned here from Tennessee, a divided state.

As you look around at the top of the hill, you see few signs of modern civilization, except for cars in the parking lot. This is rural Georgia. Prison shelters, sometimes called shebangs, have been set up in one corner of the stockade site, including a barber tent. Down the hill, a pavilion erected by the Women's Relief Corps of the Grand Army of the Republic around 1901 protects Providence Spring. During the men's confinement, clean water was even more precious than food. Stockade Branch, a small creek, was the only water source in the stockade, and it was muddy much of the time. During a rainstorm, a spring gushed out of the ground. The men attributed this water miracle to divine providence, hence the name. The spring still flows.

Star Fort sits at the bottom of the prison site. The earthworks, built to protect the prison against Union attacks, contain four cannons pointing outward. But the Confederates also had to guard against prison rebellions, so five cannons pointed inward.

80◆03

By now I'm probably numb, but I don't find Andersonville National Cemetery as depressing as the stockade prison site. At the entrance to the cemetery, a huge statue shows three men, one lame, another with a broken arm, and a third otherwise afflicted. The Old Testament engraving says, "Turn you to the stronghold Ye prisoners of hope, Zechariah 9:12."

Clara Barton, founder of the American Red Cross, worked on finding out who was buried in the cemetery. She didn't have much to go on until Dorence Atwater, a former prisoner, contacted her. Atwater, who had worked in the prison hospital, kept meticulous records of the dead. Along with other helpers, Barton and Atwater identified and marked the graves in the cemetery. Rows and rows of headstones have only a name, number, and state. Over 13,800 bodies are buried here from the Civil War.

Andersonville is one of only two open national park cemeteries, where veterans and their spouses can still be buried; the other is Andrew Johnson National Historic Site in East Tennessee. The modern section has crosses and other approved religious symbols. Some graves are as fresh as 2014.

After the Civil War, the site bounced around through several owners until the Women's Relief Corps bought the land. After making improvements, the women's group donated the site to the people of the United States. The War Department, followed by the Army, administered Andersonville before it became a National Historic Site in 1970.

Twice a year, the museum opens at night. The park illuminates the prison site by candle lanterns, allowing access to the reconstructed northeast corner of the prison site. Living history volunteers portray life in the winter of 1864–65.

Lenny and I take a full day to visit Andersonville, eating a packed lunch in the picnic area. After we leave the site, we drive across the road into the community of Andersonville to see the memorial of Captain Henry Wirz, still a controversial historic figure. I almost feel sorry for Wirz, trapped between his orders from above and his lack of resources in the prison.

ᕙ Kennesaw Mountain National Battlefield Park
On Sherman's march to Atlanta
Georgia

The battle on Kennesaw Mountain was part of General Sherman's campaign on his way to capture Atlanta and ultimately march to the sea. In 1864, three long years after the firing upon Fort Sumter, General Ulysses S. Grant took command of all Union armies and planned a coordinated strategy to end the war.

Still, the Confederate Army remained daunting. General Grant ordered William T. Sherman to inflict as much damage as possible to the heartland of the Confederacy. Sherman started his march in North Georgia and worked his way down the route of the Western & Atlantic Railroad, the Confederates' supply line.

Sherman's troops forced the Confederates to a defensive position in the Kennesaw Mountains, where opposing armies clashed on June 27, 1864. The South lost fewer men than the North, but the battle seemed to delay Sherman for only a few days. Though the battle itself could be called a stalemate, Sherman's troops got closer and closer to Atlanta and finally occupied the city on September 2, 1864.

The National Park Service has protected 2,965 acres in what is now the outskirts of Marietta, only twenty miles from Atlanta. Suburban sprawl surrounds the battlefield, but that's both good and bad. Though Lenny and I stayed only ten minutes from the park the night before, we crawl through rush hour traffic, only to misread the sign into the park and miss the turn to the visitor center—bad. When we turn around and have to make a left turn, kind and polite southern drivers let us in—good.

Still we're parked and ready to explore before the visitor center opens. Lenny and I walk up to the top of Kennesaw Mountain, climbing 700 feet in 1.2 miles. Kennesaw Mountain, at 1,808 feet, is lower than where I live. Before the war, the countryside was dotted with farms and grazing animals, but war changes the landscape. Soldiers had to tear down trees and homes to build earthworks, still visible today, for protection. Now from the top, a panoramic view of the city lies before us. Many Union soldiers were flat-landers from the Midwest who were challenged by the rocky and hilly terrain. Mountains offer an advantage to the defenders, who always understand the geography better.

Runners, exercisers, and dog walkers who may never go into the visitor center join us at the top. Fall colors are at their peak. At higher elevation in the Blue Ridge, most trees are now bare and dull, but here we're enjoying a second shot of autumn with a sunny and bright day.

We jump from the Civil War to the 1930s on our walk through Camp Brumby, a Civilian Conservation Corps site. The CCC boys built most of the eighteen miles of trails in the park. About two hundred men lived here for four years. Yet, only a few foundations are left of the original camp.

As with most Civil War battlefields, Kennesaw Mountain veterans started returning in large numbers as they got older. An Illinois veteran bought sixty acres of land and eventually trans-ferred the property to the Colonel Dan McCook Brigade Asso-ciation. However, even the association couldn't maintain the site properly and offered it to the War Department. The National Battlefield was designated in 1917; Cheatham Hill was added on in 1933.

The visitor center exhibits are almost all about the Civil War. Nevertheless, the park recognizes that many visitors come to run, walk, and look for birds. In 2014, over two million people visited Kennesaw Battlefield, double the number of visitors in 1998. I wonder how that tracks with the number of locals who use the park regularly. The park seems to be involved in the community, with a lively Facebook page that recognizes its volunteers and sister parks.

The visitor center displays three types of shoes: the Creek moccasin, the Jefferson Bootees for infantrymen, and the modern running sneaker, along with a display of energy foods for these three groups.

Michael Gillard, the ranger on duty, was intrigued by a calorie counter at the Women's Rights National Historical Park in New York State. "They only had a mile of trail," he says. "We have eighteen." Gillard created a calorie chart that shows the number of calories burned for the major trails in the park. For example, The Big Mountain Hike, which is about two miles round trip, burns 302 calories for a 130-pound person. This is one ranger's response to Mrs. Obama's Let's Move Outside campaign.

⬸ Brices Cross Roads National Battlefield Site and Tupelo National Battlefield
One-acre parks
Mississippi

My knowledge of the Civil War is growing, mostly based on visiting national parks, battlefields, and monuments. If you find yourself in Tupelo, Mississippi, you need to check out two more Civil War National Park sites: Brices Cross Roads and Tupelo. Each park is only one acre, so it's not difficult to say that I walked the whole park. Because the units are so small, the official visitor center is on the Natchez Trace Parkway, a scenic road stretching from Natchez to Nashville.

Brices Cross Roads commemorates a Confederate victory on June 10, 1864, outside the town of Baldwyn, about fifteen miles north of Tupelo in northeastern Mississippi. The one-acre park is part of a larger piece of land protected by the Final Stands Civil War Interpretive Center. This may have been the last stand of the Confederates in Northeast Mississippi.

Veterans groups have always wanted to commemorate this site, along with any other site they could justify. In 1929, President Coolidge authorized one acre for the battlefield site. Various groups worked together to choose the land that would represent the battle and designed the memorial, all for $10,000.

A month after the encounter at Brices Corner, there was another clash in Tupelo. The Confederates attacked and the Union troops stood their ground. With heavy Confederate losses, the Yankees called it a victory. One soldier, William Frederick Cody, was a young private in the Union army who just followed orders. Later, he became a scout and the creator of Buffalo Bill's Wild West shows.

The same commemorative groups worked on remembering the Battle of Tupelo. One acre was found in what was then called the community of Harrisburg, to preserve the memory of this battle. Now, Tupelo National Battlefield on Main Street is enveloped by downtown Tupelo, squeezed in between a car wash and a fast-food restaurant, with a pull-off for one or two parking spots. Both sites were preserved in 1929, as Civil War veterans were dying off.

For the first time on my national park journey, I wonder if these two sites are worthy of being part of the National Park Service. The two one-acre parks may not cost too much to operate since they share a visitor center and superintendent with the Natchez Trace Parkway. One pamphlet covers both parks. Someone still has to cut the grass and raise and lower the American flag every day, but overall, these are minimalist parks.

In Tupelo, visitors meet Elvis Presley at every turn. He was born here and businesses are quick to use his memory. Colorful metal sculptures have been placed on street corners as part of the city's downtown revival, another reason to go to Tupelo.

Andrew Johnson National Historic Site
More than his impeachment
Tennessee

As all schoolchildren know, or should know if they were paying attention, Andrew Johnson was the first American president to be impeached. For most of us, that's the only thing we know. However, there's a lot more to this complex man. Andrew Johnson National Historic Site in Greeneville, Tennessee, tells the story of the seventeenth president and the impact he had on the United States.

Andrew Johnson (1808–1875) was born in Raleigh, North Carolina. His father died when he was just three years old. Seven years later, his mother apprenticed him to a tailor, a position he was supposed to hold until he turned twenty-one. However, after a few years the young Andrew ran away and eventually settled in Greeneville in 1826, where he opened up a tailor shop and soon married Eliza McCardle.

Without formal education, Johnson depended on his wife to help him improve his basic writing and math skills. While his tailor business flourished, Johnson found time to enter civic life. He moved up the political ladder in a methodical manner: alderman, mayor, state representative, state senator, US representative, governor of Tennessee, and US senator.

Though Andrew Johnson was a Southern Democrat, he was loyal to the Union cause. When Tennessee seceded from the

Union, President Abraham Lincoln appointed Johnson the military governor for the state. Two years later, he became Abraham Lincoln's vice president. After President Lincoln was assassinated in 1865, Andrew Johnson succeeded him. As president, Johnson wasn't popular with his Republican congress, and he refused to compromise. As Ranger Daniel Luther puts it, "He wasn't one of them. He wasn't a good schmoozer."

President Johnson vetoed more bills than any other president before him. He wanted to readmit the Southern states much as they were before the war but without slavery. He battled with Thaddeus Stevens, the character played by Tommy Lee Jones in the movie *Lincoln*. His friction with Congress left his opponents anxious for an excuse to get rid of Johnson. They passed the Tenure of Office Act, which required Senate approval before a president could remove an appointee.

President Johnson, however, wasn't swayed. He declared the Tenure of Office Act unconstitutional and removed Secretary of War Edwin M. Stanton. This was the excuse that Congress needed. The House moved to impeach him. The Senate tried him but failed by one vote to muster the two-thirds majority necessary to convict him. It was certainly a close call.

During his four years in office, Andrew Johnson did more than just survive impeachment. He purchased Alaska from Russia. He started the Easter egg roll on the White House lawn. He was the voice for the working class. As a senator, he had introduced the Homestead Act, which President Lincoln signed in 1862.

But Johnson believed in the strict interpretation of the American Constitution. He vetoed the Freedmen's Bureau, which provided aid to ex-slaves. He pardoned Dr. Samuel Mudd, who was suspected as an accomplice in the assassination of President Lincoln and imprisoned in Fort Jefferson in the Dry Tortugas off the tip of Florida. This was yet another decision that didn't endear him to his Republican Congress. There was no way that Johnson was going to run for a second presidential term. He returned to Greeneville, though he later was reelected to the US Senate.

The president's great-granddaughter, Margaret Johnson Patterson Bartlett, lived in Johnson's Greeneville home until 1956. She would dress up as Eliza Johnson and give tours. She petitioned government officials to have the house preserved. The Andrew Johnson site became a national monument in 1942 and a national historic site in 1963.

Ⅴ◆Ⅼ

Ideally, you'd be able to set aside most of a day to see the site and talk to the rangers. The site consists of four separate locations: visitor center, early home, the Homestead, and cemetery. The Homestead can only be seen on a free guided tour, offered almost every hour. To start my visit, I park at the visitor center and make a reservation to tour the Homestead later in the day. Andrew Johnson's first tailor shop is a wood frame house located inside the visitor center. To preserve the structure, the State of Tennessee erected a building around it in 1926 and opened it to the public. You can peek in the tailor shop, surrounded by a railing.

After seeing the exhibits on Johnson's interaction with Congress, you can decide if he was guilty or not. You vote by putting a ticket into one of two boxes—guilty, not guilty. Once a year, the Park counts the ballots. *Not guilty* wins every time by a large margin. If you're lucky, Ranger Daniel Luther will greet you from behind the visitor desk. Ranger Luther worked in theater for thirty years and now plays Andrew Johnson at various events at the site and in town.

"What is a NPS uniform but a costume?" Luther says.

Across the street from the visitor center, I tour Johnson's early home on my own. Johnson and his family lived in this modest two-story brick home from the 1830s until 1851. The Homestead, President Johnson's later home, is a block and a half up Main Street from the visitor center. The tour starts on the porch. Ranger Kendra Hinkle grew up in Greeneville and started volunteering at the site when she was still in high school. "They couldn't get rid of me, so they hired me," she says.

As Andrew Johnson moved up in the world, he became quite wealthy and acquired a great deal of land in the area. He had a few household slaves, who stayed on as servants after the Civil War. The home has been restored to its appearance in 1869, after Andrew Johnson returned from Washington. The house has six bedrooms, a dining room, parlor, and kitchen.

Outside, the two-acre plot of land had a vegetable garden, a smokehouse, and the privy. His two daughters, three sons, and five grandchildren lived here occasionally. All three sons died early in life: one in the Civil War, one by laudanum poisoning, and one from tuberculosis. Eliza, Johnson's wife, also had tuberculosis, so she had her own bedroom, where she could rest during the day. It was a hard life, even for rich folks.

Greeneville changed hands many times during the Civil War, and both Union and Confederate forces stayed in the house. Though new wallpaper was hung after the family came back from Washington, the National Park Service exposed some graffiti written on Eliza's bedroom walls by Civil War soldiers. One pencil scrawl said, "Andrew Johnson the old traitor."

Andrew Johnson is buried on a hill on his own land, a few blocks from his home. "It was probably a cow pasture," says Ranger Jim Small. In his coffin, President Johnson was wrapped in a flag with a copy of the Constitution beneath his head. Eliza, who died six months later, is next to him. Many of his descendants are buried in the cemetery as well. The rest of the cemetery holds veterans and their dependents.

"Andrew Johnson Cemetery is only one of two National Park Service military cemeteries still open to new veterans; the other is Andersonville National Historic Site," Ranger Small explains.

One of the pleasures of going to a small historic site early on a weekday is being able to talk to the rangers.

"What's it like to have a national park site in the middle of your town?" I ask.

"Oh, most people don't know it's a national park," one ranger says.

Another differs. "Businesses in town have an overinflated idea of the number of people it attracts and the economic impact of the park site."

Almost forty-three thousand people visited the park in 2014, which seems like a small number for its location, a little more than an hour's drive from Asheville. Greeneville is named for Nathanael Greene, a Revolutionary War general, who received twenty-five thousand acres as a land grant. Though Greene never lived on this land, loyal Patriots who settled here honored their hero.

It seems that Andrew Johnson is still a controversial figure, and historians keep bringing out new books on the seventeenth president. According to Ranger Luther, the American Association of State and Local Historians criticized the historic site for portraying an image of Andrew Johnson that's too positive. It's natural to feel empathy and affection for a historical figure you're dealing with every day. After spending several hours with President Andrew Johnson, I ended up liking the guy myself.

After I visit the Andrew Johnson site, I walk a section of the Appalachian Trail, which passes Andrew Johnson Mountain, close to Greeneville. It's not much of a mountain, and the sign has fallen down. I'm sure no one else knows that the mountain is named after our seventeenth president. Altogether, a sad sight.

10

Twentieth-Century Developments

Twentieth-century national parks show hope for the future. Whether the future was technological or social, the new century was going to be better than the old stodgy, segregated, and classist society of the previous century.

Who can resist the optimism of the Wright Brothers, whose flying machine went down time after time in the Outer Banks of North Carolina? Finally, they achieved success with a twelve-second flight. Although you can categorize their achievement as technical, it was also a feat of dream over reality. Two young bicycle tinkerers with little formal education achieved what engineers in large companies couldn't.

What about the optimism of Carl Sandburg, who moved his family to North Carolina when he was in his late sixties? When most men his age slow down, he started a completely new life. President Jimmy Carter will never slow down. As I write this, President Carter, over ninety years old, is still traveling far and wide from his home in Plains, Georgia. Six different neighborhoods in New Orleans have connections with jazz. The spirit of Louis Armstrong seems to permeate the whole city.

But the twentieth century also saw the dissolution of small communities. By the 1960s, family vacation patterns had changed. People were no longer spending a whole summer in their vacation homes at Cape Lookout. Abandoned houses fell apart. Eventually, the park service took over the whole area.

The National Park Service continues to protect and interpret historic events. In December 2014, President Obama signed the National Defense Authorization Act into law, with a provision authorizing the Manhattan Project National Historical Park. Someday, three sites will open to the public, including one in Oak Ridge, Tennessee.

❧ Wright Brothers National Memorial
First in flight
North Carolina

The North Carolina license plate claims "First in Flight" while Ohio's plate promotes "Birthplace of Aviation." Can both be right? The two states lay claim to the Wright Brothers, the first to succeed in power-driven flights, and both have national parks commemorating the inventors. The Wright Brothers National Memorial at Kill Devil Hills on the north end of the Outer Banks in North Carolina interprets the site of the first flight, while the Dayton Aviation Heritage National Historical

Park tells the brothers' story from bike racers and repairers to manned flight pioneers and visionaries.

Wilbur and Orville Wright were Bill Gates's spiritual predecessors. They were tinkerers, but they were also skilled in math and science. When the brothers felt that they had nothing more to learn at school, they quit high school, but kept taking correspondence courses. First bicycle racers, they soon became bicycle repairers, and then bicycle manufacturers in Dayton. But they always dreamed of powered flight. They studied the inventions and failures of others trying to fly. They also stared at birds for a long time. They couldn't replicate the birds that continuously flapped their wings, so they studied how birds soared and stayed in the air. The Wrights were "doers with dreams."

How did the brothers end up in the Outer Banks of North Carolina? The Wrights were meticulous in their preparation. They wrote to the US Weather Bureau in Washington searching for open areas with wind, sand, and no obstacles. The Outer Banks was on the list. They then wrote to the postmaster at Kitty Hawk—Kill Devil Hill was just a hill then and not a town—and William J. Tate replied with an offer of free room and board. A letter from Orville in 1900 read, "We came down here for wind and sand and we have got them."

The Wright Brothers site is spread out with lots to do, but that's true of most parks. The visitor center tells the story of Wilbur and Orville Wright through exhibits and sketches, with the brothers always depicted wearing jacket, tie, and workman's cap. Instead of a standard theater seating arrangement, chairs surround a full-scale replica of the original 1903 Wright Brothers plane, the Flyer. The auditorium displays their kites and a sewing machine used to modify the fabric on their glider. Around the Flight Room Auditorium hang portraits of other famous flyers, including President George H. W. Bush and Amelia Earhart.

Steve Jones, a full-time volunteer, relates the human side of the Wright brothers. Jones emphasizes that the brothers' mother went to college, which was very unusual in the nineteenth century. She taught her children mathematics, languages, and kite flying. At the time, their father, an itinerant United Brethren bishop, wasn't home much.

Jones also demonstrates how the plane worked by pushing and pulling on controls. The brothers used bike pieces and principles of body motion as in a bicycle. Jones believes that "The Wright brothers' story is not just about planes, but about family and faith in each other and perseverance."

I walk the grounds to the First Flight Boulder, where in 1928, the National Aeronautic Association erected a memorial plaque set in stone to mark the take-off spot. The big day was December 17, 1903, when Orville Wright's first flight carried him 120 feet in the air in 12 seconds. The day's last flight, by Wilbur, covered 852 feet in 59 seconds. If you just see these markers, you miss a big part of the story: the many unsuccessful flights that dove into the ground.

I climb up to the Wright Brothers Monument on Kill Devil Hill to enjoy the view of the Atlantic Ocean to the east and Albemarle Sound to the west. Here the inventors experimented with hundreds of glider flights before they succeeded with powered flight. The path around the monument has a life-size stainless steel sculpture of the first Flyer. Statues of the men and boys who helped the Wright brothers drag and position the plane correctly stand behind the plane. The reconstructed hangar and living quarters show a well-supplied and outfitted kitchen; the Wrights were not camping out. A sign quotes Wilbur on November 23, 1903: "We intend to be comfortable while we are here."

After 1903, the Wright brothers tried to get a patent in the United States, but there was a great deal of skepticism about their flying machine. They went to Europe, where they were more successful in obtaining patents. Wilbur died of typhoid fever in 1912. In 1915, the aviation industry really took off; Orville became a multimillionaire. Orville saw their invention bloom through two world wars. He lived in Dayton, where he continued to be a tinkerer and inventor until his death in 1948.

The average visitor stays ninety minutes. I was there almost five hours. While on the Outer Banks, I read *The Outer Banks*, a travel narrative by British author Anthony Bailey. One incident sent chills down my spine.

As a child, Bailey spent four years during World War II living in Dayton, a few blocks from the Wright home. While visiting the Wright Brothers Memorial in 1985, he realized his connection with Orville Wright. He writes that he was dimly aware of an old man who puttered in his garage. When Bailey and his friends went out on Halloween night and knocked on Wright's door with "Trick or treat, Mr. Wright?" he didn't realize that the hand that gave each boy a silver dollar was the same hand that had worked the controls of the first powered aircraft.

❧ New Orleans Jazz National Historical Park
Birthplace of American music
Louisiana

With the creation of the New Orleans Jazz National Historical Park in 1994, the National Park Service has come a long way from its original idea of protecting outstanding natural vistas. This park tells the history of jazz throughout the city.

It's impossible to separate New Orleans from jazz. The music was born at the beginning of the twentieth century from many origins such as African drumming, blues, and ragtime. I'm here to visit the national parks in New Orleans and the rest of the state.

Usually, I go to the park visitor center, get my bearings, and walk through the battlefield or preserve. However, at the Jazz Park, the sites are everywhere. The National Park Service publishes a self-guided walking tour, but Lenny and I hear jazz and see history in many other places. Until this visit, jazz was background music for me, but not music that I would choose to add to my playlist.

Our first stop is Jackson Square in the heart of the city, where a pick-up band plays for tips. In front of the St. Louis Cathedral, a large statue of Andrew Jackson on a rearing horse commemorates his victory at the Battle of New Orleans in 1815. I go in the official New Orleans Visitor Center to ask them where the Jazz Visitor Center is located. The fellow behind the desk has never heard of the site and pulls out his cell phone to look it up. This is a test to see if anyone other than National Park groupies has heard of the Jazz Museum. He fails it.

We walk up Conti Street with a map that I printed off the web. Two friendly residents, about to enter their apartment, stop us. "You look lost," the woman says.

"No, we're looking for the Tango Belt at 1026 Conti." I show them the map.

"There's nothing farther up the street. We've been living here for five years," the woman says. "Well, there might be a plaque."

She was almost right. The attached house at 1026 is a conventional three-story home. The upper two floors have a balcony with ornamental black railing. A sign says, "The historic parlor house of Madam Norma Wallace." The house had been a brothel, last run by Madam Wallace. This madam earned $100,000 a year as a successful businesswoman in the 1920s, hosting prominent politicians and tycoons.

Basin Street Station, the next stop, is much easier to find. The building had belonged to the Southern Railway for over fifty years, but is now a privately owned visitor and exhibition center.

One section is devoted to the jazz gumbo that is New Orleans, a mixture of African, European, Caribbean, and American music.

At Armstrong Park, jazz thrives in both the sculpture and music. In the southern corner of the park, Congo Square, where slaves once danced, drummed, sang, and traded goods on Sunday afternoons, is now an open event space. A detailed sculpture shows a man and woman dancing in front of a smiling crowd of musicians and spectators.

We're here on a Thursday afternoon, where a weekly party is going on, but there's always activity on the city streets. Today people set up food and souvenir stalls in the park. A huge standing statue of Louis Armstrong dominates the area. A free jazz concert starts at five p.m., and a crowd has already claimed seats an hour ahead. Instead of sitting and waiting, we follow the Sudan Social Aid and Pleasure Club, a group of African-American musicians in red pants, gold T-shirts, and red suspenders, who weave their way through the park. The men hold decorative baskets, fans, and parasols as they dance, strut, and charm the ladies they swing around.

Social aid and pleasure clubs have deep roots in the nineteenth century, when they provided insurance and burial services to recently freed African-American communities. As insurance became available to a larger segment of society, social aid clubs started to focus on the pleasure part. These clubs specialize in second-line parades that traditionally follow a funeral procession. Now you can see them behind a wedding party, through the street, or just on their own with no first line.

Though these destinations may seem disconnected, they're all part of the Jazz Museum. Not bad for a day in the Crescent City.

80✦CZ

໒ Cape Lookout National Seashore
Walking to an abandoned village
North Carolina

Everyone claims to want solitude. However, as I walk through a deserted village at Cape Lookout National Seashore, I wonder why I don't see anyone. On a beautiful Sunday afternoon, with sunny skies and a gentle breeze, I have the village to myself.

It's not easy to visit Cape Lookout, in the eastern corner of North Carolina, located south of Cape Hatteras National Seashore. Cape Lookout has many attractions, including a lighthouse, cabin and tent camping, Shackleford Banks, wild ponies, and Portsmouth Village, most requiring a separate ferry trip. Only the visitor center is accessible by road.

A ferry, really a skiff that can hold ten passengers, drops me off in front of the lighthouse and keepers' quarters. Most visitors stay close to the lighthouse area, but a walk down the beach reveals a world of old, vacant houses from an intriguing past. The village offers a quiet place to wander. I carry a pack with water, snacks, insect repellant, and sunscreen and wear hiking boots. You can't walk barefoot or with flip-flops through the village because you'll encounter concrete and stone paths.

Farther south on the beach, toward the point of the cape, you'll find a relocated keepers' quarters, a historic Coast Guard station, a US Lifesaving Service station and boathouse, fishing cottages, and other buildings that were home to crew members, fishermen, construction workers, and summer residents. Les and Sally Moore built a house and dock complex between 1950 and 1971, where they rented out vacation cabins and ran a store that became the heart of the community. The Moores planted various ornamental bushes and flowering perennials and bulbs, mostly nonnative plants.

The two-mile walk to the village takes about forty-five minutes, longer if you stop to identify birds. A squadron of pelicans flies overhead. A great egret stands in the sand. Oystercatchers, with their characteristic red beaks, strut on the beach. Black-headed laughing gulls have been following me since the picnic area in front of the visitor center. These birds aren't shy. I'm a haphazard birder, but I printed out the park's bird list before I came to get an idea of what's flying out here.

I continue on the beach to the Barden House. In the early 1900s, it was the Principal Keeper's Quarters, but it was sold and relocated in 1958. Here, a dirt road takes me away from the water and into the village proper. Old structures don't die, they just keep moving around. Islanders reused buildings. Another house was repurposed from the original lifesaving station, built in 1888.

In 1915, the Lifesaving Service and the Revenue Cutter Service merged to become the US Coast Guard. The house was absorbed into the new organization and then moved to accommodate a new station. A few years later, it was used as barracks for Navy radio operators. In 1957, the house was sold as surplus and moved again by the new owners, who converted it into a private residence. Eventually, the park probably will relocate it to the Coast Guard area farther up the road for interpretation downstairs and staff or volunteer housing upstairs.

Right now, only one house is fit and approved for human habitation. The Gordon Willis House provides lodging to volunteers and staff members working in the village. From the outside, it doesn't look much better than the other abandoned houses. Without a sign alerting you that people live here, the only other clue might be the shells neatly laid out on the picnic table. Farther on, the main building and kitchen of the Coast Guard station, built in 1916–1917, have survived. Other structures shown in a picture on the information board have been moved or demolished.

The National Park Service installed plaques in front of most structures explaining the history of the buildings. I wander around the village, imagining what it was like to live here or spend the summer fishing, repairing a roof, and installing screens on windows. Even in the 1950s and '60s, families spent the whole summer on the Cape in houses with names like the Coca-Cola House and Casablanca.

In the village, redwing blackbirds flit from tree to tree. Blue-eyed grass and Robin's plantain cover the ground. It's an idyllic pastoral scene, if you ignore the structures that are falling apart. A front door hangs on by one end. Vines crawl up the outside walls. Barns and outbuildings have holes in their roofs. The wooden houses haven't been painted in years.

Gordon Willis, who was born on Cape Lookout in 1916, remembered, "The Cape proved to be quite a lively place during the summer months after Mrs. Carrie Arendel Davis built a house big enough to take in boarders, as well as house a dance hall complete with snack bar. Weekend parties, at the Cape, were attended by young people from other communities, as well." The Davis House was demolished in the late 1940s.

Although there is plenty of information on the lighthouse and lighthouse keepers, little has been written about life in this village. In contrast, numerous books and articles are available about Portsmouth Village, located on the northern end of Cape Lookout. Portsmouth Village was a more cohesive community that still holds homecomings every two years. Reaching Portsmouth takes a little extra effort, including a ferry ride from Ocracoke.

Congress authorized Cape Lookout National Seashore in 1966. Later, the park entered into a twenty-five-year lease agreement with the property owners of the village to ensure that the dwellings would be occupied and used. When the leases were close to expiring, the National Park Service commissioned a Cape Lookout

Village Cultural Landscape Report to look at the history and condition of the structures in the village. The 446-page report was published in 2005, followed by an assessment of historic structure reuse. But unfortunately, according to a roving ranger, nothing has been done to the buildings because the park just doesn't have the money to implement these recommendations.

ᘀ Carl Sandburg Home National Historic Site
Poet of the people
North Carolina

Fog

The fog comes
on little cat feet.

It sits looking
over harbor and city
on silent haunches
and then moves on.

Carl Sandburg

I'm at Glassy Mountain Overlook at the Carl Sandburg Home National Historic Site, with a view of a distant mountain range and houses below. No fog today and certainly no cat feet. Connemara, Sandburg's home, is a beautiful, peaceful place with a historic house, gardens, goat barn, and five miles of trail.

Since the early 1800s, Flat Rock had been a summer haven for rich Charlestonians who wanted to get away from the heat and malaria of the lowcountry. The village of Flat Rock is on the National Register of Historic Places, though you won't be able to admire most of these palatial houses from the road since they're set back behind tall bushes. In 1838, Christopher Memminger, a Charleston lawyer and the first Secretary of the Treasury for the Confederate States of America, built the house that became Sandburg's home. Ellison Adger Smyth, the next owner, named the estate Connemara, after an area in Ireland.

Carl Sandburg, a reporter, writer, biographer, folksinger, lecturer, and poet of the people, provided a unique American voice for working men and women. He spoke out, wrote against exploitation of workers, and called for the end of child labor practices. Born in Illinois of Swedish immigrant parents in 1878, Sandburg's roots were in the Midwest. In 1945, when Sandburg was sixty-seven years old, he and his wife, Lilian, moved their family to Flat Rock, North Carolina. They came with three adult daughters, two grandchildren, and more than fourteen thousand books. Sandburg was looking for more privacy to continue his writing. He had already won a Pulitzer Prize for history and received honorary degrees from several universities. Lilian Sandburg, a prominent goat breeder, liked the milder climate and the pastureland available in Western North Carolina.

From the parking lot, a short path goes up to the house. Today Ranger Katie Dotson gives a tour through the three-story house. The Sandburg home is arranged as if the family had just stepped out for a moment. Books are everywhere, many with slips of paper inserted between pages where Carl Sandburg found something interesting. The writer had two offices. In his business office, on the main floor, he worked with a secretary and dealt with his correspondence. Cardboard boxes are stacked high, and letters and manila envelopes fill his inboxes.

He did his creative work in his second office on the third floor. The room is dark and cluttered. Sandburg had a private bedroom next to his office. Ranger Dotson emphasizes that the room arrangements are a reflection of Sandburg's writing schedule. He preferred to write in the evening, going far into the night. He slept until noon and joined the family for lunch in the dining room. Maybe separate bedrooms explain the success of their marriage, which lasted almost sixty years until Sandburg's death in 1967.

Most visitors now come to hike or run the trails, the same trails that Sandburg walked to think and find stillness and inspiration. Lenny and I have brought our two granddaughters, Hannah, eleven, and Isa, five, to climb Glassy Mountain. Hannah runs up the 1.2 miles to the overlook, Lenny right behind her. Meanwhile Isa and I walk, talk, and sing our way to the top. She doesn't complain or say she can't do it. She just walks at a steady pace. Both girls know that when they visit, they'll go hiking with us. I like to think they look forward to it.

We pass and are passed by adult hikers, runners, and dog walkers, but we don't see other children. Where are all the kids? At the top, Isa wanders around with a granola bar in one hand and trail mix in the other. Lenny sits on the bench, conveniently placed to face the western view out to Mount Pisgah.

It's getting chilly and we head back down. Isa now flies down the mountain, Lenny chasing after her. He catches her just before a side trail to Little Glassy Mountain. We don't realize that Little Glassy doesn't have a view and blow right past the top. In winter, it's obvious how close the trail comes to private property. Carl Sandburg wasn't isolated. He could see his neighbors' houses when the trees were bare.

Soon we're back at the Sandburg home and visitor center, where most of the people have congregated. The children and their adults are listening to music, playing with toys at the bookstore, and generally hanging around. Why weren't they on the trail?

Nature-deficit disorder is such a popular topic of conversation that I hesitate to add to the discussion. Getting children to enjoy the woods is not that complicated. Children aren't out on the trail because their adults aren't here either. When parents and grandparents are eager to get up early, prepare lunch and snacks, and fill water bottles, they'll spread the excitement to the kids. Adults need to check that children have proper fitting daypacks, boots, and the right socks before they start out. Coaches insist that children come to their sports field suitably equipped. Why is it different for the outdoors?

I don't share any of this with my granddaughters. Instead, we wander toward the goat area. Today the barn is empty because all the goats are in the field, patiently being petted. Children play tag—with each other, not the goats. There's no shortage of children in this national park, but they could have been on any farm.

At its peak, Mrs. Sandburg had more than two hundred goats. Her breeding work made her a famous figure in the world of dairy goats. She believed that goat milk was healthier than cow's milk. She sold milk and cheese to dairies in the area until North Carolina passed pasteurization laws in the mid-1950s. Now the park maintains about twenty goats for historical accuracy and still breeds them. Local volunteers help with cleaning out the stalls and doing other farm chores.

Carl Sandburg died in 1967 at the age of eighty-nine. To preserve her husband's memory, Mrs. Sandburg sold the property to the National Park Service and donated the furniture and effects. She moved to Asheville with her two oldest daughters, who still lived at home. Connemara became a historic site the next year.

Every piece of writing about Carl Sandburg seems to include this piece of sage advice from the man himself:

> *It is necessary now and then for a man to go away by*
> *himself and experience loneliness; to sit on a rock in the*

forest and ask of himself, "Who am I, and where have I been, and where am I going?"

However, I prefer "Arithmetic," a poem that shows Sandburg's playful spirit.

Arithmetic is where numbers fly like pigeons in and out of your head. . . .
If you ask your mother for one fried egg for breakfast and she gives you two fried eggs and you eat both of them, who is better in arithmetic, you or your mother?

⚜ Jimmy Carter National Historic Site
Back in Plains
Georgia

George Washington had Mount Vernon, Thomas Jefferson had Monticello, and Franklin Delano Roosevelt had Hyde Park. But to me, no town in the United States is as tied to a president as Plains, Georgia. President Jimmy Carter was born and raised in Plains, worked most of his life in Plains, and returned after his years in the White House. He and Rosalynn Carter are still here today as an active, visible presence in the community.

The Jimmy Carter National Historic Site, established in 1987, tells the story of our thirty-ninth president's humble rural beginnings and his life during and after his presidency. Lenny and I start at the visitor center in the old Plains High School. When President Carter attended school, it was the only school in town, spanning from first to eleventh grade. Georgia didn't have a twelfth grade at the time. A film, narrated by fellow southerner Charles Kuralt, introduces the historic site. Many friends and relatives reminisce about President Carter's life in Plains and his presidential campaign. The principal's office has been recreated along with five classrooms. Reproductions of the president's paintings hang in the hallway.

In segregated Georgia, Plains High School served white students only. Eventually, a school for African-American students opened up in the area. Plains High School integrated in 1966 and closed in 1979 when Georgia went to a county school system. Students now ride the bus to Americus, the large city ten miles down the road.

No doubt, President Carter's life growing up in Plains affected his future goals. Miss Julia Coleman was a cherished teacher in Plains. Her classroom has been restored to 1937, when she was Jimmy Carter's seventh grade teacher. She encouraged all her students to learn about the world beyond Plains and opened their horizons. President Carter's dream was to attend the Naval Academy, and he succeeded. In 1946, he graduated from the Academy and married Rosalynn Smith. He became a naval officer and looked forward to a bright future in the military.

When his father died in 1953, President Carter decided to return to Plains to take over the family peanut business. Rosalynn Carter wasn't happy. By her own admission, she pouted for a year. She thought her life was over and that they would never travel again. They became full partners when she took over the financial side of the business.

President Carter started working his way up the political ladder, first on the Sumter County Board of Education, then state representative and governor. He championed racial integration when that was still an unpopular position to take. An exhibit lists his accomplishments as president. He's probably best remembered for the Camp David Accords that brought peace between Egypt and Israel. An environmentalist would laud him for the Alaska National Interest Lands Conservation Act, which now protects over one hundred million acres of federal land, including increasing the size of Denali National Park. An educator would note that President Carter created the Education Department in 1979. To my Taiwanese daughter-in-law, President Carter will always be remembered as the president who dropped recognition of Taiwan as a sovereign country when he established diplomatic relations with China.

No other former president has been as active after leaving the White House as President Carter. In 1982, he created the Carter Center, best known for sending out election observation teams to countries that request them. The Center also works on preventing and resolving conflict around the world and tackling preventable diseases. The president's work hasn't gone unnoticed. In 2002, he was awarded the Nobel Peace Prize "for his decades of untiring effort to find peaceful solutions to international conflicts, to advance democracy and human rights, and to promote economic and social development."

The Carters still live in the house they built in 1961. Though they've donated the house and 2.4 acres to the park site, you can't visit their home while they still live in it. According to park rangers, it will take at least five years for the house to open to the public after it becomes vacant. The National Park Service will have to inventory all the household effects, and let the family take the ones that they've inherited. The park will need to figure out how they're going to protect the house and accommodate the public. Parking and bathrooms will be added.

The train depot sits across the street from the one row of tourist shops in downtown Plains. It served as the presidential campaign headquarters because, as a plaque explains, it was the only building in town with a public bathroom. The exhibits depict his campaign for president. He introduced himself to voters with, "Hello. I'm Jimmy Carter and I'm running for president." The townspeople volunteered to work on his campaign. His family pitched in, and it certainly helped that he had a big family.

As Mrs. Carter said, "Once we got married, we were kin to everyone in town." The depot was the symbol of small town America. At a $5,000-a-plate dinner, Plains volunteers cooked the food. Jimmy Carter won the presidential election "one handshake at a time."

80◆CR

Jimmy Carter's boyhood home stands in the community of Archery, about three miles out of town. The farmhouse has been restored back to its appearance in 1937, a year before the Carters installed electricity.

"Not putting electricity in the house is saving the Park Service a lot of money," an interpretive ranger explains.

The family got running water in 1935 when they installed a windmill purchased from a catalog for a hundred dollars. But the kitchen didn't have running water.

"Why put running water in the kitchen when the pump was right outside?" Earl Carter, Jimmy Carter's father, thought. "It's a waste of money." The bathroom had a bucket for a showerhead, which dripped only cold water. Still, moving to an indoor bathroom was a big event and an improvement in the family's lifestyle.

Working train tracks run behind the Carter farmhouse. The family was used to the train noise. However, girls who were invited to an overnight by the Carter sisters panicked when a train passed by in the middle of the night because it sounded like the train was going to hit their bedroom.

The farm hired help and paid cash wages because Earl Carter didn't believe in sharecropping. The farm had a commissary, a store for people who worked on his land and in the surrounding area. The recreated store displays cans, slabs of meat hanging from a hook, and sewing notions. These were necessities for tenant farmers who might have a difficult time getting to town and obtaining credit. The store was open all day on Saturday and on request during the week.

Jack Clark managed much of the farm. The modest tenant house had a kitchen / dining room and bedroom with a cornshuck-filled mattress that he and his wife, Rachel, shared. Newspapers were used to insulate the walls. You can also see the blacksmith shop, barns, and other outbuildings on the farm.

The National Park Service now grows peanuts, sugar cane, and corn on the seventeen-acre farm. A huge vegetable garden is similar to what was planted in the 1930s. The farm also keeps chickens for eggs. President Carter, with the Secret Service tagging along, still brings groups and guests to show them his old boyhood home. He comes around to pick up some vegetables and eggs.

"Is it weird to have a living president visit a national park named in his honor?" I ask the ranger roving the site.

"Yes, it is a little."

Back in town, we go into antique shops, buy peanut butter ice cream cones, and talk to the residents. We spend the night at the Plains Historic Inn, located over an antique mall on Main Street. Seven rooms are named for seven decades, from 1920 to 1980, with the 1970 room as the presidential suite. Each huge room is furnished in the style of its decade. President Carter helped to put up the walls and Mrs. Carter picked out the period furniture. The inn, opened in 2002, is owned by the Plains Better Hometown Program.

If you want to hear President Carter preach Sunday school, check out the Maranatha Baptist Church website for his schedule. Time permitting, you'll be able to have a picture taken with President Carter. It's part of the visit and the fun of Plains, Georgia.

11

Fighting for Equality

African-Americans have always fought for equality—first for the most basic right, freedom from slavery, then for equal rights to education, training, and civic life.

For a small town of fewer than nine thousand people in central Alabama, Tuskegee evokes strong feelings and opinions. Tuskegee is the site of two national historic sites. Booker T. Washington headed the Tuskegee Institute, which offered a basic education to African-Americans, encouraging economic independence through hard work and practical skills. The same small town was the training site for the Tuskegee Airmen, who showed the world that black men had the intelligence, courage, and discipline to fly fighter planes in World War II. Twenty years later, the march from Selma to Montgomery highlighted the need for voting rights for African-Americans. The Martin Luther King Jr. birth home in Atlanta interprets the early influences of the civil rights leader.

ᴥ Tuskegee Institute National Historic Site
Booker T. Washington's school
Alabama

Tuskegee Institute National Historic Site interprets the educational aspirations of newly freed African-American people. Lewis Adams, a former slave, encouraged a white politician from Alabama to push legislation for a Normal School for Colored Teachers. Adams hired Booker T. Washington, a twenty-five-year-old Hampton Institute graduate, to design and teach in the school. When it opened in 1881, thirty men and women crammed into the African Methodist Episcopal Zion Church. The school was coeducational from the start, but males and females learned different skills.

By the next year, the school moved to a one-thousand-acre abandoned plantation, thanks in large part to Washington's fundraising abilities. This land became the nucleus of the school and the present-day Tuskegee University, a historically black college. Now, the park unit encompasses almost the whole university campus, including the George Washington Carver Museum.

Booker T. Washington believed in teaching practical skills as well as academic subjects. Students made the bricks used in the building, did the woodworking, cooked the meals in the school kitchens, and built most of the original buildings on campus.

Today, I wander about the campus, an attractive mix of historic and new buildings. To visit The Oaks, home of Booker T. Washington, I've signed up for the nine a.m. tour along with a group of students from Carroll University in Wisconsin, studying civil rights.

The Oaks was built in 1899 and the Washington family moved in the next year. The house is dark and the furniture is heavy, in the style of the day. It had electricity and steam heating, a sign of success. Washington and his second wife, Margaret, took a European trip and brought back many decorating ideas. Margaret was very short, and much of the house and furniture was designed with her size in mind. Frieze murals encircle several rooms. The dining room has an Italian theme. Margaret Washington was Lady Principal, the person who watched over female students. After she died, the family sold the original furniture, but kept the house until the 1940s, when they sold it to the university.

Booker T. Washington was the school's principal from the start until his death in 1915. He attracted the best African-American faculty, hiring George Washington Carver as the school's agricultural director. Armed with a master's degree in agriculture from Iowa Agricultural College, Carver, also born a slave, became the second famous name many people associate with Tuskegee Institute. He taught progressive methods in farming, nutrition, and food preservation. The Carver Museum holds a dizzying array of Carver's accomplishments. The building is also the visitor orientation center, where most people start their visit. Tuskegee Institute donated The Oaks and the Carver Museum to the National Park Service in the 1970s.

Carver saved the southern economy by finding over three hundred uses for peanuts and another one hundred uses for the sweet potato. This helped the south wean itself from cotton. Peanuts add nutrients to the soil while cotton depletes it. Both Booker T. Washington and George Washington Carver are buried on campus.

The park, along with the university and town of Tuskegee,

opened the George Washington Carver Nutrition Walking Trail, which weaves through the city streets for two miles. Along the route, motivational signs keep walkers moving. One sign says, "The USDA Food Guide Pyramid recommends eating fats, oil, and sweets sparingly. A healthy diet and an active lifestyle builds a strong heart."

For many Americans, Tuskegee evokes only one thought: the Tuskegee experiments. From 1932 to 1972, the US Public Health Service conducted an experiment to study untreated syphilis in men, even though by the 1940s, doctors recognized that penicillin cured syphilis. The government offered free medical care and burial services if men participated in the experiment. The men were never told that they had the disease. The shocking experiment led to the creation of institutional review boards, which now set rules for researchers working with human subjects. You can visit the Legacy Museum on the Tuskegee University campus to learn more about the Tuskegee experiments.

Over 95 percent of present-day Tuskegee town residents are African-American. Yet, a statue of a Confederate soldier stands in the town square park. The pedestal reads, "Erected by The Daughters of the Confederacy to the Confederate Soldiers of Macon County."

ᕦ Tuskegee Airmen National Historic Site
Training Red Tails
Alabama

Tuskegee Institute and Tuskegee Airmen National Historic Site, a couple of miles down the road, are intimately connected in history. Though aviation was growing in the 1900s, most African-American men didn't have a chance to learn how to fly. And they certainly were excluded from military flight programs.

In 1939, Congress wanted to increase the number of civilian

pilots who could be quickly turned into military personnel. The Army Air Corps, the forerunner of the Air Force, looked to expand its reserve of military pilots and contracted with civilian flight schools. Because Tuskegee Institute had a good Civilian Pilot Training program, it was selected as a primary flight school for the army. The mild Alabama weather made year-round flying possible, and the Tuskegee Institute knew how to work within a segregated environment. African-American cadets came from all over the country to train in Tuskegee. As soon as they reached the Mason-Dixon Line, they had to travel on segregated trains.

At this time, there weren't any black military flight pilots. Many whites felt that African-American men weren't suited for the rigor and discipline of flying. Moton Field, named after the second president of Tuskegee Institute, was built as the only place where African-Americans could obtain primary flight instruction. With pressure from civil rights organizations, the segregated 99th Pursuit Squadron was established. All support personnel, such as mechanics, radio operators, and nurses were considered Tuskegee Airmen.

Eleanor Roosevelt provided the star power to the program. The first lady visited Tuskegee in March 1941 and asked to be taken on a flight. Pictures show Mrs. Roosevelt sitting in the back of a J-3 Piper Cub, wearing her distinctive hat and frilly blouse. Chief Civilian Flight Instructor Charles Alfred Anderson, at the controls, took her on a one-hour flight. Anderson, known today as the "Father of Black Aviation," trained pilots until his death in 1996. Recently, he was honored with a postage stamp.

The Tuskegee Airmen proved that black men could fly with distinction. Their combat record helped pave the way for integration of the military by President Truman in 1948. The historic site consists of several buildings, but only the two hangars are open to visitors. Hangar #1, an original building, contains a PT-17 Stearman and J-3 Piper Cub, both training planes. The cadet sat in front with an instructor in back. A side room shows a library, called the war room, with aeronautical magazines, *Time* and *Life*, and posters of German uniforms. Pilots needed to keep up with current events. Cadets were also trained to instantly recognize over a hundred planes and ships under low light conditions.

Hangar #2 was opened a couple of years ago. The *Duchess Arlene*, the showpiece of this room, is a P-51D Mustang reproduction. The plane, suspended from the ceiling, has a red tail, red nose, and yellow bars on its wings. They painted the tails of their planes red because they had a lot of extra red paint. The Tuskegee aviators became known as the Red-Tail Angels.

Today, a civilian worker who doesn't know much staffs Hangar #1. She refers all questions to the ranger in Hangar #2, the only one on duty. He keeps his friendly demeanor as he answers visitor questions, opens the auditorium, and starts the movie. The control tower, the only historic section of Hangar #2, should be open, but I have to ask the ranger to unlock it. He also watches over the bookstore where I stamp my national park passport.

The site has a Skyway Club, an old officers' club that has been refurbished but is still closed. There just isn't enough staff. What a shame that this site isn't given the funding to interpret the Tuskegee experience properly. If it sounds like I've complained before, and I have, it's because I'm visiting small historic sites. We can't forget them.

❧ Selma to Montgomery National Historic Trail
Marching for voting rights
Alabama

Don't go to Selma, Alabama, on a Sunday afternoon expecting anything to be open. The small town of about twenty thousand residents is shut tight, but that's when I arrive. I don't have to fight for a parking space downtown. I'm here to visit the Selma to Montgomery National Historic Trail, which commemorates the 1965 historic fifty-four mile walk to demand equal voting rights for African-Americans. Most of the trail is on US 80, a four-lane divided highway. However, I want to do it right, by starting at the beginning.

I walk to the Brown Chapel African Methodist Episcopal Church, the start of the Selma to Montgomery march. Still an active church, the building is across the street from an apartment complex where children play ball and ride bikes on the quiet street.

Monday morning, I show up at the Selma Interpretive Center, a downtown storefront at the foot of the Edmund Pettus Bridge, as the building opens up. The ranger is eager to recount the story of the iconic civil rights march from here to Montgomery, the Alabama state capital. Just as fascinating is the story of volunteer Henry Allen, who walked part of the route when he was in high school. Allen, a Selma local, became the first African-American firefighter in Selma in 1972, and worked his way up to become its first black fire chief. After a successful career, Allen now works as a park volunteer and tour guide.

Allen explains that African-Americans had been systematically denied the right to vote by imposing literacy tests, poll taxes, and plain old-fashioned intimidation. African-Americans also had an identifiable enemy in county Sheriff Jim Clark, a violent but predictable man. In a peculiar way, the struggle needed the hot-tempered Clark to garner national attention. The Dallas County Voters League had added a few voters by holding voter registration classes, but the bulk of the black population was still disenfranchised. Bernard and Colia Lafayette, longtime Student Nonviolent Coordinating Committee (SNCC) organizers, came to Selma to work with potential voters. They looked at voting as a basic right.

The march also needed Martin Luther King Jr., who brought money and the national media. Sheriff Clark and his men thwarted several early attempts at assembling and marching. On March 7, known as Bloody Sunday, marchers walked slowly up to the Edmund Pettus Bridge, where a sea of state troopers and volunteer officers of the local sheriff's department blocked the road. When the marchers didn't move, troopers hit them with nightsticks and kicked them. They released tear gas and chased the marchers through the streets of Selma. This barbarism was on national TV, and Selma stood in the spotlight around the world.

Finally, a judge allowed the march. President Johnson nationalized Alabama guardsmen and dispatched protection for the potentially thousands who planned to walk to Montgomery.

"There were a lot of youth and college students who were going to march," Allen recalls. "They didn't have jobs on the line and were critical to the movement."

Supporters started their third trek on Sunday March 21, 1965, from the Brown Chapel A.M.E. Church. From the many photos in the interpretive center, you can see that marchers wore their best clothes. Men had on suits, ties, and leather dress shoes. Women were in dresses and sandals. They walked three abreast in one lane, keeping the other lane clear for traffic on US 80. The march took five days and four nights.

"Reverend King didn't walk the whole time," Allen says. "He was in and out of the march."

The road narrowed to two lanes in Lowndes County. Only three hundred people were allowed to continue the march because the guardsmen didn't think they could protect more walkers. When the road widened again, hordes came by bus. At the fourth camp, at St. Jude Church in Montgomery, Joan Baez, Harry Belafonte, and other music stars performed for the crowd. The next day, they walked the four miles to the state capitol building. Over twenty-five thousand gathered to listen to speeches and sing "We Shall Overcome." President Johnson signed the Voting Rights Act on August 6, 1965.

After I leave the Selma Interpretive Center, I drive slowly on US 80, stopping at each place where the marchers camped for the night, on land offered by sympathetic and courageous African-American farmers. Organizers provided food and tents.

One man stands out in every photo and website dealing with the march. He's also portrayed in a life-size sculpture of marchers. A burly, middle-aged, one-legged white man from Michigan walked the entire way on crutches. On the park website, Lynda Lowery, at fifteen the youngest marcher, remembers him.

> *There was a guy named Jim Letterer. Jim was a white guy with one leg. He walked on crutches all the way from Selma to Montgomery. He carried a flag sometimes and I am in some of the pictures with him now. But Jim said before he let anything happen to me, he would lay down and die. But the fact that this man would die for me, and he didn't even know my name kind of thing, you know. He was there; he would die for me. That made me go all the way from Selma to Montgomery.*

The Lowndes Interpretive Center sits about halfway on the route off US 80, where a tent city has been recreated on the site. At the time of the march, white landowners evicted black tenant farmers who had registered to vote or helped others register. Some African-American families had no place to go, so SNCC erected a tent city for families. A few stayed as long as two years.

Congress designated the historic trail in 1996. Fifty years after the fateful march, the movie *Selma* chronicled the brutality, negotiations, and hopeful spirits of the times. The film put the historic events in front of the American public, even if the starring actors were all British.

But now the rest of the story.

In 2011, the Alabama State Legislature passed a voter ID law. Effective June 2014, every voter needs a photo ID. If you have a driver's license, that's your identification—no problem. If you're not a driver, you can show several other documents or get a nondriver ID. However, how do you prove who you are to get an ID that proves who you are? You can go around in circles, trying to decipher the seventeen-page Alabama Photo Voter ID Guide. And how do you get this pamphlet if you don't have access to the web? Most nondrivers aren't going to persevere.

"Is that a step backward?" I ask Henry Allen.

"It's not just an African-American issue," Allen said. "It will hurt the old, poor, and young who are less likely to drive." I wonder what Martin Luther King would have to say about this rush to require an approved identification document in order to vote.

☙ Martin Luther King Jr. National Historic Site
A leader and dreamer
Georgia

Oh my gosh. Am I so old that I can remember events that have since resulted in national park units? That's the way I feel visiting the Martin Luther King Jr. site in Atlanta. The March on Washington (1963), the shooting of Martin Luther King Jr. in Memphis (1968), the creation of the federal holiday honoring his life (1981)—all these events are explained at the site.

The Martin Luther King Jr. National Historic Site, created in 1980, is located along several blocks in downtown Atlanta. The buildings, gardens, sculptures, and walkways recount Dr. King's life, achievements, and the changes in race relations that occurred during his lifetime. The designers have done a terrific job of incorporating historic and modern features to tell the story.

The King Birth Home explains how the civil rights leader's upbringing and extended family shaped his life and work. King was born on Auburn Avenue in 1929 in the home of his maternal grandparents. A. D. Williams, his maternal grandfather, was an early architect of the civil rights movement in Atlanta. In 1956, *Fortune* magazine called Sweet Auburn "the richest Negro street in the world." The whole block, part of the national park site, has been restored to what it looked like in the 1930s. The King Center still owns the birth home, which it leases to the National Park Service.

The home and furniture have been restored to their 1930s appearance, with about 50 percent of the pieces still original. The house had electricity and running water. All the major utilities were available in this neighborhood by 1900. The Kings were a comfortable, educated, upper-middle-class family. When formal visitors came, they were received in a parlor, complete with a piano and gramophone. The family relaxed in the den and played Monopoly and Chinese checkers. A radio and telephone are prominently displayed.

The dining table is set formally and ready for dinner with a pitcher of iced tea in the center. This room was not reserved just for Sunday but used for breakfast and dinner every day. The children were expected to recite a Bible verse from memory at the dinner table. In the kitchen, a box of Wheaties, Dr. King's favorite cereal, sits on a small table. The huge second-floor hallway was used for extra bedroom space.

Ranger John Jenkins, a retired paratrooper with the 82nd Airborne, gives a lively, personal tour. He reminds visitors that before desegregation African-Americans couldn't stay in a motel or eat in most restaurants. Travelers had to find willing black folks like the King family to rent them a room. The house was unusual as it had central heating, an innovation at the time. One of young Dr. King's jobs was to feed coal into the furnace. Ranger Jenkins points out that if the young man didn't do his chores, there was no time-out in those days. Instead, the tour visitors respond with one voice, "He got a whupping."

The family moved to a brick house when Dr. King was twelve years old, which Martin Luther King Sr. considered an important step up the social ladder. An entrepreneur who built modest homes for cotton mill workers in the neighborhood owned the house next door, now the bookstore. The young Dr. King played with the neighbor's children, exposing him to kids from all different backgrounds and races. The tour ends at the bookstore where Jenkins encourages you to buy a book on the Birth Home because you can't take photographs inside.

We had lined up for the tour before nine a.m. and were glad we had. Free tickets are available for the Birth Home tour at the visitor center on a first-come, first-served basis only on the day of the tour. Since only fifteen persons can go through the house at one time, tours fill up quickly.

Dr. King Jr. spent a considerable amount of time during his youth at the Ebenezer Baptist Church, where his father and grandfather preached in favor of desegregation and voting rights for all. At the time, the church was one of the few institutions that African-Americans could control. Dr. King delivered his first sermon here when he was eighteen years old. The church, built in 1914–22, has stained glass windows on which the names of donors have been inscribed. The large, ornate church held 529 worshippers. In 1999, the Ebenezer Church opened the modern Horizon Sanctuary opposite the old building, and turned over the original church to the National Park Service.

Peace Plaza lies between the visitor center and Auburn Avenue.

The I Have a Dream World Peace Rose Garden is part of a land-scaped area that includes a flowing fountain. In the plaza, the *Behold* statue depicts the baptism of the infant Kizzy, by her father Kunta Kinte, characters from Alex Haley's 1976 novel *Roots*.

The King Center, though not a part of the national park, is integral to the visit. The reflecting pool with gently cascading water encircles the tombs of Dr. and Mrs. King. An eternal flame burns in front of the tombs. While visitors admire the gardens, they can hear Dr. King's speeches broadcast onto the street.

The visitor center concentrates on the major contributions of Dr. King using film, audio recordings, and photographs. The displays start with segregation in the South. In 1955, Rosa Parks sat down on a city bus in Montgomery, Alabama. Dr. King, one of the leaders of the bus boycott, received national attention for his civil rights work. In 1963, more than 250,000 people of all races gathered in front of the Lincoln Memorial in Washington, DC, to demand passage of civil rights legislation. At the time, it was the largest demonstration in the United States, where Dr. Martin Luther King Jr. gave his historic "I Have a Dream" speech.

Opposite the visitor center, a large mural depicts scenes in Dr. Martin Luther King's life: Dr. King as a child, at Morehouse College, police dogs going after demonstrators. The mural is peppered with Peace Now, We Shall Overcome, and No More War signs. The more you look at the mural, the more incidents you can recognize.

80 ◆ 03

Parks are usually in the countryside or in small towns. But national parks also pop up in the middle of big cities, and they aren't immune to big city challenges. The site shows the effects of budget cuts. Tours of King's Birth Home are now offered six times a day. In earlier years, they were available every thirty minutes in the summer. As I walk around the several city blocks that make up the site, I remind myself that I'm in a national park. The visitor center didn't open exactly on time. The ranger in the Ebenezer Baptist Church kept her flat hat on indoors, breaking NPS protocol. Ouch!

This casual approach has its positive side. When I ask the ranger on desk duty where we could walk to lunch, he makes a restaurant recommendation, something that most rangers are reluctant to do, since they don't want to appear to favor one business over another. Also, here rangers seem to speak their mind a lot more freely.

"Where are your volunteers?" I ask.

"It's tough to get volunteers, especially on Sundays."

"Volunteers?" another ranger says. "Everyone has bills to pay."

I would have thought that in the Atlanta metropolitan area, residents would fall all over each other to volunteer at such a prestigious historic site.

12

THE GREAT OUTDOORS: THE LOWLANDS

While many of the national parks of the South were created to preserve complex history and artifacts, other southeastern parks protect natural habitats, as we saw in Chapter 1. Here in the lowlands, we won't see rhododendrons lining trails or juncos darting through coniferous forests. With the exception of Congaree National Park, all the great outdoor parks in the lowlands are on the coast. What these parks have in common is water. Congaree protects the largest intact expanse of old growth bottomland hardwood forest remaining in the southeastern United States. Here, water from the Congaree and Wateree Rivers brings nutrients to this distinct ecosystem of plants and animals. The highest point of Congaree is 120 feet.

The other parks have a combination of fresh, salt, and brackish water habitats, attracting big birds such as herons, egrets, ibis, and vultures that even I can recognize. Many of these parks are best explored on the water. Biscayne National Park is the largest marine park in the National Park Service, with more than 95 percent of the park covered by water.

Each park also has a human history. We can thank the space program for donating the land that became Canaveral National Seashore. The Everglades and Big Cypress were created after development threatened the river of grass.

In the mountains, I ordered the parks by their maximum altitude. But if I did the same with the lowlands parks, I'd be splitting hairs over a couple of feet or maybe inches. In these low-lying areas, just a few inches in elevation can bring a host of different species and habitat types. Here, the parks are ordered from north to south.

ᕮ Cape Hatteras National Seashore
Climbing Bodie Island Lighthouse
North Carolina

A few years ago, I walked a thousand miles on the Mountains-to-Sea Trail across North Carolina, including eighty-four miles on the Cape Hatteras beaches. The trail passes the Cape Hatteras Lighthouse, which I stopped to climb. At the time, the Bodie Island Lighthouse was closed for repairs, and I had to bypass it. Now it's open, and I'm going to the top.

The Bodie Island Lighthouse has been standing on Oregon Inlet in the Outer Banks since 1872, still with its original first-order Fresnel lens; Fresnel is the most powerful and expensive type of lens. The striped lighthouse is 165 feet tall, shorter than the one down the coast at Cape Hatteras (198 feet), its more famous cousin. But the Bodie Island Lighthouse offers something that the Hatteras Lighthouse doesn't have—a guided tour given by an enthusiastic ranger.

Ranger Joel Proper first assembles the group in a room at the bottom of the lighthouse, where he asks children the reason for lighthouses.

"Imagine my feet are Florida, my waist is Charleston," he explains as he uses his body to go up the Eastern Seaboard. Then he sticks his elbow out. "And this is Cape Hatteras. Warm air goes up the coast. In the meantime, cold water is coming down from Canada. Where they meet is known as the Graveyard of the Atlantic, a region where shallow waters and converging currents make for tricky sailing and navigation. Lighthouses were built and staffed to guide sailors around these treacherous waters with their strong beaming signals.

"But a lighthouse also told mariners that they weren't alone. Someone cared about them," the ranger adds.

Our group starts climbing. The staircase is freestanding, not bolted to the wall. Even after much study, the park staff isn't quite sure how much weight it can hold. "After all," Ranger Proper says, "the staircase was designed for one man to go to the top twice a day." The 214 steps are divided by seven cast-iron landings. Every second landing, Ranger Proper stops to let everybody catch up and breathe. He takes the opportunity to tell the history of the lighthouse and to answer questions.

"Why are there guided tours here and not at the Cape Hatteras lighthouse?" I ask.

"At Cape Hatteras, the steps are wider and people can pass each other. Here there's no passing. Also, this is a new offering. Maybe these Bodie tours will change."

Once we get to the top, the group is speechless, and not because we're worn out. The view is, well, breathtaking. As we walk around the outside viewing deck, Ranger Proper orients us to the ocean east and sound side to the west.

"Way out there, beyond the ocean, you can see England," he jokes.

Before the area became a national seashore, the local duck club dammed up the small streams to create ponds. The brackish water attracts waterfowl and, back then, hunters to shoot them. The National Park Service has left the dams and duck ponds in place. Now the area attracts birders, photographers, and still some waterfowl hunters. To help negotiate the marshy area, park crews built a walkway and observation platform. Once on top, we're now free to spend as much time up here as we want and come down at our own pace.

The current lighthouse is the third Bodie Lighthouse. The first one, built in 1847, leaned so much that its lamps were out of sync. After ten years, it was declared useless. The second lighthouse was built just before the Civil War. After Federal troops captured Hatteras Inlet in 1861, retreating Confederates removed the lens and blew up the lighthouse, leaving the area in total darkness. Both previous lighthouses are now underwater. On the tour, the ranger shows us a bump, way out in Oregon Inlet, where the first lighthouse sank.

The current lighthouse is north of Oregon Inlet, halfway between the ocean and the sound. The US Coast Guard, the previous owner of the lighthouse and lens, wasn't so sure it wanted to give up the lighthouse and, more importantly, the lens. The transfer of the complete site to the National Park Service occurred only in 2005.

Plans for restoration of the lighthouse started almost immediately after that. But there were lots of setbacks. Federal funding was requested but not received. Once renovations started, they found significant structural problems, requiring more money. But hopefully this is all behind us. Visitors can now climb the lighthouse.

Is it Body or Bodie? Spelling was more fluid in the past than it is now. The name of the island has changed spelling over the years. It used to be Body but now is Bodie. A sign in the visitor center is adamant that the pronunciation is like the word *body*. A marble plaque high up the wall just before you start the climb reads: "Body's Island Lighthouse Erected A.D. 1872 Latitude 35–48 Longitude 75–33."

The bookstore offers a certificate for this great feat, which reads, "I climbed the Bodie Lighthouse." I didn't see any T-shirts, yet.

⟿ Congaree National Park
Floodplains and cypress knees
South Carolina

Ask a camping family to list national parks in the South, and you'll likely hear about Great Smoky Mountains National Park, Shenandoah National Park in Virginia, and the Everglades in Florida. Most people have never heard of Congaree National Park in South Carolina. That's not too surprising when you consider that only a little more than 120,000 folks visited the park in 2014. It seems that most visitors to South Carolina want to hit the beach.

Congaree, less than twenty miles from Columbia, the state capital, was turned into a national park from Congaree Swamp National Monument in 2003. The park is small, a little more than twenty-six thousand acres, with about twenty-five miles of hiking trails. But visitors don't go to Congaree to hike. Even the park literature calls it walking.

They come to see the huge bald cypress and loblolly pines considered champion trees, and the largest remnant of old growth, bottomland hardwood forest on the continent. Congaree is a floodplain, not a swamp. A floodplain is a low-lying area near a river, covered by water periodically throughout the year, while a swamp is permanently covered with water. Birding is outstanding, especially in the spring and fall when birds use the area as a migration flyway.

A couple of years ago, I organized a group of Carolina Mountain Club hikers from Asheville for an early spring weekend visit to the park. Mid-April is the perfect time to enjoy Congaree, warm enough so you only need a T-shirt, but before the infamous mosquito season. Right now, the mosquito meter hung above the breezeway at Harry Hampton Visitor Center shows only a mild chance of bugs.

Almost all the offerings in Congaree—camping, canoeing, and ranger programs—are competitive, especially if you're bringing a group. Only primitive camping is available, and it's really primitive (you need to bring all your own water). The Longleaf Campground only has ten sites and several group campsites. Two vault toilets service the whole campground.

Since you can't reserve a campsite, you need to get here early on a Friday to snag a spot for your tent. Rangers say that some group leaders arrive at the park on a Wednesday and stay until the weekend to get sites for their whole group. If you can't get into the Longleaf Campground, you'll probably be able to find a place at Bluff Campground, though that entails a mile walk from your car. And there are no toilets there.

Several in our group start out at seven a.m. Friday for the three-hour drive from Asheville. We're able to score a couple of sites for the whole group. I feel victorious and relieved. The tent sites are flat, spacious, and free of roots and rocks, with a picnic table each. Most campers will gravitate to one of the four shady sites, but the ones in full sun have more room for children to run around.

On some evenings, rangers offer an Owl Prowl, a guided walk around the park's 2.4-mile boardwalk. Today you can make reservations online, but getting a spot is still extremely competitive since the park only takes twenty-five people. We each brought a flashlight and now wrap the lens in red cellophane. "Not pink. Red!" the ranger emphasizes. Covering a light with red cellophane protects your night vision and makes animals less aware of your presence.

The planning is worth it. Ranger Fran Rametta, who's been at Congaree for almost his whole career, is a wealth of scientific information, lore, and just good fun. He answers serious adult questions and engages young children. Each time youngsters answer a question, Rametta gives them a high five. With a crowd, we don't see owls or any wildlife, but it doesn't matter. We learn a lot about Congaree's floodplain environment. Rametta points out the huge bald cypress, called bald because the tree is a conifer that loses its leaves in the winter. The characteristic knees, parts of the root system that stick up out of the water, support the tree. Nothing says swamp better than cypress knees.

Canoeing is where the competitive spirit really kicks in. Whenever staffing levels allow, the park offers free guided canoe trips on Cedar Creek. They provide canoes, life jackets, and instructions. The ranger greets us in uniform, along with three volunteers in jeans and T-shirts. After she checks us in, the ranger makes a big point of saying "We couldn't do this without our volunteers." Ranger Rametta had said the same thing on Friday evening.

We drive to a locked put-in spot, passing the public put-in. After listening to a short safety lecture and getting a PFD vest and paddle, we drag the aluminum canoes down to Cedar Creek. The ranger and volunteers are in kayaks, the ranger in front, one volunteer in back and the other two intermingled with visitors.

First safety question: What do we do if a snake falls in our canoe? Answer: Don't fall in the water. Most of the snakes in trees aren't poisonous. Just paddle to the shore and then tip the canoe over and let the snake drop out.

Cedar Creek is not a whitewater experience. The water is brown, and so still that we paddle down to a tree obstructing the creek and paddle back upstream. We go at our own speed, taking care not to pass the ranger's boat. We're too spread out for the ranger to talk to the group. But she and knowledgeable volunteers answer questions if you sidle up to their canoe.

Most visitors are content to drift quietly, look at trees, and spot snakes in the water or on the shore. The whole trip takes about three hours. If you have your own canoe, you're free to paddle Cedar Creek and the Congaree River any time you want, although there's no vehicle access to the river in the park. Recently, the reservation system went online, but getting a place in a park canoe is still a challenge.

Hiking is one activity that doesn't require reservations or competing for a spot. Whew! For mountain folks, the flat trails are almost a guilty pleasure, like finding out that chocolate is good for you. The first afternoon, we head for Oakridge Trail, hiking ten miles without racing or feeling tired. The only way to reach most backcountry trails is to walk on the boardwalk and repeat other sections of trail. Unlike most national parks, dogs on leashes are allowed on backcountry trails in Congaree, a decision made by a prior superintendent. The Sims Trail, taken by dog walkers, bypasses the boardwalk and connects to backcountry dirt trails.

The River Trail leads to the Congaree River, which forms one border of the park. Crayfish burrow in the soft mud, creating little raised fairy castles, each with a hole in the center. The rough green snake looks like a lime green contour in the dirt. Barred owls are easy to photograph with an amateur camera because the birds seem frozen on a tree branch. Pileated woodpeckers, heard but not usually seen in the mountains, look for insects in snags, standing dead trees. I even identify a prothonotary warbler.

The habitat is supposed to be right for the legendary ivory-billed woodpecker, but no one was looking for the Lord God Bird because there are too many actual birds to identify. Three feral baby hogs run right in front of me. They don't spend any time rooting around or posing for pictures. This turns out to be the highlight of my weekend. I've hiked in the Smokies for years without ever seeing a hog.

In the visitor center film, a man says, "You can almost hear the trees grow." It sounds lyrical until I get on the trail. I hear a wonderful chorus of birds, without the overwhelming sounds of crows. Though Carol Gist, the VIP at the visitor center desk, assures me that she's seen crows in more remote parts in the park, none are squawking overhead today. Crow mobs are the gangs of the bird world.

Like every other piece of ground in the Southeast, people have been here since prehistoric times. First, the Congaree Indians hunted game. De Soto, the Spanish explorer, passed through the area. Europeans settled here, though it was a tough place to farm and keep livestock. Francis Marion hid out from the British during the American Revolution, earning him the nickname Swamp Fox. African-Americans, who escaped slavery on nearby plantations, created maroon settlements. The impenetrable tangles of roots and trees provided a feeling of safety from slave owners. Later, moonshiners found refuge in those same trees to make illegal booze.

Logging wasn't easy here, but trees in this bottomland hardwood forest were valuable. Francis Beidler, whose lumber company owned most of the good-quality land, only cut down trees for about ten years, ending in 1915. But in the late 1960s, as lumber prices shot up, landowners started harvesting trees again. Harry Hampton, a local journalist and outdoorsman, had been advocating for the protection of the majestic bald cypress and flood-plain environment since the 1950s. Finally, the Beidler family sold their land to the National Park Service, and other owners followed suit. A few private inholdings are still shown on the Congaree map, including a hunting club on the far eastern side of the park.

Over 80 percent of the park is now federally designated wilderness area. That means that the park can't build roads or structures. Once you park your car, the only way to get around is by foot or boat. Less than a half-hour's drive from Columbia, forested wetlands, creeks, champion bald cypress, and the critters that live in them are forever protected.

ᲚᲦ Canaveral National Seashore
Thank you, NASA
Florida

I continue to marvel at Florida's natural beauty. From Fort Caroline in Jacksonville to the Dry Tortugas in the tropics, the national park units are as diverse as the state itself and provide a much more fascinating look at the state than the "other Florida."

In Central Florida, Indian River, best known for its citrus fruit, is also the home of hammock forests, estuaries, and Canaveral National Seashore. Located at the end of New Smyrna Beach, you can reach the park by getting off I-95 and driving thirteen miles on A1A through a residential area. How did this stretch of land resist development, and how did the National Park Service get this jewel?

For that, we can thank the space program. In the 1950s, NASA bought land to "buffer their activities." In other words, they didn't want a housing development next to their launch pads. In 1963, they turned over some of their land to Merritt Island National

Wildlife Refuge. Other parcels became Canaveral National Seashore in 1975. Both agencies manage the land according to their mission, but most visitors would have a hard time figuring out where the park ends and the refuge begins. Yet, if you think preservation, you'll see that human artifacts are under the auspices of the National Park Service. Wildlife viewing areas are in the refuge.

Continuing on A1A, we find most of the human artifacts. At fifty feet above sea level, Turtle Mound boasts the tallest shell mound in Florida. It's a midden, a refuse pile of oyster shells left by Timucua Indians. Archaeologists use this mound to learn about the Timucuan people because not much else is left of their civilization. Most other oyster mounds were used for filling in roadbeds. The park has built an elaborate boardwalk so visitors can climb the mound without disturbing it.

European-American settlers moved in starting in the 1870s, attracted by the climate. Eldora, a small community served by steamboats, was a prosperous place for a short spell, with a school and post office. Farmers grew pineapple, citrus fruit, and olives, which were shipped up north. By the turn of the twentieth century, the population may have reached two hundred. By the time railroads arrived on the mainland, dependence on steamboats became obsolete. Two years of killing frost, which wiped out the orange crop, convinced most homesteaders to move on.

The area turned to gentlemen farmers and winter visitors. Only Eldora State House, built by an early landowner in 1913, remains today, though it was abandoned for thirty years. Friends of Canaveral renovated the two-story house and now offer regular interpretive tours. Behind Eldora house, Castle Windy, another shell mound, looks like a garbage dump.

A half-mile Castle Windy Trail goes from the road to the shores of Mosquito Lagoon. Native Americans used saw palmetto, with its thick roots and fronds, as nourishment and medicine. Majestic live oaks form an overhead canopy. Yaupon, a plant related to the American holly and used to brew a black tea, grows here.

Heading south on Kennedy Parkway, we stop at Seminole Rest, a large mound of shells dating back to 2000 BCE. The modern-day owners of this property refused to sell their shells for road construction. Instead, they built two houses on the mound, one for themselves, and the other for a caretaker. Both houses are now protected by the park.

In Merritt Island Wildlife Refuge, the manatees seem to have arrived on cue below the observation deck on the northeast side of Haulover Canal. The manatees, attracted by warm water, lounge in the lagoon. They come to the surface just long enough to take their next breath, but don't show much of their bodies.

The Black Point Wildlife Drive, a seven-mile drive through a prolific wildlife viewing area, is one of the best places to see Florida birds, from sparrows to roseate spoonbills, the latter, large shore birds with pink, punky stripes on white bodies. The refuge raises and lowers the water in the impoundments to lure the right birds at the right time, but the area feels natural.

The one-way road attracts serious birders with large scopes on tripods. We have quality binoculars, but they just can't compete with their professional equipment. Even so, we're able to identify over thirty bird species; the area boasts over 320 species. You need to take the drive slowly and stop often, so often that it might be easier just to walk the seven flat miles.

It's always a dilemma to decide on how much time to leave for such a visit. We spent a full afternoon at Cape Canaveral, concentrating on human history, and several hours the next day for birds and manatees, but it wasn't enough time. And if you want to swim and boat as well, you could make this area the anchor for a week's vacation.

⚷ Biscayne National Park
An underwater oasis south of Miami
Florida

Only an hour south of crowded, noisy Miami, Biscayne National Park is an oasis of blue water and bluer skies. Even in November, it's hot. We arrive at the Dante Fascell Visitor Center just as it opens. We had made reservations weeks ago to take a boat ride to Boca Chita Key, but now it seems like our trip is in jeopardy. The concession that runs the boat trip wants a minimum of eight people and so far only has four. Not a good start.

I stifle the desire to ask, "What else is there to do around here?" Instead, we watch the movie promising us birds, turtles, manatees, and more. But it's just a movie; I want to see the real thing. When the movie ends, the boat driver is able to scare up four more interested visitors, so we're off, only fifteen minutes late. If the National Park Service ran the trips, they would start on time. But here in tropical Miami, things are casual. Why doesn't the National Park Service run these boats? Private enterprise can probably run it cheaper, but it's not the same experience. The first mate charged with giving us a talk does a superficial job.

The ride to Boca Chita takes almost an hour, with herons, egrets, cormorants, and brown pelicans on the way. The tiny island has a half-mile trail through the mangrove swamp where we get close to black vultures. If we had rented a canoe and paddled ourselves, we could have explored around and gotten a more up-close-and-personal look at the vegetation and birds.

We climb the lighthouse to observe blue waters as far as the eye can see, as well as the Miami skyline. Mark Honeywell, who founded Honeywell, the engineering and aerospace company, owned Boca Chita in the 1940s. He built the ornamental lighthouse and added the cannon. We think of the Florida Keys starting at Key Largo because the highway starts there. Geographically, Boca Chita is the beginning of the Florida Keys.

I realize that without our own boat, we're at a disadvantage at Biscayne National Park. It's like coming to Great Smoky Mountains National Park and saying, "I don't have hiking boots."

Everglades National Park
Saving a river of grass
Florida

Everglades National Park was the first traditional national park that I ever visited, soon after we were married. Lenny wanted to show me his home state of Florida. Mostly we stayed around Miami Beach, where he grew up, and where his parents still lived. We went down to Homestead and the Everglades for a day trip at the end of August. I knew about national parks, though the label didn't mean much to me then. I remembered the alligators and the mosquitoes. August may not be the best time to visit the Everglades, but you go to a national park when you can go. I've been back several times, each time with new eyes and expectations.

Now we're here with our granddaughters and their parents during the Christmas break, and I'm concerned. How are you going to keep them down on the farm after they've seen Paree? In this case, how am I going to get the girls excited about a national park after they've seen animals up close at a zoo? I'm sure the professionals working to get children to appreciate the outdoors worry about this. A zoo isn't a natural habitat for animals, but a safe, approved place for adults to take kids.

The day before, we went to Jungle Island, a private zoo in Miami. It was an expensive disappointment, but the caged animals were labeled and easy to see. The zoo did all the work for us. Today we drive into the Everglades, where we have to find the wildlife and figure out what they are. I'm worried about taking children to a natural place, where the animals are not on display.

When Marjory Stoneman Douglas published *The Everglades: River of Grass* in 1947, no one thought of the Everglades as worthy of saving. The swamps were drained because early settlers saw the area as farmland and potential home sites. The river of grass was drying up. Cattails, a native invasive, replaced saw grass. Not all invasives come from another continent; sometimes they're our own nuisance plants.

Before 1880, water flowed from the Kissimmee River to Lake Okeechobee in the center of the state and eventually down to Florida Bay. Now cities, roads, levees, dams, locks, and pumps have interrupted the flow. The Everglades must compete with people and agriculture, and it's not doing well. Only rain can flood the Everglades and move water downstream. As Douglas described it, "Where there had been the flow of the river of grass, there were only drying pools, and mosquitoes."

Douglas is credited with saving the Everglades, but she didn't spend much time in the area.

"I hardly ever go to the Everglades," she wrote. "It's too buggy, too wet, too generally inhospitable. . . . I know it's out there, and I know its importance. I suppose you could say the Everglades and I have the kind of friendship that doesn't depend on constant phys-ical contact." She knew what worked for her. I have to see, feel, walk, and sweat in a place to understand it.

The Everglades has now been recognized as America's tropical rainforest, an iconic region on par with Yellowstone and Califor-nia's redwoods. The park, dedicated in 1947, protects the ecolog-ical diversity of the animals and plants. The thick mangroves, marshes, and gigantic palm trees make it feel like a jungle. South

Florida is the only place where you can see alligators and crocodiles living side by side.

Fifty years later, Randy Lee Loftis, in an epilogue to Douglas's
classic book, writes, "Natural places, ecosystems, are not fragile.
They are, in the main, tough as an old tire." The Everglades wilderness system protects the recharge area, where water goes from the
surface into the ground for South Florida's drinking water.

We know the park for its alligators, but it protects a long list
of threatened and endangered species, including the Everglades
mink and Florida panther. The snail kite, a medium-size raptor, is
a picky eater, depending almost only on apple snails, themselves
requiring flooding wetlands. In the Everglades, the cascading
environmental dependencies are clear.

On the Anhinga Trail, we're astonished by the teeming wildlife
that congregates during the winter dry season. This area of Florida
only has two seasons, wet and dry. You want to come here in the
winter, the dry, when it's mostly free of bugs. If water is scarce in
other parts of the park, animals move to the Taylor Slough. We
may think of slough, which rhymes with *two*, as another word for
wetlands, but the park defines it as a deep body of slow-moving
water.

What a place! The trail is packed with birds, turtles, and of
course, alligators. Anhingas sit on a tree branch, drying their
wings. We feel that we can almost touch the alligators and turtles
sunning themselves. Countless numbers of herons and egrets
parade around the water. Gallinules, colorful birds with long toes,
appear to walk on water. Our granddaughters have completely
forgotten yesterday's zoo and marvel at the wildlife being wild. Isa,
who's five years old, points to alligators stock-still in the water and
keeps asking, "Are they real?"

Walking this trail is not a solitary experience. Busloads of
people come here because this is where the alligators are. But we're

not concerned and neither are the animals. They want to be in and around the water.

ॐ✦ॐ

On another visit, my husband and I drive to the Flamingo Visitor Center, thirty-eight miles south of the park entrance. The Everglades is otherworldly. I'm not much of a birder because I don't have the patience to stand around waiting for that warbler hiding in a tree on the side of the mountain. But here birds are big and identifiable. Egrets, herons, ibis, vultures . . . If I can photograph a heron with a small point-and-shoot camera, you know the bird is close by.

In the morning, we have the tourist boardwalks to ourselves. The trails almost seem to be ordered according to altitude. The pine and hammock ecosystem reaches a height of seven feet. We move down to a river of grass, considered the true Everglades, followed by mangrove swamp, and ending at Florida Bay at Flamingo. In this subtropical paradise, the difference between these ecosystems is a foot or so, and each foot brings different plants and animals. This park is made for canoeing, not hiking, but we walk all the boardwalks that we find.

When we get on the Christian Point Trail, a real dirt trail, the mosquitoes dive into us. They may not have enjoyed another warm-blooded creature for a while. We turn back after about ten minutes. We're the Christians and the mosquitoes are the lions. We didn't turn around quickly enough, and I scratch for days.

On the way to Flamingo, we pass a sign: "Rock Reef Pass, Elevation 3 feet." Another identifies the dwarf cypress forest at four feet.

"If these places are not underwater by 2100, they will be soon afterwards," Lenny says. A chemical engineer by training, Lenny has been working as a climate change expert for more than twenty-five years, since way before the public had heard of the topic.

"I realize that when our granddaughters are our age, about sixty years from now, none of what we're looking at is likely to exist. Yes, there will be an area defined as Everglades National Park, but most of it will be underwater," Lenny says.

He's read all the reports, and knows intellectually that sea level will rise one to four feet by 2100. He also knows that storm surges and saltwater intrusion will dramatically change areas that aren't directly flooded.

"But there's a difference between knowing something intellectually and feeling it in your gut. Today, I felt the future impacts of climate change in my gut," he says as we explore the boardwalks.

When sea level rises two feet, the effects are dramatic. The western area of the park, now covered by mangroves, would be underwater. The mangroves would move north and east, displacing the pinelands and shallow marsh now covering the eastern and central parts of the park. The American crocodile would thrive, but many birds and land animals that live in the Everglades today would have to migrate. The sea of grass would be gone forever.

With all its wonders, Everglades National Park still works hard to attract visitors. A free trolley ride is available on weekends from Homestead, the gateway town, to three destinations: the Everglades Visitor Center, Biscayne National Park, and a local beach. Because it's a joint venture with the city of Homestead, it's well advertised. The park itself doesn't advertise.

Once in Flamingo, the park also worries about your car. It seems that vultures will eat the rubber around the car doors and windows. The park won't shoo away the birds, but it can try to protect your car by offering tarps to put over your vehicle. I guess that they realize that most visitors find the Everglades a strange and even frightening place. So the park tries to smooth the experience, all in the name of attracting visitors to their national park.

South Florida is a world unto itself and much more than the excesses of Miami. The tropical setting, palm trees, and wildlife are like no other in the United States. Those who dismiss going to Florida because of the reputation of its cities should spend a few days in the Everglades.

∽ Big Cypress National Preserve
Alligators and wildlife artist
Florida

It doesn't take much orientation to see why almost 1.2 million visitors came to Big Cypress National Preserve in 2014. Lenny and I are on a visit with our older granddaughter, Hannah, during the Christmas holidays. We watch the drama happening outside the visitor center.

On the boardwalk, a cormorant has a catfish, still very much alive, in its mouth. The catfish is struggling to free itself. It flounders and flaps, but the bird has the fish clamped tight in its mouth. The cormorant has its own trouble. The bird is struggling to hold on to the fish while egrets and other cormorants approach and want to share its booty. Maybe the cormorant can't just swallow the fish whole. But it doesn't want to put it down and take the chance of a competing bird swooping it up. Finally, the cormorant flies away with the wriggling fish.

Big Cypress is named for its large expanse of land (729,000 acres), not for its trees. Most cypresses are of the dwarf pond variety, not the massive trees you see in Congaree National Park. Ecologically, the preserve is considered an extension of Everglades National Park along with Fakahatchee Strand Preserve State Park, made famous by the 2002 movie *Adaptation* with Meryl Streep.

Two east-west roads trisect the preserve. Alligator Alley (Interstate 75) is a four-lane road without an alligator in sight. Drivers have little chance of seeing any wildlife through the tall fences on the roadsides. The Tamiami Trail, US 41, gives visitors access to all the outdoor activities in the preserve. The road from Miami to Tampa was completed in 1928. Soon after, major logging started in Big Cypress Swamp. Great bald cypress trees were turned into coffins, gutters, and pickle barrels.

This land has been threatened since the completion of the Tamiami Trail and the real estate boom. But in 1968, construction of a large jetport was started. This got the attention of environmentalists, including Marjory Stoneman Douglas, author of *The Everglades: River of Grass*. In 1969, when she was seventy-nine years old with failing eyesight, Douglas became an activist and started Friends of the Everglades. She had advocated for saving and restoring the Everglades all her life. The jetport was stopped and Big Cypress became a preserve in 1974. Douglas lived to be 108 years old and was able to see both the Everglades and Big Cypress protected through her efforts.

At the visitor center, the film highlights the endangered Florida panther. Only about twenty years ago, the Florida panther population was estimated to number between twenty and thirty. The park imported Texas cougars, another subspecies of panther, to mate with the Florida panther, increasing the gene pool. Now there are about one hundred animals, and they are all considered Florida panthers. Along with being perhaps the most endangered mammal in North America, Florida panthers are an umbrella species. By protecting their habitat, many other species, such as black bears, will also benefit.

The Everglades Association, the cooperating association that runs the bookstores in Big Cypress along with the three National Parks in South Florida, must have had a run on Junior Ranger books today. When we ask for one for Hannah, the sales clerk says,

"We only have them in Spanish and Creole. We've run out of the English language books."

I suggest that she gives Hannah some alternate challenge so she can work on a Junior Ranger badge. When Hannah visited Great Smoky Mountains National Park, we took her to several sections of the park where she really had to put some effort to earn her badge.

Here, without a booklet, the ranger asks Hannah to find five things: cypress trees, saw grass, bromeliads, insects, and water. She directs us to the Florida Trail. Before we leave, I have to fill out a backcountry permit. If you plan to walk more than a mile on a trail, you need a backcountry permit.

The Florida National Scenic Trail extends more than 1,300 miles across the state of Florida, from Big Cypress to Gulf Islands National Seashore at the western end of the Florida panhandle. The trail is lined with slash pines, a long-needle pine commonly found in the swamps. Cypress trees with their characteristic knees are everywhere, along with cabbage palms, the Florida state tree. The land is full of saw grass, long, sharp-edged grass that inspired the phrase "river of grass." We find a few late-blooming flowers, the light violet glades lobelia, and tiny white asters. Hannah recognizes the five required things she had to find on a three-mile hike from the visitor center.

A brown carsonite sign showing location coordinates and the altitude marks off each mile of trail—here it's twenty-eight feet. I don't think my hiking GPS could register such a low altitude. The trail is so flat that even a five-foot elevation change gives you a different perspective. Here it's easier to see animals than in the mountains. The system of canals that parallels the roadways attracts wildlife.

In winter, animals have less cover and all animals gravitate toward water. Large birds are easy to spot: great blue heron, wood stork, cormorant, tricolored heron, black vulture, little blue heron, moorhen, and cattle egret. We find several turtles and an iguana. But all those animals pale before an alligator.

The literature says that the H. P. Williams Roadside Park is a good place to see alligators, and we're not disappointed. From the boardwalk, we watch large alligators lazing about in the swampy water contained in a canal tied into the Turner River. With a quick glance, you might think they were floating logs. Past the boardwalk on Turner River Road, smaller alligators sun themselves half out of the water and in the grass. During the dry season, alligators eat only once a week. Alligators and crocodiles appear to be connected to dinosaurs. They even look prehistoric with their huge jaws and menacing teeth.

Big Cypress is not Everglades National Park. As befitting a preserve, you can hunt and drive off-road vehicles. Much has been written about the controversy of allowing more ORVs in the preserve. Big Cyprus Preserve also has commercial businesses, private communities, hunting cabins, and the small community of Ochopee. Every town needs a post office. The current building, formerly a tomato farm irrigation shed, became a post office in 1953, after a fire burned the general store and post office. The lone postal clerk also sells Trailways bus tickets and keeps busy with stamp collectors who seek out the postmark.

While we're here, the Miccosukee Indians hold their annual arts festival just outside the preserve. They've put up signs within the preserve, advertising the festival at regular intervals on the road, something I couldn't imagine being allowed in a national park.

Big Cypress boasts another treasure that Everglades National Park doesn't have: the photographer Clyde Butcher. Now well over seventy years old, Butcher has been called the Ansel Adams of Big Cypress. He and his wife moved here in 1992 and soon opened the gallery located a quarter mile east of the visitor center on US 41.

Butcher exhibits marvelous black-and-white photographs taken with large-format cameras. He's built a system in his darkroom that can handle up to 12 x 20 negatives. Clyde also takes visitors on swamp walks. Until recently, they lived on the property behind the gallery. Now that they've moved to Venice, Florida, they rent out their two cottages to tourists wanting a quiet vacation. What a wonderful retreat that would be.

ᕦ Buck Island Reef National Monument
It's five o'clock somewhere
St. Croix, Virgin Islands

I'm lying face down in the water as waves splash all around. I have to remember to breathe through my mouth while staring at the coral below. It looks artificial, but everything is real at Buck Island Reef National Monument in St. Croix. Elkhorn coral really does look like the antlers on an elk. I feel I can reach out to the brain coral, but the lagoon is more than twelve feet deep. Besides, touching anything in the water is illegal.

This is my first time snorkeling from a boat instead of close to the shore, and I'm hesitant. Though I'm in the lagoon between the coral reef and the shore, land seems very far off. Fish float around me, not bothered by my presence. My boat companions have long moved past the boat and follow signs for an underwater trail, but I'm in no rush to be first on this trail.

The island is only 176 acres of land, but the monument includes almost nineteen thousand acres of protected submerged coral reef system. Buck Island was proclaimed a national monument in 1961 and expanded in 2001 to "preserve one of the finest marine gardens in the Caribbean Sea." We're at the easternmost national park unit in the system.

The Danes owned this island along with the rest of the US

Virgin Islands from 1733 until they sold it to the United States in 1917. There are several theories of how the island was named. The official park publication refers to a corruption of the Danish or German *Pocken-Eyland*, after the green lignum vitae tree, a heavy, dense tree that covers the island.

Though we travel seven miles from Christiansted to the west side of the island in about forty minutes, Buck Island lies only one and a half miles away from the St. Croix mainland. Today, the boat people have trouble with their sailboat. So they put us on a motor boat and we arrive on the island earlier. A sailboat might take ninety minutes for the same trip.

The captain pretends to be on island time, but the day is carefully choreographed. After everyone has their fill of snorkeling, the boat moves from the west side of the island to the designated anchorage area. We make sandwiches from an array of cold cuts and vegetables and eat on the boat because the crew doesn't want to take a chance of leaving garbage on the island. There's no camping, fishing, or shell collecting on the island.

The boat anchors in a sandy spot, but still offshore. To get to land, I have to swim, though taller people can walk out. Wes, the captain's assistant, takes my camera off the boat. With a camera in one hand and a bottle of water in the other, Lenny and I take the walking loop up to the observation tower.

The trail starts on the beach at Diedrich's Point, named after Johann Diedrich, the town clerk for Christiansted in the 1700s, who built a house on top of the island. The trail is lush with trees and cactus. Tan-tan, an exotic tree with prodigious pods, grows everywhere. We're warned about the poisonous manchineel tree, which produces a sap that can burn the skin and cause temporary blindness if it finds its way to your eyes. But we also steer clear of the acacia, a wattle tree with sharp pointy thorns protruding from its trunk.

Buck Island was sparsely settled over the centuries, but no one lives here now. The Danes imported the Indian mongoose, a weasel-like rodent, to the Virgin Islands in the hope it would eat rats. However, mongooses are active during the day and tree rats come out at night, so that scheme didn't work out as planned. Both rats and mongooses are pests, feeding on turtle eggs. The National Park Service was able to get rid of both exotic animals on Buck Island, and reintroduced the native St. Croix ground lizard.

From the observation tower, about three hundred feet above sea level, I can see the outline of the reef through the blue-green water. An automated Coast Guard signal light warns boats to stay off the reef, but there's no trail to the very top of the island. Our trail down is dry and lined with organ pipe cactus. Red-tailed hawks, pelicans, and magnificent frigatebirds soar overhead. Park information states that brown pelicans are locally endangered, though they seem plentiful to me, even in the Christiansted Harbor.

Once on the beach, we can walk on the sand, but every once in a while, the water goes right up to the rocks. We follow the inland trail and bump into an archaeology team that just started work today. Their mission is to study the remains of the Taino Indians, who used the island as a temporary fishing camp. Without fresh water, it's unlikely that they would have lived here permanently. The native people left a mound of shells, a midden like the ones in Canaveral.

A three-person team consisting of an archaeologist, a natural resource specialist, and a student intern sets up a research site on the side of the trail. The research questions ask: Is there anything worth preserving, and how do we study it without endangering the lizard?

Before the team can dig up and study Indian artifacts, they have to ensure that they aren't harming the ground lizard in the process. So the two women, down on their hands and knees, stick their index fingers deep in the burrow to check for lizards. This is in preparation for their real study.

On the trip back, the boat crew offers us unlimited rum punch. After all, "It's five o'clock somewhere."

Epilogue

"I've been everywhere, man. I've been everywhere." This Johnny Cash song keeps swirling in my head. Cash's song rattles off places from Alaska to Winslow, Arizona, but doesn't mention national parks. I started to spend serious time in Southeastern parks about six years ago, first on the way to other places. Later, I focused on going to parks that were destinations on their own. By the time Lenny and I flew to Puerto Rico and the Virgin Islands, I knew I was committed to this project.

"When you went to the Virgin Islands, did you check out St. Thomas as well?" a friend asked.

"No. No national parks there," I said.

I completed my journey through national parks of the Southeast, though I'll keep visiting national parks everywhere. I went to the iconic Everglades and Mammoth Cave several times, though I haven't explored every corner of these parks. I found the one square block of Tupelo National Battlefield in the center of Elvis Presley's hometown.

My husband and I spent a day among the memorials and graves at Andersonville Historic Site, the saddest place I've visited. The Battle of Cowpens in South Carolina took less than an hour, much less time than I spent at the national battlefield. But the Southeastern parks aren't just about war. I saw manatees in Canaveral National Seashore, climbed the refurbished Bodie Island Lighthouse at Cape Hatteras, and walked a beach in St. Croix where Christopher Columbus's men landed. The National Park Service preserves and protects not only the scenery and views but also our history. I had an excuse to go to New Orleans and learn about jazz, the quintessential American music. Visiting Tuskegee allowed me to learn more about our civil rights history.

Each visitor center may seem the same, with its movie, exhibits, and brochure, but they differ physically, from a modest one-room building to imposing edifices with multimedia presentations. Every national park has a unique story. I visited six Revolutionary War battlefields, but somehow managed to keep them straight in my head.

It's important to separate the event from the park unit. The National Park Service was not involved in the event or where it happened. As a popular expression goes, "It is what it is"—or better, "It was what it was." The colonists won the Battle of Kings Mountain. The Creeks lost to General Andrew Jackson at the Battle of Horseshoe Bend. The Wright brothers came to an out-of-the-way, unpopulated beach to test out their ideas about human powered flight. However, now the question is "How do you interpret the resource?"

Park rangers are the best when it comes to interpreting that history and making it come alive. Rangers may differ in their approach from precise to casual. Most are talkative; they really wanted me to understand the story and were excited to have an appreciative listener. One of the major tenets of visiting national parks is that there are no secrets. If you read and ask questions, you can find every feature in every park. From the Hall Cabin in the Smokies to the statue *Fame* in Shiloh, it's all out here for visitors to explore. So you can forget articles that claim to tell you about secrets of the national parks.

Parks are not crowded. Even in Great Smoky Mountains National Park, the most visited traditional national park in the country, only the roads and visitor centers are busy. Walk a mile from the trailhead and you'll see almost no one. Arrive at a visitor center at nine a.m. and you'll have the ranger's full attention.

More funding needs to be available for full-time interpretive rangers. As the face of the parks, rangers make the history or science relevant to the rest of us. Visitor centers in all units should be open every day of the year, except maybe Christmas Day. This all takes money.

When I talk about my national park experience, the most common question is, "Which one did you like the best?"

Each park is unique. Did I say that already? There's a reason why each unit is part of the National Park Service, which I've tried to explain here.

My most memorable visits are the ones where I was able to engage a ranger or VIP. Ranger Barney Schoby in Natchez was steeped in William Johnson's story. Ranger Aleutia Scott at Barataria was so passionate about saving the Louisiana delta. Ranger Daniel Luther made Andrew Johnson, a third-rate American president, come alive. Without Ranger Brittony Beason's clear instructions, I would have never found the trailhead for the Hensley Settlement at Cumberland Gap.

This is my national park story. Go out and make your own.

WHAT PEOPLE WANT TO KNOW
ABOUT NATIONAL PARKS

1. Why can't I take my dog on trails in most national parks?

This is probably the number one question I seem to get, at least in the Smokies. Large national parks with extensive backcountry areas, such as Yellowstone, Yosemite, Grand Canyon, Glacier, Rocky Mountains, and the Smokies, as a rule, don't allow dogs on trails. Here are some reasons from the various park people and rangers I've talked to.

Dogs can carry disease into the park's wildlife populations, as well as chase and threaten wildlife, scaring birds and other animals away from nesting, feeding, and resting sites. The scent left behind by a dog can signal the presence of a predator, disrupting or altering the behavior of park wildlife. Dogs bark and disturb the quiet of the wilderness. Pets may become prey for larger predators such as coyotes and bears.

2. What's the difference between national parks, national forests, wildlife refuges, and Bureau of Land Management (BLM) holdings?

National parks, such as Great Smoky Mountains National Park, were created to protect and preserve public lands. In general, you can't hunt, gather plants, or mountain bike on trails. They have better facilities, maintain trails well, and are usually more user-friendly than National Forests. Parks preserve not only the landscape, but also historic structures and battlefields. You can say that the National Park Service is our country's public historian. The folks in green and gray try to keep our natural and historic resources "unimpaired for future generations."

Wildlife refuges help conserve wildlife, fish, and plant resources and their habitats. Most of the time, refuges allow hunting, fishing, wildlife observation, photography, interpretation, and environmental education. In general, parks are for people and refuges are for wildlife.

BLM holdings lie mostly in the western states. BLM allows mining, timber harvesting, mountain biking, and other activities usually not allowed in national parks. BLM also has national monuments and scenic and historic trails. The three services are under the Department of the Interior.

National Forests, operated by the Forest Service in the Department of Agriculture, focus on conservation. Forests are multi-use areas. In practice, this means that forests allow hunting by the public, logging by timber companies, road building, gathering plants, and mountain biking on hiking trails, even ATVs, all with the proper permit. Conservation at its best is the careful utilization of a natural resource in order to prevent depletion. Recreation is only one mission of national forests.

3. Who sells all the books and T-shirts in national parks?

It's not the government.

From the first, national parks visitors had questions such as, "What is that flower that I saw on the trail?" In 1923, the Yosemite Association, now the Yosemite Conservancy, was established as the nation's first cooperating association with the National Park Service. Cooperating associations are park partners that manage the bookstores. In Great Smoky Mountains National Park, the Great Smoky Mountains Association (GSMA) also publishes trail guides and maps. Associations donate part of their profits to national parks. Cooperating associations are not advocacy groups and don't take positions on park issues as an association. Almost all national parks have cooperating associations. Eastern National manages the bookstores on the Blue Ridge Parkway and in many small eastern parks that could not sustain their own association.

Cooperating associations are different from Friends groups, such as Friends of the Smokies. Friends groups are purely fund-raising organizations. Almost every park has a Friends group. Look for their donation boxes in the visitor center.

4. Who owned all this land before it became part of the National Park Service?

Every piece of land has a different history.

In the Smokies, the states of North Carolina and Tennessee bought each individual parcel from families and logging companies. They then turned the land over to the National Park Service. Daughters of the American Revolution and Colonial Dames of America preserved a lot of historic battlefield land before turning it over to the federal government. In some cases, Friends groups were able to buy the land, and later, donated it to the government. Prominent individuals and their families, including Carl Sandburg and President Jimmy Carter, sold or donated their homes to the National Park Service, knowing that they would be preserved and protected.

5. How do I find the official website for a particular park?

The official websites all start with www.nps.gov.

If the park name is one word, like Congaree, the first four letters are used. So the website is www.nps.gov/cong.

If the park name is two or more words, you use the first two letters of the first word and the first two letters of the second word. For example, Blue Ridge Parkway is www.nps.gov/blri.

There are exceptions in case the algorithm ends up with the same abbreviation. Castillo de San Marcos reduces to CASA. Carl Sandburg Home does as well. So the Sandburg website is www.nps.gov/carl.

6. What is the difference between all those park designations?

There are national parks, national seashores, national monuments, national memorials, not to mention national historic sites and national historical parks. The Southeast region has almost all the classifications for park units. When Congress authorizes a park unit, it chooses a designation. A president can proclaim a national monument under the Antiquities Act of 1906.

Most people are familiar with national parks, large, spectacular natural places that may also have historic significance. You can't hunt or log in a park. As you would expect, a battle was fought in a national military park, battlefield, or battlefield park. A historic site contains one main feature, such as the Carl Sandburg Home, while a historical park, like Natchez National Historical Park, has more than one. If the park includes the word preserve, it usually means that hunting is allowed somewhere on the premises. Recreation areas protect land to provide outdoor recreation for large numbers of people. Depending on the area, you might be able to mountain bike or hunt on that land.

The nuances between these designations are probably not as important as the fact that each area is now protected on the federal level.

Helping Out the Parks:
More Than Writing Letters

Occasionally, Congress decides to make a statement and shuts down the nonessential services of our government. In October 2013, our national parks were closed for sixteen days as part of a partial government shutdown. I was outraged. Why are national parks considered nonessential?

Letters, emails, newspaper columns, and Facebook comments were flying, and the message was clear: Open up the parks. Finally, Congress appropriated money and our parks reopened. However, the outrage seemed to die down, even though our national parks are so underfunded.

A recent poll shows that voters think parks are very important. Somehow, Congress isn't getting the message. We, national park lovers and visitors, aren't helpless. We can show Congress that parks are important to us—and we vote.

We can write to our Congressional representatives and urge them to work on a real budget. During the shutdown, that was the standard advice. But are they getting letters and emails about our national parks now? Write to your representative and two senators. You do know who they are, right? Let them know that you would like them to restore full funding to national parks.

There's more that we can do to demonstrate that national parks and public lands are important, though it will take some effort on our part. So here goes:

- As they say, 90 percent of life is showing up. Visit your local national park. Everybody has a park unit reasonably close by. Hike the trails, walk the battlefield, study that monument. Thank the rangers or volunteers behind the desk for being there. Ask about the closed trail or facility. Chances are that your park made some difficult choices because of their budget problems. Let your friends on Facebook and Twitter know what park you've visited.

- Almost every park has a Friends Group. For $35 or so a year, you can show solidarity with your park, help it financially, and meet like-minded people. If the number of members suddenly shot up, our legislators would notice. You can find information about Friends groups on national park websites; click the Support Your Park link. Even joining or liking the group's Facebook page and Twitter feed says to the world that this park unit is important. Friends of the Smokies has over 120,000 likes. What if they all became members?

- Even I can't join the friends group from every park I visit, so I drop a few dollars in the donation box at the visitor center. Look at it this way. Compared to amusement parks, national parks provide low-cost entertainment. A one-day pass to the Magic Kingdom in Disney World costs over a hundred dollars, and they don't even have hiking trails.

- Buy something from the park bookstore, which offers authoritative information on the site. Cooperating associations that manage bookstores in the park donate part of their sales to their national parks. Think Christmas and birthdays and buy your gifts from the park store. We can all use a calendar, a fresh T-shirt, or some jam and honey to make life a little sweeter. Every purchase helps your park.

- If your car says a lot about you, somebody somewhere realized that your license place could show what's important to you and what you support. So look at your license plate. Does your car believe in anything, or is it naked? Most states have specialty plates that help support a driver's cause. In North Carolina, we can support Great Smoky Mountains National Park, the Blue Ridge Parkway, and the Appalachian Trail. Revenue from the

Everglades Trust Fund goes to conservation and protection of natural resources and abatement of water pollution in the Everglades. Check out your state's Division of Motor Vehicles. Usually $20 a year from the sale of each specialized license plate goes to the nonprofit Friends group. In addition, more people become aware of your support for the national park. As advertising goes, this is really cheap.

- Volunteer time at your park. Almost every park could use enthusiastic people to answer questions behind the desk, take visitors on walks, or maintain trails. The park provides all the training and, best of all, you get to wear a uniform.

- If your park needs a champion, try involving a famous person in your national park. That's a reach, but why not try? When Oprah Winfrey visited Yosemite, visitations and visibility went up tremendously. Dolly Parton was the ambassador of the seventy-fifth anniversary celebration of Great Smoky Mountains National Park, but we haven't heard much from her in connection with the park recently. Whom can you get to be a mascot or proponent of your national park?

- You may notice that I haven't yet mentioned donating money directly to your national parks, but that wouldn't be a bad idea. Usually, you give through the individual park's Friends group, but if there's no Friends group, you can donate directly to the park. Again, look at the Support Your Park link on the national park website. The parks need our private money because our taxes aren't enough.

THANK YOU, READERS

Thanks for reading my book. I hope it motivated you to get out there. Visit and support your national parks.

I'd love to hear from you. Let me know where you went and what you thought. You can find me at www.hikertohiker.com.

I'm available to speak at your book club or outdoor group. Again, contact me through my website.

If you liked the book, leave a review on the book site of your choice.

Thanks and see you in a park!

Bibliography

I mention the following books and films in my story.

Books

Bailey, Anthony. *The Outer Banks*. Chapel Hill: University of North Carolina, 1999.

Barr, Nevada. *Endangered Species*. New York: Berkley, 2008.

Barr, Nevada. *Flashback*. New York: Berkley, 2004.

Bartram, William. *The Travels of William Bartram*. Mineola, NY: Dover Publications, 1955.

Buchanan, John. *Jackson's Way: Andrew Jackson and the People of the Western Waters*. Hoboken, NJ: Wiley, 2001.

Chambers, Thomas. *Memories of War: Visiting Battlegrounds and Bonefields in the Early American Republic*. Ithaca, NY: Cornell University Press, 2012.

Cox, William E. *The Hensley Settlement*. Fort Washington, PA: Eastern National, 2005.

Douglas, Marjory Stoneman. *The Everglades: River of Grass, 50th Anniversary Edition*. Sarasota, FL: Pineapple Press, 1997.

Haley, Alex. *Roots: The Saga of an American Family*. 30th Anniv. Ed. New York: Vanguard Press, 2007.

Harlan, Will. *Untamed: The Wildest Woman in America and the Fight for Cumberland Island*. New York: Grove Press, 2014.

Horwitz, Tony. *Confederates in the Attic: Dispatches from the Unfinished Civil War*. New York: Vintage, 1999.

Horwitz, Tony. *A Voyage Long and Strange: On the Trail of Vikings, Conquistadors, Lost Colonists, and Other Adventurers in Early America*. 2008. Reprint, New York: Picador, 2009.

Irving, Washington. *The Legend of Sleepy Hollow*. EBook #41: Project Gutenberg, 2008.

Kantor, MacKinlay. *Andersonville.* 1955. Reprint, New York: Plume, 1993.

McCrumb, Sharyn. *King's Mountain.* New York: Thomas Dunne Books, 2013.

Moore, Francis. *A Voyage to Georgia Begun in the Year 1735.* St. Simons Island, GA: Fort Frederica Association, 1983.

Muir, John. *A Thousand-Mile Walk to the Gulf.* New York, Mariner Books, 1998.

National Park Service. *The Civil War Remembered.* Fort Washington, PA: Eastern National, 2011.

National Park Service. *The War of 1812.* Fort Washington, PA: Eastern National, 2012.

Ray, Janisse. *Ecology of a Cracker Childhood.* Minneapolis, MN: Milkweed, 2000.

Smith, Timothy B. *The Golden Age of Battlefield Preservation: The Decade of the 1890s and the Establishment of America's First Five Military Parks.* Knoxville, TN: University of Tennessee, 2008.

Tidwell, Mike. *Bayou Farewell: The Rich Life and Tragic Death of Louisiana's Cajun Coast.* New York: Vintage, 2004.

Tilden, Freeman. *Interpreting our Heritage.* Chapel Hill: The University of North Carolina Press, 2008.

Watkins, Andra. *Not Without my Father: One Woman's 444-mile Walk of the Natchez Trace.* Charleston, SC: Word Hermit Press, 2015.

Whitman, Walt. *Leaves of Grass, 150th Anniversary Edition.* New York: Oxford University Press, 2005.

Films

Adaptation. Directed by Spike Jonze. Culver City, CA: Columbia Pictures, 2002.

Andersonville. Directed by John Frankenheimer. California. Turner Pictures, 1996.

Lincoln. Directed by Steven Spielberg. Glendale, CA: Dream-Works, 2012.

Moonshine. Directed by Kelly L. Riley. Highproof Films, 2008. DVD.

Mystery of the Mounds. Directed by Gray Warriner. Seattle: Camera One, 2014.

Selma. Directed by Ava DuVernay. Hollywood, CA: Paramount Pictures, 2014.

Sergeant York. Directed by Howard Hawks. Burbank, CA: Warner Brothers, 1941. DVD.

The Andersonville Trial. Directed by George C. Scott. Burbank, CA: Community Television of Southern California, 1970.

The Obed: Find Yourself Here. Directed by Donald O'Brien. Chicago: Silver Fir Media, 2014.

The True Meaning of Pictures: Shelby Lee Adams' Appalachia. Directed by Jennifer Baichwal. New York: New Video Group, 2003. DVD.

The Wizard of Oz. Directed by Victor Fleming. Beverly Hills, CA: Metro-Goldwyn-Mayer Studios, 1939.

Wizards of Waverly Place: The Movie. Directed by Lev L. Spiro. Burbank, California: Disney Channel Original, 2009. DVD.

NATIONAL PARKS BY STATE

National Park	Chapter Heading
Alabama	
Horseshoe Bend National Military Park	The War of 1812
Little River Canyon National Preserve	The Great Outdoors—The Mountains
Russell Cave National Monument	Prehistoric America
Selma to Montgomery National Historic Trail	Fighting for Equality
Tuskegee Airmen National Historic Site	Fighting for Equality
Tuskegee Institute National Historic Site	Fighting for Equality
Florida	
Big Cypress National Preserve	The Great Outdoors—The Lowlands
Biscayne National Park	The Great Outdoors—The Lowlands
Canaveral National Seashore	The Great Outdoors—The Lowlands
Castillo de San Marcos National Monument	The Europeans Are Coming
De Soto National Memorial	The Europeans Are Coming
Dry Tortugas National Park	Coastal Defense
Everglades National Park	The Great Outdoors—The Lowlands
Fort Matanzas National Monument	The Europeans Are Coming
Gulf Islands National Seashore (and MS)	Coastal Defense
Timucuan Ecological and Historic Preserve	The Europeans Are Coming
Georgia	
Andersonville National Historic Site	The Civil War
Appalachian National Scenic Trail (and NC to Maine)	The Great Outdoors—The Mountains
Chattahoochee River National Recreation Area	The Great Outdoors—The Mountains
Chickamauga and Chattanooga National Military Park (and TN)	The Civil War
Cumberland Island National Seashore	Young America
Fort Frederica National Monument	The Europeans Are Coming
Fort Pulaski National Monument	Coastal Defense
Jimmy Carter National Historic Site	Twentieth-Century Developments
Kennesaw Mountain National Battlefield Park	The Civil War

Martin Luther King Jr. National Historic Site	Fighting for Equality
Ocmulgee National Monument	Prehistoric America
Kentucky	
Abraham Lincoln Birthplace National Historical Park	The Civil War
Cumberland Gap National Historical Park (and VA, TN)	Young America
Mammoth Cave National Park	The Great Outdoors—The Mountains
Louisiana	
Cane River Creole National Historical Park	Young America
Jean Lafitte National Historical Park and Preserve	The War of 1812
New Orleans Jazz National Historical Park	Twentieth-Century Developments
Poverty Point National Monument	Prehistoric America
Mississippi	
Brices Cross Roads National Battlefield Site	The Civil War
Natchez National Historical Park	Young America
Natchez Trace Parkway (and AL, TN)	The War of 1812
Natchez Trace Scenic Trail (and AL, TN)	The War of 1812
Tupelo National Battlefield	The Civil War
Vicksburg National Military Park	The Civil War
North Carolina	
Blue Ridge Parkway (and VA)	The Great Outdoors—The Mountains
Cape Hatteras National Seashore	The Great Outdoors—The Lowlands
Cape Lookout National Seashore	Twentieth-Century Developments
Carl Sandburg Home National Historic Site	Twentieth-Century Developments
Fort Raleigh National Historic Site	The Europeans Are Comingg
Guilford Courthouse National Military Park	Revolutionary War in the South
Moores Creek National Battlefield	Revolutionary War in the South
Wright Brothers National Memorial	Twentieth-Century Developments
Trail of Tears National Historic Trail (and AL, AR, GA, IL, KY, MO, OK, TN)	The War of 1812

Underground Railroad Movement (and many other states)	The Civil War
Puerto Rico	
San Juan National Historic Site	The Europeans Are Coming
South Carolina	
Charles Pinckney National Historic Site	Young America
Congaree National Park	The Great Outdoors—The Lowlands
Cowpens National Battlefield	Revolutionary War in the South
Fort Sumter National Monument	Coastal Defense
Historic Camden Revolutionary War Site	Revolutionary War in the South
Kings Mountain National Military Park	Revolutionary War in the South
Ninety Six National Historic Site	Revolutionary War in the South
Overmountain Victory National Historic Trail (and NC,TN,VA)	Revolutionary War in the South
Tennessee	
Andrew Johnson National Historic Site	The Civil War
Big South Fork National River and Recreation Area (and KY)	The Great Outdoors—The Mountains
Fort Donelson National Battlefield	The Civil War
Great Smoky Mountains National Park (and NC)	The Great Outdoors—The Mountains
Obed Wild and Scenic River	The Great Outdoors—The Mountains
Shiloh National Military Park (and MS)	The Civil War
Stones River National Battlefield	The Civil War
Virgin Islands	
Buck Island Reef National Monument	The Great Outdoors—The Lowlands
Christiansted National Historic Site	The Europeans Are Coming
Salt River Bay National Historical Park and Ecological Preserve	The Europeans Are Coming
Virgin Islands Coral Reef National Monument	The Europeans Are Coming
Virgin Islands National Park	The Europeans Are Coming

ACKNOWLEDGMENTS

First, thanks to all the national park rangers and many other National Park Service staff who protect and preserve our national resources. Without your work, insight, and concern for visitors, we wouldn't be able to enjoy these treasures.

Earlier versions of certain pieces were published on the National Parks Traveler website, owned by Kurt Repanshek. Thanks, Kurt, for your guidance.

Thanks to all those who helped me brainstorm this book: Mary Ammerman, Hannah Bernstein, Lenny Bernstein, Neil Bernstein, Patrick Cumby, Holly Demuth, Stuart English, Holly Scott Jones, Kathy Kyle, Maggie Marshall, Brent McDaniels, Steve Pierce, and Anna Lee Zanetti. Beth Ransom accompanied me on several national park visits and graciously allowed me to use a photograph of her on the book cover.

Lenny Bernstein, Bill Hart, Holly Scott Jones, and Cyn Slaughter read and commented on earlier versions of the manuscript. Each provided great insight.

Thanks to Terry Maddox, Executive Director of the Great Smoky Mountains Association, for his thoughtful foreword.

Thanks to Nicole Ayers for her careful editing and Susan Ferentinos, a public historian, for checking my facts and providing insight on historical matters. Diana Wade designed a great cover as well as interior design. Maya Packard edited the formatted copy of the book. Rowe Copeland, the Book Concierge, is publicizing not only this book, but in the process, the 100th anniversary of the National Park Service. You're all a pleasure to work with.

And always, to Lenny, my husband, who visited many parks with me, stood patiently while I asked the same questions again and again at visitor centers, walked some of the trails, read numerous drafts of this book, and has always been my supporter-in-chief.

ABOUT THE AUTHOR

Danny Bernstein's mission is to get people out of their cars and walking.

She's been a committed hiker for over forty years, completing the Appalachian Trail, all the trails in Great Smoky Mountains National Park, the Mountains-to-Sea Trail, and many other hiking challenges.

Danny hikes and leads hikes for the Carolina Mountain Club, Friends of the Smokies, and other outdoor groups. She's on the Board of Directors of the Great Smoky Mountains Association and Friends of the Mountains-to-Sea Trail.

She's written two hiking guides, *Hiking the Carolina Mountains* and *Hiking North Carolina's Blue Ridge Mountains*, and a narrative on her MST hike, *The Mountains-to-Sea Trail across North Carolina*. She blogs at www.hikertohiker.com.

In her previous life, she worked in computer science for thirty-five years, long before computing was cool, first as a software developer, then as a professor of computer science.

Her motto is "no place is too far to walk if you have the time." She plans to die with her boots on.

CPSIA information can be obtained at www.ICGtesting.com
Printed in the USA
LVOW11s1046120616

492276LV00001B/151/P